MEDIA'S SHIFTING TERRAIN

Media's Shifting Terrain

Five Years that Transformed the Way India Communicates

Pamela Philipose

Orient BlackSwan

MEDIA'S SHIFTING TERRAIN: FIVE YEARS THAT TRANSFORMED THE WAY INDIA COMMUNICATES

ORIENT BLACKSWAN PRIVATE LIMITED

Registered Office
3-6-752 Himayatnagar, Hyderabad 500 029 (Telangana), India
e-mail: centraloffice@orientblackswan.com

Other Offices
Bengaluru, Bhopal, Chennai, Guwahati,
Hyderabad, Jaipur, Kolkata, Lucknow, Mumbai,
New Delhi, Noida, Patna, Visakhapatnam

First published by Orient BlackSwan Private Limited 2019

ISBN 978-93-5287-534-4

028736

Typeset in
ITC Giovanni Std 10/13
by Le Studio Graphique, Gurgaon 122 001

Printed in India at
Yash Printographics, Noida

Published by
Orient BlackSwan Private Limited
3-6-752, Himayatnagar, Hyderabad 500 029
e-mail: info@orientblackswan.com

for

ACHIN

CONTENTS

List of Abbreviations ix
Preface xi
Acknowledgements xv

1. Changing Journalism 1
New Media Shapes, New Mediascapes

2. Framing Corruption in Today's Times 28
Media Discourse and the Anna Campaign

3. Reverberations in the City 89
Delhi Gang Rape Protests and Media Convergence

4. Scripts, Tweets, Posts, and Verdicts 147
Electoral Discourse in a Mediatised Age—I: Narendra Modi

5. Scripts, Tweets, Posts, and Election Outcomes 211
Political Discourse in a Mediatised Age—II: Arvind Kejriwal

6. Multiple Changes, Manifold Impacts 262
The Conundrums Facing a Mediatised India

Bibliography 275
Index 294

ABBREVIATIONS

3G services	Third-generation services
AAP	Aam Aadmi Party
ADR	Association for Democratic Reform
AI	Artificial Intelligence
AIPWA	All India Progressive Women's Association
AVAM	AAP Volunteer Action Manch
AVUT	Association of Victims of Uphaar Tragedy
BJP	Bharatiya Janata Party
CAG	Comptroller and Auditor General
CBI	Central Bureau of Investigation
CII	Confederation of Indian Industry
CSDS	Centre for the Study of Developing Societies
CVC	Central Vigilance Commission
CWG	Commonwealth Games
DTH	Direct-to-home
ECI	Election Commission of India
FDI	Foreign direct investment
FYUP	Four-Year Undergraduate Programme
IAC	India Against Corruption
IAMAI	Internet and Mobile Association of India
ICC	Indian Chamber of Commerce
INC	Indian National Congress
INSAT	Indian National Satellite System

IPC	Indian Penal Code
JNU	Jawaharlal Nehru University, New Delhi
MKSS	Mazdoor Kishan Shakti Sanghathan
MMRDA	Mumbai Metropolitan Region Development Authority
NCPRI	National Campaign for People's Right to Information
NCR	National Capital Region
NDA	National Democratic Alliance
NOFN	National Optical Fibre Network
NSSO	National Sample Survey Organisation
OBC	Other Backward Classes
OBVs	Outdoor broadcasting vans
OECD	Organisation for Economic Co-operation and Development
PIL	Public Interest Litigation
PSA	Public Safety Act
PwC	PricewaterhouseCoopers
RIL	Reliance Industries Limited
RSS	Rashtriya Swayamsevak Sangh
RTI	Right to Information
RWAs	Resident Welfare Associations
SIT	Special Investigative Team
SMS	Short Messaging Service
TI	Transparency International
TRAI	Telecom Regulatory Authority of India
TRPs	Television Rating Points
UPA	United Progressive Alliance
VCR	Video Cassette Recorder

PREFACE

When I began working on this book, in June of 2014, the Sixteenth Lok Sabha election had delivered a verdict that was to constitute a turning point in the affairs of this country of subcontinental proportions. The media, in their variegated avatars, had in that election played the role of an empathetic *sutradhar* in propelling Narendra Modi, the erstwhile chief minister of Gujarat, on to the centre-stage of national politics. The moment forced introspection. It raised questions about the nature of mediatisation in India and its social and political consequences.

This book grew out of those questions and they helped to trace a chronological pathway through contemporary developments and mass mobilisations that had played out over the earlier three years. In the end what came into view was a spiral of mediatisation, with its ever-widening gyres, which took shape in the half-decade from 2011 to 2015, beginning with the India Against Corruption mobilisations (2011) and the public protests against the gang rape of Jyoti Singh Pandey (2012), to the Delhi elections of 2013 and 2015 and the general election of 2014. I go on to argue that this period has put an indelible stamp on the way India and Indians seek to communicate in contemporary times, not only during protests and elections, but also in their everyday interactions.

Those years saw a sharp spike in global capital flows into the country; an emphatic consolidation of market presence achieved by home-grown corporate behemoths, which then invested heavily in the media space; and the never-ending expansion and influence of global internet giants, like Google, Facebook and Twitter, within the country. The period witnessed not only the further augmentation of mainstream media—in terms of the rising circulation figures of newspapers and increases in the number of television channels—but also an unprecedented proliferation of path-breaking communication technologies and social media platforms. New geographical spaces, some of which had hitherto remained unaffected by the influences of mediatisation, now began to be included within its sphere, even as new discourses seeped in communal rhetoric emerged.

The research I did was largely qualitative, based on detailed readings on the media and related subjects, which included a close scrutiny of the content generated by newspapers, television, and social media of the time, supplemented by the occasional supporting interview to understand a nuance here, or a prevailing reality there. The Delhi-centricity of the research could be faulted, but I would argue that given the pole position occupied by the city-state as the country's political capital, it emerges—almost by default—as the primary site of pan-national media engagement.

In order to contextualise the five mass mobilisations dwelt upon within these pages, an attempt has been made to provide a detailed pre-history for each. This back story, to my mind, is important in order to understand how, for instance, the India Against Corruption (IAC) campaign could draw its relevance from the fact that corruption as a theme had been a major trope in Indian journalism since independence; how gender-based violence—long dismissed as soft news—came to be framed as a story of exceptional 'national interest' during the protests over Jyoti Singh Pandey's gangrape; or why this particular gangrape, and no other, received the kind of attention it did; or how an unknown political entity like the Aam Aadmi Party (AAP), which had debuted in late 2012, catapulted itself to power in Delhi a year later; or how Narendra Modi's use of the media has been shaped by the Gujarat pogrom of 2002; or, indeed—how did a party that evoked universal condemnation for being a quitter in 2014 come back to win sixty-seven of the seventy seats in the Delhi assembly in 2015, in spite of a hostile mainstream media?

The events dealt with in these pages, given their high-level mediatisation, suggested themselves. The IAC protests of 2011 were considered a seedbed of innovative strategies of communication, including emerging technologies like mobile telephony. The coverage of, and response to, the gang rape of Jyoti Singh in December 2012, saw both continuity and change in the mass communication and self-communication methods adopted a year earlier, during the IAC protests. I also tried to demonstrate how the material put out by older and newer media influenced and fed off each other, by citing samples of the coverage from that period. In researching the three elections—those to the Delhi assembly in 2013 and 2015, as well as the general election of 2014—that are dealt with in Chapters 4 and 5, efforts have been made to cite contemporary media content extensively. For instance, the pattern of tweeting that leaders adopted established how self-communication of one-to-many had become the prevalent model.

The book, even as it acknowledges that the media was a crucial factor in these discrete events, is careful not to essentialise this role. To argue, for instance, that elections can be won by the assiduous and strategic harnessing of media convergence would be a wrong surmise. There is really no guarantee that the media strategies that a Kejriwal or a Modi adopted in 2013, 2014, or 2015 would lead to similar electoral outcomes in the future. This is a particularly important cautionary note to strike, given the homogenisation that is now increasingly marking the electoral strategies of variegated political parties. Indeed, in a political field marked by great heterogeneity of communities along lines of religion, caste, class, culture, location, and ethnic background, this adoption of modular media practices is a disturbing trend, and could potentially hollow out democratic politics. Related to this is a major conundrum inherent in many mediatised societies: technological inclusion is easier to achieve than social inclusion. Media information can only contribute to change if other social, political, and economic conditions exist that are conducive to enabling people to receive such information and act upon it for their own self-interest.

There were moments while writing this book when I rued the fact that I had chosen this particular topic for study. A sector in constant flux seemed to move faster than I ever could, and playing catch up all the time was no fun. Sometimes, material drawn from Facebook posts and the like would vanish overnight, as fresh avatars of these pages, controlled by new teams, cropped up. But despite these constraints, if I have managed to capture some of the action and contextualised it to an extent, I would consider my job done.

New Delhi, September 2018 PAMELA PHILIPOSE

Acknowledgements

This book began as a research project supported by the Indian Council of Social Science Research (ICSSR) in the form of a two-year senior fellowship. The fellowship allowed me to temporarily leave the world of active journalism and do something that I have always wanted to do—try and make intellectual sense of the media, a field that I have been involved in ever since I joined *The Times of India* as a trainee journalist over three decades earlier. To ICSSR, which has a provision for awarding fellowships to non-academics, therefore, I owe many thanks. I especially wish to express my gratitude to the then member secretary, Ramesh Dadhich, and the independent jury that vetted my proposal and accepted it. I need to also acknowledge the uniformly polite and helpful manner in which those who headed ICSSR's unit for research fellowships discharged their responsibilities, as also that of their supporting staff.

In many ways, this book has been influenced by the insights of academics and interactions with friends. I am extremely indebted to the Jawaharlal Nehru University (JNU). That an institution of this kind, with its rich legacy of scholarship and array of world-class academics, actually exists in our midst should be a source of pride for every Indian. The attempts being made to undermine, even destroy, it is therefore disturbing. JNU was the affiliating institution for my research, according to ICSSR norms, and I wish to thank its administrative staff for the professional way in which they handled the process.

The Centre of Comparative Politics and Political Theory, JNU, was the department where my research was located. Two outstanding academics, Kamal Mitra Chenoy and Nivedita Menon, happened to be chairs of the Centre—the latter succeeding the former—through the duration of my study. My interactions with them were extremely helpful. In this context, I also need to acknowledge the role of Anuradha Chenoy, the then Professor and Chairperson of the Centre for Russian and Central Asian Studies, School of International Studies, JNU, who was among the first to encourage me to write a book and was always ready with timely advice. Thanks are due to Sanjay Kumar, Professor and Director at the Centre for the Study of Developing Societies, for allowing me to cite figures from his election data, while Pooja Bakshi helpfully tabulated data for purposes of this book.

I have engaged in conversations on this work with Zoya Hasan, a noted political scientist who has always taken a lively interest in the media, as well as with Tanika Sarkar and Sumit Sarkar, whose insights into the public sphere of nineteenth-century India are exceptional. Completing the circle of conversation are friends Antara Dev Sen, Pratik Kanjilal, and Parsa Venkateshwar Rao Jr, all former *Indian Express* colleagues; Rajeev Bhargava, Tani Bhargava, Ritu Menon, A. G. K. Menon, Suneeta Dhar, Seema Mustafa, Amrita Chhachhi, Sheba Chhachhi, Harsh Kapoor, Anil Chaudhury, Preeti Mehra, Ajith Pillai, Geeta Seshu, M. J. Pandey—and, of course, the exceptional Suresh Grover and Balvinder Gill.

I also had the good fortune to present parts of this book to communities of scholars and mediapersons. The first was at a seminar on 'The Power of Communication: The Media, Public Space and Participatory Democracy', convened by Sukumar Muralidharan in October 2015 at the Indian Institute of Advanced Study (IIAS), Shimla. The second was at 'Diginaka 2016', an event organised at the School of Media and Cultural Studies, Tata Institute of Social Sciences (TISS), Mumbai, in January 2016, and anchored by Anjali Monteiro and K. P. Jayasankar, Professors at the School of Media and Cultural Studies at TISS.

The ultimate phase of publishing this book has created its own circle of friends, including Nilanjana Majumdar and Roopa Sharma, senior executives with Orient BlackSwan, and my conscientious editor, Proteeti Banerjee.

Home has always been a primary site of discussions, which have ranged from the scholarly to the inane, so how can I not acknowledge the wonderful conversations we have had as a family? For this, my everlasting gratitude and love is due to Anish Vanaik and Samar Vanaik, both situated in different fields, but always engaged. Working on edgy research in the field of literature, Megha Anwer has also often joined in, as also my brother Prakash Philipose and sister-in-law Anna Philipose.

Finally, this book would never have been written if it was not for the constant and informed support of Achin Vanaik, life partner, comrade, sounding board, and sharer in life's tribulations and celebrations.

one

Changing Journalism

New Media Shapes, New Mediascapes

Changes in communication technologies and media platforms are transforming the world around us in ways that often seem sharply contradictory and with consequences that are simultaneously tangible and amorphous, predictable and unintended, disturbing and elevating. We realise that our social environment is being altered radically by new communication technologies and yet, not being endowed with the gift of hindsight, we are clueless about where all this is leading us.

We recognise that the media are often ideologically and commercially linked to existing social, economic and political systems and serve to reflect them in order to extend these spheres of influence. Both digital conglomerates and large media houses exercise power in all its forms, whether social, economic, political, or symbolic, and strike osmotic relationships with governments and elites in order to further mutual interests. So perceiving communication technologies and the media they support as socially and politically liberatory in and of themselves, as is often done, would betray a determinism that overlooks the manifold contexts of their uses, many of which conform to the worst extractivist aspects of capitalism.

At the same time, we also know that these technologies are potentially able to 'make possible new forms of social interaction, modify or undermine old forms of interaction, create new foci and new venues for action and interaction, and thereby serve to restructure existing social relations'.[1] They lend themselves to the articulation of counter-hegemonic narratives and help individuals, social activists and collectivities—constituting the public—to gain visibility and voice.

The word 'public' has been theorised a great deal over the twentieth century. Jurgen Habermas put it across in a seemingly simple introductory sentence in his classic work, *The Structural Transformation of the Public Sphere*: 'We call events and occasions "public" when they are open to all in contrast to closed or exclusive affairs ....'[2] Habermas then brings the media into the frame by delineating the public sphere which allows people within a society to exercise their capacity to arrive at a common understanding of their best interests. The public sphere, Habermas recognises, is itself restructured and dominated by the mass media. Inherent in the word 'public' is also the keyword 'community', which Raymond Williams traces to some of its original meanings: the 'commons', or the common people; 'a sense of common identity and characteristics'.[3] This takes us to another keyword of Williams—'society'—the primary meaning of which, as he puts it, is companionship or fellowship.[4] Then we come to 'culture' which, according to Williams, is one of the two or three most complicated words in the English language. What concerns us here is 'culture' in one of the modern senses of the term that Williams delineates: a noun describing 'a general process of intellectual, spiritual and aesthetic development'.[5] Neither community nor society, nor indeed culture, would have been possible without 'communication', which derives from 'communicate', which was about 'making common to many, impart'.[6] But, as Williams points out, it is in the twentieth century, given new means of 'passing information and maintaining social contact', that the term communications came into currency and was predominantly used in reference to the press and broadcasting industry.[7]

Communications, it could then be said, is one of the central building blocks of human sociality, or the capacity of human beings to develop social links and live as a community. Christian

Fuchs provides a clear understanding of the links between these various aspects when he observes that

> Information (cognition), communication and co-operation are three nested and integrated modes of sociality (Hofkirchner 2013). Every medium can be social in one or more of these senses. All media are information technologies. They provide information to human beings. This information enters into the human realm of knowledge as social facts that shape thinking.[8]

Benedict Anderson recognises that it was 'print capitalism'—one of the early capitalist enterprises of book publishing—that helped to create the 'embryo of the nationally imagined community',[9] and advances in communication technology could conjure up the imagined community to illiterates and those who speak other languages.[10] India's national movement saw the media, ranging from newspapers—some of which were owned by elites within the Indian population and possibly influenced decision-making during the national movement for independence—to the more plebian-focused posters and pamphlets of the day, play just such a role. In post-independent India, as in many other parts of the world, it could be argued that print media, followed by television, became important interpreters of quotidian realities and emerged as important sites of an imagined consumer-centric community, a role enhanced dramatically with the unprecedented flows of global capital that came into the country following the opening up of the markets in 1991 in the wake of the paradigm-shifting liberalisation of the Indian economy.

Economic liberalisation saw the majority of the country's mainstream media houses, whether print or television, adopt a business model that was advertisement-oriented, and where the target audience of the media shifted from readers/viewers to advertisers. It was not just advertisements that linked mainstream media directly and intimately to the market. Indian corporate bodies, some of them with deep political connections and ambitions, also began to invest directly in the media businesses to promote their business interests and influence policymaking by buying over existing newspaper houses and television channels, or setting up new ones.

The markets and the media thus came to be linked in a feedback loop, with the markets ploughing in capital and drawing profits made through the media's capacity to create and propagate demands, dreams and desires for the goods and services offered by the markets. The growing synergy of the media and the market created more than profits for shareholders; it also fashioned a distinct category of people who benefited disproportionately from economic liberalisation and who expressed their euphoria over, and appetite for, the goods and services offered by global markets. It was also a category that sought to be upwardly mobile and ambitious, not just for themselves but for India as 'their' country. In his exposition of the 'great Indian middle class', Pavan K. Varma argues that this is a category of people who are 'convinced that India's destiny is about to change, and that the country is at last set to get its due in the international arena'.[11] The religious identity of this category—primarily Hindu—and its caste composition—primarily upper caste—could be seen as factors that fuelled the onward march of Hindu nationalism from the late 1990s onwards.

Such an enthusiastic embracing of consumerism, globalisation and nationalism was the zeitgeist of the times for middle-class India. It led to those who constituted this class to actively disengage themselves from those who were not like them, who happened to be 'different', either because of their religious, caste or tribal identity, or marginalised in some way. Media personnel, themselves largely drawn from the more privileged sections of society and overwhelmingly upper caste,[12] were closely imbricated in a process that deepened class distinctions and urban–rural divides, fed off these popular attitudes, and furthered them in equal measure. The demand to retain emerging readers by valourising their life choices, the pressure to accommodate advertisers, the increasing consumerism that marked urban lifestyles, and the need to fend off competition impacted decisively on editorial content, as observed by academics like J. V. Vilanilam, Daya Thussu, and

Arvind Rajagopal.[13] There was a conspicuous narrowing of themes, lightening of treatment, segmentation of information, and corporatisation of content. In her exposition of the new middle class, Leela Fernandes notes changes in media content, which included television talk shows that 'specifically target a middle class audience and address a range of issues such as the cultural effects of consumerism, changing youth attitudes, problems of small investors, and changing gender roles'.[14]

With profit becoming a major determinant of media content, mass newspaper readerships—to take one media form—were consciously fragmented into identifiable, homogeneous sub-groups, which were then marketed to potential advertisers looking for target audiences to place their products. So markedly market-centric had the mainstream media grown over the first ten years of the twenty-first century that a 2011 survey found that, on an average, only 2 per cent of coverage in the country's top circulating newspapers dealt with rural issues, and even within that category, 36 per cent focused on non-agrarian issues like crime, violence, and politics.[15]

This book is an attempt to critically analyse the role of new communication technologies and the media in general in shaping some important historical moments that have played out in this country on a mass scale over the first five years of the second decade of the twenty-first century. This period, from 2011–15, is termed here as the 'mediatised half decade', with the sharp rise in the use of the internet and mobile telephony. It was a point where the country saw a simultaneous efflorescence of older media, comprising largely print and television, as well as the emergence of newer media, representing a mélange of communication technologies, interactive digital platforms, and communication modes and practices. Both categories were simultaneously attracting investments, market traction, and public involvement in this period.

Older and newer media are often regarded as binaries, but there is a fallacy in such a perspective. Each category may have its distinct ways of functioning and spheres of influence, but no single media platform in contemporary times exists in a vacuum. This is also why the argument that digital media does not impact those outside urban, networked spaces is unsustainable. The digital divide does exist in terms of millions of people not being able to access the use of new communication technologies because of their geographical and social location, but the content generated by digital media does not remain confined to merely digital spaces, going on to permeate newspaper and television content as well as general conversations.

One of the laws of communication technologies, according to John Naughton, is that newer media are generally additive rather than substitutive, 'which is a fancy way of saying that new technologies generally don't wipe out older ones',[16] although the arrival of newer media does change the media ecosystem. What typically happens, according to him, is that as newer media emerge, they challenge the existing media, which then either adapt to the newcomer or fade into irrelevance. To illustrate this trajectory, he cites the example of how the arrival of broadcast television in Britain in the 1950s led to two distinct transformations in the newspaper market in that country. While the mass circulating tabloids adapted to the change by becoming parasitic on television content, the 'quality' broadsheets responded by offering the public more commentary and features, rather than just news.

In India, too, evidence of such media convergence emerged at various junctures and the consequent inter-media links thus went on to transform public culture in decisive ways. Take, for instance, the thread of consequences, intended and unintended, that was unspooled in 1982 with the decision to broadcast the Asian Games in colour through State-run Doordarshan using INSAT 1A. It brought together a cluster of new communication infrastructure, tools and technologies—satellites, transmitter networks, outdoor broadcasting vans (OBVs) and, a little later, VCR and cable. It also resulted in a convergence in content and commercial intent, with television programming now privileging entertainment a great deal more than earlier. There also came about a widespread infusion of cinema into television; a new focus on making celebrities out of showbiz and sports personalities; and in rendering news as 'infotainment' for media 'consumers'.

If the old media had created the prospect of large numbers 'moving from peasant to couch-potato in a single generation,'[17] the couch potato was soon to turn into a mobile phone and internet addict within a few short years, thanks to the explosion of Wi-Fi broadband services at relatively affordable rates. It was into this altered media landscape that new communication technologies and internet media found their way, shaped by flows of global capital that had earlier changed the mainstream media scene.

When the internet in India was thrown open to private players in 1996, with the government issuing licenses for those operating net-based services, unsurprisingly it was the urban, educated, largely English-speaking middle classes who embraced it the fastest. The earliest years of this phase saw a few dedicated bloggers waving the flag. One ardent blogger put out an interesting self-definition of his cohort in 2006: 'For the urban twentysomethings with intellectual pretentions and the hope of being spotted by the commissioning editor of a publishing house, it's the new P3, or rather the virtual world's own India International Centre.'[18] By the following year, the number of bloggers in India was estimated at over 100,000,[19] and what was particularly striking about Indian bloggers around this period was that they had become both politically confident and localised. An early initiative called 'BlogathonIndia, April 2008' was staged to influence voters during the Karnataka assembly election of that year, and one of its intentions was to encourage people to go beyond English and blog in regional languages.[20]

Yet it was only in 2010, with the coming of 3G services, that the relationship between the internet and the Indian middle classes really deepened. Communication academics Sunetra Sen Narayan and Shalini Narayanan note that the introduction of third-generation (3G) services in 2010 was a prime factor in the growth of the internet in India and the creation of what they term as 'Media 2.0'. The number of internet users was to grow from seven million in 2001 to twenty-five times that number over the next twelve years.[21] The compact was sealed by the increasing popularity of social media like Orkut and MySpace, which gave way in time to later-day variants like Facebook, Twitter, and Instagram.

It is important to observe here that the radio, which could potentially have addressed the information needs of people living in the periphery, could not do so because of the strict control the governments of the day exercised on it. The experiment to create an independent public broadcaster has failed conspicuously, and to this day news cannot be broadcast on radio platforms that are independent of government.

While the internet could not breach the urban–rural, rich–poor divides in those early days, the nifty mobile phone could and did. It went on to ring out to the world that India had become, in the words of Robin Jeffery and Assa Doron, a 'cell phone nation'. Introduced in 1995–96, the mobile phone ownership in India overtook fixed connections by 2004, allowing large sections of the population to leapfrog over the landline technology phase. Fuelling this unstoppable growth were several factors, including a telling rise in the average incomes of the urban middle class, as well as the plummeting user costs, which came down from Rs 16 per minute in 2000 to Rs 1.20 per minute in 2005.[22] Another significant reason for the popularity of the mobile phone was that it helped to enhance the incomes and livelihood options of those at the bottom of the economic pyramid, who found it worth their while to invest in a cheap model. Meanwhile, for those at the higher end of the income spectrum, mobile phones with their ever-advancing operating systems were the new gizmos in town, allowing their users to not only project status, but also download music, play video games, navigate city spaces, take photographs, and browse through their Facebook posts and Twitter feed on the hop.

2010 AS SPRINGBOARD

It is against this period of reverberating change in technologies and social media practices that we should look at 2010 anew. It could be considered as the year that served as a springboard for the mediatised half-decade on which this book focuses. The entertainment and media sector was facing a profitable future at this juncture, if we are to go by the cautiously optimistic assessment of PricewaterhouseCoopers (PwC). It noted that in 2010, India had recorded one of the highest growths in the entertainment and media sector, with its value standing at INR 646 billion, even as most countries were emerging from the recession that had begun in 2008. The report also pointed out that the largest chunk of profits had come from the non-digital segment, largely from television, print, and film, and expressed the hope that once digital infrastructure was shored up, digital media too would catch up. As international auditors and consultants to industry, PwC's interest in the Indian media and entertainment sector was itself a reflection of how central this sector had become, not only for the Indian economy, but also for international media and communications conglomerates.

Such keenness was by no means misplaced. Indian markets were expanding at a brisk pace as new communication technologies and media came to play a decisive role in the lives of millions. The Census of 2011 underlined this, reporting that while a little less than 47 per cent households in the country had toilets within the premises, 47.2 per cent households possessed television sets and 63.2 per cent had telephones.[23]

Those faithful television sets squeezed into modest abodes had a significant part to play in shaping many historical processes in post-liberalisation India, from patterns of consumption and assertions of citizenship to defining family politics, national politics, and sexuality. More importantly, television became an important avenue through which 'new modes of exercising power'[24] were practised. By 2010, the moving images on the television screen were touching almost every life in India, even in the deep rural hinterland, and doing so twenty-four hours a day, seven days a week. An estimated fifteen million new TV sets were sold that year.[25] The 2010 global Deloitte study on 'Media Democracy' revealed that

92 per cent of Indian respondents ranked 'watching television' as their top media source, with revenue in the industry growing at 15 per cent in 2010, attributed to the massive DTH (direct-to-home) expansion at that point.[26]

Newspapers—television's older counterpart in the mainstream media category—were also displaying a surprising resilience when compared to their Western counterparts. Newspaper circulation had fallen in twenty out of thirty countries of the Organisation for Economic Co-operation and Development (OECD) between 2007–09, with the UK and the US reporting declines of 25 and 30 per cent, respectively.[27] In India, by contrast, where a generation of neo-literate newspaper readers was emerging, the newspaper industry as a whole was estimated at INR 178.7 billion in 2010, a rise of 10.7 per cent from the previous year. In north India, it was the Hindi newspapers that were establishing a distinct presence, with a growth rate in 2010 of 9 per cent, as compared to 3 per cent in 2009.[28] In her book, *Headlines from the Heartland*, Sevanti Ninan quotes a 2004 interview where Suresh Dubey, a circulation manager of Hindi daily *Nava Bharat*, observed how twenty to twenty-five copies of a newspaper were now being sent to a village, instead of the one copy that used to be the case a decade earlier. He attributed this to two factors: the spread of education and the awareness that the electronic media had created.[29] Vanita Kohli-Khandekar, writing in 2012, also noted the 'aspirational value of newspapers' in the Hindi language, adding that the fact that they accounted for only 20 per cent of the market where literacy was about 65 per cent also meant that there was significant 'headroom for growth'.[30] Important to flag here too is a secondary impact: the emergence of an Hindi-speaking elite that could, and did, replace the post-colonial English-speaking one.

It needs to be noted here that while such a proliferation of television channels and newspapers should have contributed towards creating a pluralistic and vibrant media scene, it did not do so. Instead, by the end of the first decade, there was conspicuously greater monopolisation of media presence and homogenisation of media content, with the big players having successfully expanded their market presence through acquisitions and mergers. The numbers, as Paranjoy Guha Thakurta observes, 'often conceals the fact [that] there is dominance over specific markets and market segments by a few players—in other words, the markets are often oligopolistic in character.'[31] As an example of this kind of growth, Thakurta cites the case of the Hindi language daily, *Dainik Bhaskar*. It began as a single edition newspaper in 1958, but by 2010 it had seven newspapers, two magazines, and seventeen radio stations running under its banner. To take another example, by 2010, Bennett Coleman & Co., which owned India's biggest English language daily, also had a strong footprint in the radio, television, and digital sectors as part of its vertical integration business strategy, with content from one very often making its way to the other.

The real transformations, however, were taking place in mobile telephony and digital media. The mobile phone was fast becoming the vector of change, providing 'access to global flows of knowledge; altered local cultural practices; mobilised political and social movements; and challenged gender dynamics'.[32] Sales of mobile phone handsets had touched new highs with 223 million having been sold in 2010 alone, and there were no less than twenty-eight mobile phone manufacturers, several of them Indian, jostling for presence in the market.[33] As for mobile subscriptions, it was now an estimated 791 million—of which 500 million were characterised as 'active' mobile users. In terms of penetration, mobile telephony had overtaken television by 50 per cent. The mobile phone and the humble short messaging service (SMS) were to play a decisive role in the India Against Corruption (IAC) mobilisations, as we shall see, and by 2010 sending an SMS had become a way of life for many. Airtel reported that in 2010 alone, 90 billion such messages had been sent via its network, which worked out to something like 2,850 messages every second.

Social media was gaining traction simultaneously. In 2010, Indian social media users numbered around 33.2 million, with the average browser estimated to be spending twenty-six minutes online every day, with most of this activity being conducted through internet cafes. Facebook claimed a user base of 23.9 million, with 79 per cent of them below thirty years of age and 71 per cent male. Orkut, now defunct, was also popular in India, and in fact 35 per cent of its global traffic was in India, with the number of users estimated at 18.7 million. Twitter, which was to expand its wings dramatically by the time of the Delhi gang rape of December 2012, had a modest footprint of around 2.7 million users in 2010.[34]

A striking aspect of the youth cohort emerging from the liberalisation years was their immersion in the market economy, leading a media academic to comment that while the youth growing up in the media-saturated environment in the West half-a-century earlier had successfully 'rebelled out' from their parents' generation,

> the youth in Asia, influenced by marketing strategies of the globalized media, are in the process of 'rebelling in' to the middle class. In fact, they are being transformed by the agency of a powerful and persuasive advertising industry and the media in general to become 'aggressive consumers'.[35]

Commercial interests recruited the support of young social media users in a concerted manner. The sales strategy of US restaurant chain, Pizza Hut, to draw in young corporate professionals, is a case in point. They were encouraged to 'like' its Facebook page and access discounts. In 2010, Pizza Hut's Facebook page had one of the largest number of followers in the restaurant category, indicating how digital presence and advertising could now work in a seamless way to create networks of market allegiance.

By 2010, India was among Facebook's top five countries, with the number of users having shot up from eight million to 15.5 million within six months from March to October that year, most of whom were urban, male (70 per cent), and young—80 per cent being below thirty years of age.[36] We will be considering in Chapter 2 how Facebook was used in the IAC protests. The unprecedented growth it had in the country prompted Facebook to choose India as the site for its first offices in Asia that year.[37] It was a relationship that grew with the years, and among the factors persuading Facebook to clinch an US$ 19 billion deal to acquire the messaging service WhatsApp in 2014 was the fact that 10 per cent of the messaging application's 450 million subscribers was Indian.

This was the early genesis of the intimate relationship that Facebook–WhatsApp was to have in the country, influencing greatly not only patterns of life and consumer choices, but also electoral exercises. As we shall see, the 2014 general election provided abundant evidence of the nexus. This is a trend that will be further accentuated in the 2019 general election, given the base of an estimated 250 million Facebook and 200 million WhatsApp users.[38]

It was not just as consumers that young Indians embraced available communication technologies. In each of the mass mobilisations dealt with in this book, youth constituted a critical cohort, with their comfort with new communication technologies contributing towards throwing up new forms of social and political engagement. A newspaper report, capturing the prevailing mood during Anna Hazare's fast at the Ramlila Maidan in August 2011 in Delhi, illustrated this eloquently. It noted how, even after darkness fell and most of the protesters had left the site, 'the young, the urban and the restless' continued to roam around the *maidan*, photographing themselves compulsively on their camera phones.[39] This raw, youthful, mediatised presence was to be replicated in the social mobilisations that followed, whether it was the gang rape protests of December 2012 or the electoral campaigns which were soon to change the country's political landscape.

Twitter was also making a modest appearance on the firmament, having been tested for the first time during the Mumbai attacks of late 2008, although it had a convoluted form of dispatching messages with tweets having to be sent across as short mail messages. Yet, despite this, Twitter became a source of real-time information so rapidly that it prompted the authorities to prohibit its use while security operations were on. By 2010, Twitter had around two million users in the country. Although Twitter was a long way behind Facebook in terms of Indian users, they still constituted the world's third highest number of users, after those in the US and Germany.[40]

That the majority of social media users were located in the five major metros of the country was to be expected, but evidence of their capacity to permeate into regions beyond the mainstream also kept surfacing. In mid-2010, during the interregnum that came to be known as the 'summer of the stone pelters', popular anger over the use of force by the Indian security forces rapidly spread across the Kashmir Valley with local people, including young children, hurling stones at them. By August that year, there were at least 120[41] casualties, mostly caused by police firing. This was a phase marked by mass arrests of both political leaders and 'stone pelters' under draconian laws, including the state-specific Public Safety Act (PSA), in a scenario of unending curfews and strikes. Despite the clampdown on mainstream media and suspension of mobile telephone services, thousands of young people across Kashmir kept returning to the streets, time and again, leading to speculation that social media was playing a significant role in fomenting such activism. Some dismissed the possibility of any direct link between street protesters and social media users, given that laptops and computers were accessed by only a minuscule section of the elite.[42] The fact, however, remained that Kashmir had higher literacy and income levels than the rest of the country and a younger demography: 48 per cent of its population falling within the age group of 15–35 years. These were factors that made the region a hospitable ground for social media platforms, more so given the prevailing censorship regime in the state.

A clearer picture of this pattern emerged in a survey commissioned by the Government of India's Ministry of Home,[43] which found that there were more than 100 Facebook accounts that existed in 2010 with names like 'Free Kashmir', 'Freedom for Kashmir', 'Free United Kashmir', 'Mission Free Kashmir', 'We Want Free Kashmir', 'Pakistan-India Go Back, We Want Free Kashmir', and so on. A year after that fateful summer, it became clearer that the use of Facebook as a tool of protest had increased dramatically in the Valley, with the platform now enjoying a support base running into the thousands.[44]

TECHNOLOGIES COALESCE

By the beginning of the second decade of the twenty-first century, with digital media changing the media ecology even more emphatically than television had in the last decade of the twentieth century, it became clear that media content, practices and technologies were coalescing in innumerable ways.

India was now witnessing media convergence, which was bringing together older and newer media in various ways on a scale never hitherto imagined. The rapid spread of communication technology in a disparate, heterogeneous, unequal country like India over the first decade of the twenty-first century allowed it to join the ranks of the most mediatised societies in the world. It is the mobile phone and the internet that acted as the enablers of this leap. If the mobile phone allowed convergence between socially and geographically disparate communities and individuals, the internet engendered technological convergence through a range of functionalities. The internet provided '(i) *communication* services such as email and Internet telephony (ii) *broadcasting* services, such as webcasting and electronic community services (iii) *publication* services such as publishing electronic journals, e-books and electronic manuals on the World Wide Web and (iv) *electronic commerce* and electronic business services'.[45] It is because of their capacity for enabling such wide convergence that mobile telephony and internet media have far deeper impacts than television did two decades earlier, potentially creating 'a cornucopia of new possibilities'.[46]

Newspapers, to take one example, could no longer remain untouched by digital media, and set up their own interactive websites and Facebook pages in order to survive. In much the same way, content from newspapers and television were hyperlinked by users to social media platforms, circulating not just in the brick-and-mortar space, but in the digital one as well. Ownership changes underlined content convergence, as large mainstream media houses aggressively embraced cross-media ownership.

Media convergence, or variations thereof, has been understood in various ways, depending on whether it is technology, the political economy, or the behaviour patterns of media users that is being privileged in such theorisation. Technology creates convergence by allowing voice, data, and video messages to be transported through a single physical telecom infrastructure.[47] But while there can be no disputing the centrality of technology in creating media convergence since it forms the material basis for the phenomenon, others have viewed convergence from the vantage point of content. Henry Jenkins defines media convergence as 'a situation in which multiple media systems coexist and where media content flows fluidly across them'.[48] He links media convergence with two other concepts, participatory culture and collective intelligence, and argues that internet-mediated convergence cannot take place without the user's active participation in seeking out new information, making connections, and dispersing media content. Manuel Castells argues that convergence is 'fundamentally cultural and takes place primarily in the minds of the communicative subjects who integrate various modes and channels of communication in their practice and in their interaction with each other'.[49]

The concept of a 'hybrid media system' has been posited by Andrew Chadwick in the context of political news, while emphasising the need to understand how newer media practices adapt and integrate the logics of older media practices, and vice versa. Actors within the hybrid media system, Chadwick argues, 'create, tap, or steer information flows in ways that suit their goals and in ways that modify, enable or disable others' agency across and between a range of older and newer media settings'.[50] The term 'media assemblage', which has its origins in art and literary studies, has also been employed in this context. Amit S. Rai, in his theorisation of media assemblage from the vantage point of the media spectator, cites the observation made by Jay David Bolter and Richard Grusin:

'Our culture conceives of each medium or constellation of media as it responds to, redeploys, competes with, and reforms other media. In the first instance, we may think of something like a historical progression, of newer media remediating their predecessors.'[51] What is emphasised in this reading is the organic linkages between older and newer media.

In their 2008 editorial, 'Convergence Culture', Jenkins and Mark Deuze capture the early perplexity over media convergence, noting that alongside the corporate-controlled broadcast or mass media channels, there is also the bewildering array of community and alternative media, from pirate radio and the SMS to pictures taken on a phone. They also point to the new 'hybrid spaces' of corporately created platforms, such as Flickr or YouTube, which 'provide a common environment for grassroots media makers, both individuals and groups, to come together and share what they have created with each other'.[52] Today, the scene is even more densely converged than it was when Jenkins and Deuze wrote that editorial. Facebook, for instance, which brought all these activities on to a single platform, had still not acquired its present status as a digital leviathan. Convergence of this kind had many contradictory aspects: on the one hand, 'this "democratization" of media use signals a broadening of opportunities for individuals and grassroots communities to tell stories', and on the other, media companies sought to extend their reach by 'merging, co-opting, converging and synergizing their brands and intellectual properties across all of these channels'.[53] Convergence, they argued, had thus both a top-down corporate-driven process and a bottom-up consumer-driven process. The concern that the former process could overtake the latter was one that grew with time.

The fact, of course, is that some interests and entities stood to gain enormously from media convergence. Media academic Robert W. McChesney terms it the 'marriage of the internet to really existing capitalism', and highlighted how the internet, supposed champion of increased consumer power, has today become one of the greatest generators of monopoly in economic history, with new digital industries going from being 'competitive to oligopolistic to monopolistic at breakneck speeds'.[54]

In India, the Reliance Industries Limited's 2014 takeover of Network 18 Media and Investments Ltd could be seen as a classic 'marriage of the internet to existing capitalism'. With that one acquisition, India's biggest business house also became the country's largest media entity. The press release issued by RIL, which was also on the threshold of launching its fourth-generation (4G) wireless broadband network, was clear about the company's ambitions: 'The acquisition will differentiate Reliance's 4G business by providing a unique amalgamation at the intersection of telecom, web and digital commerce via a suite of premier digital properties.'[55]

With political actors and social elites pushing for and achieving even greater integration of the Indian economy with markets, media convergence has had serious repercussions, including extremely negative ones, for media pluralism, unbiased content, freedom of expression, and information, all the more so because the country's mass media in their varying forms have always constituted a major site on which the Indian nation-state has been imagined and contested, and where power is decided and legitimised.

MEDIATISED HALF-DECADE

This book seeks to explore the social and political impacts of the cascading dynamic of media convergence in India in what is termed the 'mediatised half-decade'. Organised within a partially chronological framework, the main conceptual argument offered here is that the years between 2011 and 2015 were central to the mediatisation of contemporary India, witnessing as they did five major media-driven mobilisations that changed the nature of India's public culture.

Each one of these discrete developments saw a wide range of actors make optimum use of variegated media platforms, leading to the creation of an inflection point in the mediatisation of the country, its society and politics. The term 'mediatisation' has been widely used in communications theory. It has been defined as a general process by which transmission of symbolic forms (linguistic expressions, gestures, actions, works of art, and so on) 'becomes increasingly mediated by the technical and institutional apparatus of the media industries',[56] and the rapid proliferation of institutions of mass communication is viewed as one of the key transformations associated with the rise of modern societies.

Which, then, were these five developments? The first was the 2011 India Against Corruption (IAC) protests, which were arguably one of the largest and most prolonged civil society mobilisations in India's post-independence history. Chapter 2 focuses on this interlude in contemporary history. The protests, which were driven by the promise of ridding the country of corruption, while being framed as a 'social movement', had immensely significant political consequences that have directly led to the creation of one political party—the Aam Aadmi Party (AAP)—and powered another (the Bharatiya Janata Party [BJP]), to rule at the Centre.

Given their scale and pan-India impact, the IAC protests proved to be a seedbed of new communication ideas and practices. This chapter begins with an exploration of how corruption as a major theme had played out in the mainstream newspapers of post-independent India, partly because it fed into the everyday conversations of the newspaper-reading middle classes of the day, and partly because exposing corruption provided media entities with the moral ballast they needed to shore up credibility. What is also striking is that over the years, newer media platforms successfully kept the theme of corruption alive for middle-class audiences, whether through films, news channels, internet platforms, or social media.

The IAC protests also reflected a change in the manner in which the media was used for public mobilisation and political articulation on corruption. For the first time, interactions between the IAC team and the Government of India were made public in near real time through regular media briefings, and correspondence between Anna Hazare and the government was deliberately leaked to the media. Also for the first time, one event—the Hazare arrest on 16 August 2011—flooded out all other news on mainstream platforms for at least twenty-four hours, indicating that the media had simply shed their responsibilities as impartial observers and become participants in the action.

Chapter 3 focuses on the gang rape of Jyoti Singh Pandey in a public bus in New Delhi on 16 December 2012, noting that this outpouring of public outrage this time had no identifiable leadership to speak of, with people appearing to have 'spontaneously' thronged the sites of protest led largely by the convergence of content across a range of media platforms. One of the factors for the deep, wide-ranging, geographically spread-out public scrutiny given to this particular incident was, it is argued, directly linked to the unprecedented longevity the mainstream media and social media had accorded it. The book critically examines the content generated in this period in order to understand how this unique moment in the history of the Indian media actually came about and how it impacted popular notions of sexual violation, gender rights, and cultural resistance. The media's understanding of rape culture is also interrogated in this chapter.

The year 2013 was marked by the unprecedented arrival on the political scene of a new political party, the Aam Aadmi Party (AAP), which went on to assume power in Delhi through a coalition government. The year 2014 saw the Bharatiya Janata Party (BJP) notch a victory in the sixteenth Lok Sabha elections that no political party had achieved in three decades, and made a party founded on the notion of Hindu nationalism as the prime pole of Indian politics. Finally, in 2015, we saw AAP return to power in Delhi, winning an unprecedented sixty-seven seats in a seventy-member assembly. These three highly mediatised elections, which took place over consecutive years, are dealt with in Chapters 4 and 5.

Beginning with a brief examination of the various theories of media election coverage, Chapter 4 considers the Obama elections, particularly the one of 2008, considered the 'first twenty-first century campaign' in the US and a template for many electoral battles, both in the US and the rest of the world thereafter. Before focusing on the BJP-led NDA parliamentary election victory of 2014, which gave the BJP a full majority for the first time in its thirty-five years of existence as a party, it revisits the BJP's innovative media strategies for the general elections of 2004 and 2009. There can be no denying the formidable standards in mediatised electioneering that the BJP had set in these two elections, but the 2014 campaign represented a quantum leap in its use of the media and the presidential-style projection of its prime ministerial candidate, Narendra Modi, fuelled by seemingly unending reserves of financial support.

The chapter also traces the evolution of Modi's understanding of media deployment for political purposes from the early days of his political career and stints as Gujarat chief minister, and argues that this personalisation of the 2014 campaign was key to his party's handsome victory. A detailed examination of the Modi election strategies of that period reveals that many of them borrowed not only from the Obama election campaigns of 2008 and 2012, but also from the AAP's campaign of 2013, where alternative media was employed along with alternative ways of using social media.

The next chapter explores how AAP's media outreach, crafted by Arvind Kejriwal, paved its way to power in the Delhi state assembly elections in December 2013, but failed when it came to delivering on its promises largely because of continuous public scrutiny. It goes on to delineate AAP's preparations for the Delhi election of 2015, which saw a re-gigging of the party's media strategies by expanding its volunteer base and involving many young technocrats in the campaign. The BJP, as the principal rival, was taken on frontally in a manner that resonated with Delhi's aspirational middle class, especially the youth, some of whom would have undoubtedly voted for the BJP in the 2014 general elections. The sheer scale of the 2015 victory was particularly notable, given the less-than-friendly mainstream media reportage that had dogged the party throughout this period.

The final section of this chapter looks at the commonalities between the Modi campaign of 2014 and the two that Kejriwal conducted in 2013 and 2015, respectively. Taken together, they would seem to indicate that elections can indeed be won by the assiduous and strategic harnessing of media convergence. Such a conclusion, it is argued, would be overly facile. The very fact that the BJP, despite its array of mediatised election strategies and the personal campaigning of Prime Minister Modi in the Delhi election of 2015, did not go on to win it would indicate that even heavily mediatised election strategies can fall apart if they do not resonate with people, and external political factors can militate against such an outcome.

Chapter 6, the last chapter of this book, examines certain international and national trends. The age of satellite television during the 'roaring nineties' shaped all media in distinct ways, as we have seen. The difference between the churn unleashed by satellite television and that by digital media, is that while both created pathways that allowed global capital to access markets across the world and in India, the latter have been able to achieve this more optimally and at a far more bruising pace. This has been made possible thanks to the emergence of large internet monopolies that are decisively shaping the media universe and a common human future. As one academic perceptively observed, digital corporations 'take advantage first and foremost, of network effects which tend to produce "winner-takes-all" markets with almost no middle class of midsized firms'.[57] Against this macro-environment, an attempt is made to understand how newer media technologies have changed forever the way Indians communicated and understood the world, and why media content has begun to mutate in unexpected, even confusing, ways.

The truly interesting aspect of the times we live in, as will be seen in the forthcoming pages, is the deceptively discreet way in which mediatisation has brought about such tectonic shifts in our lives. Robin Jeffery and Assa Doron write about how a new device like the mobile phone, despite initially meeting with ambivalence, even resistance, from ordinary people, became so intrinsic to their daily existence over a period of time that they could no longer imagine life without it. When hundreds of thousands of protesters are urged to converge at a particular spot in real time through a short mail messages or a tweet; when campaign speeches can be consumed in multiple ways—at the venue itself, as a report in a newspaper or television channel, as a video on a mobile phone, as a Facebook post, a Whatsapp message, or an Instagram image; when the smartphone screen becomes the sole communications site on which day-to-day negotiations are transacted, we are talking about radical transformations in the use of the media and the way society relates to the information they impart. It is not just mass action or an electoral foray that have become so crucially dependent on multiple media, but the very fabric of human-to-human interaction is increasingly being woven on the looms of communication technologies.

NOTES AND REFERENCES

1. John B. Thompson, 1990, *Ideology and Modern Culture* (Cambridge: Polity Press), 225.

2. Jurgen Habermas, translated by Thomas Burger, 1989, *The Structural Transformation of the Public Sphere: An Inquiry into a Category of Bourgeois Society* (Boston: MIT Press), 1.

3. Raymond Williams, 1976, *Keywords: A Vocabulary of Culture and Society* (Britain: Croom Helm), 75.

4. Ibid., 291.

5. Ibid., 90.

6. Ibid., 72.

7. Ibid., 90.

8. Christian Fuchs, 2017, *Social Media: A Critical Introduction* (London: Sage Publications, 2e), 45.

9. Benedict Anderson, 1991, *Imagined Communities: Reflections on the Origin and Spread of Nationalism* (London: Verso, rev. edn), 44.

10. Ibid., 135.

11. Pavan K. Verma, 1999, *The Great India Middle Class* (New Delhi: Penguin Books), xxxv.

12. 'Survey Reveals Upper Castes' Domination in Media', *People's Democracy* XXX (24), 11 June 2006. Available at http://archives.peoplesdemocracy.in/2006/0611/06112006_media%20survey.htm (accessed January 2016).

13. J. V. Vilanilam, 2005, *Mass Communication in India: A Sociological Perspective* (New Delhi: Sage Publications).

14. Leela Fernandes, 2007, *India's New Middle Class: Democratic Politics in an Era of Economic Reform* (New Delhi: Oxford University Press), 68.

15. Vipul Mudgal, 2011, 'Rural Coverage in the Hindi and English Dailies', *Economic and Political Weekly* XLVI (35), 27 August.

16. John Naughton, 2012, *What You Really Need to Know about the Internet: From Gutenberg to Zuckerberg* (London: Quercus), 138.

17. Robin Jeffrey, 2000, *India's Newspaper Revolution—Capitalism, Politics and the Indian Language Press, 1977–99* (London: C. Hurst), 52.

18. Trvivek.blogspot.com, *Outlook*, 9 January 2006. Available at http://www.outlookindia.com/article/trvivekblogspotcom/229721 (accessed April 2015).

19. Sudhir Gore, 2007, 'The write way to earn', *Business Today*, 17 May. Available at http://businesstoday.intoday.in/story/the-write-way-to-earn/1/6327.html (accessed April 2015).

20. Prasun Sonwalkar, 2009, 'Citizen Journalism in India: The Politics of Recognition', in Stuart Allan and Einar Thorsen (eds), *Citizen Journalism: Global Perspectives* (New York: Peter Lang), 80.

21. Sunetra Sen Narayan and Shalini Narayanan, 2016, 'An Overview of New Media in India', in Sunetra Sen Narayan and Shalini Narayanan (eds), *India Connected: Mapping the Impact of New Media* (New Delhi: Sage Publications), 11.

22. S. K. Singh, 2006, 'The diffusion of mobile phones in India', Seminar paper.

23. C. Chandramouli, 2011, 'Houses, Household Amenities, and Assets Data 2001–2011'. Available at http://censusindia.gov.in/2011-Common/NSDI/Houses_Household.pdf (accessed May 2016).

24. Arvind Rajagopal, 2014, 'On the Unexpected Parochialism of Media Studies', in Biswarup Sen and Abhijit Roy (eds), *Channeling Cultures: Television Studies from India* (New Delhi: Oxford University Press), 297.

25. Nalin Mehta, 2015, *Behind a Billion Screens: What Television Tells us about Modern India* (New Delhi: HarperCollins), 4.

26. Deloitte/ASSOCHAM India, 2011, 'Media & Entertainment in India: The Digital Road Ahead'. Available at http://www.deloitte.com/assets/dcom-india/local%20assets/documents/me%20-%20whitepaper%20for%20assocham.pdf (accessed May 2015).

27. James Robinson, 2010, 'UK and US see heaviest newspaper circulation declines', *The Guardian*, 17 June. Available at https://www.theguardian.com/media/2010/jun/17/newspaper-circulation-oecd-report (accessed May 2016).

28. PwC, 2011, 'India Entertainment & Media Outlook 2011'. Available at https://www.pwc.in/en_IN/in/assets/pdfs/publications-2011/India_Entertainment_and_Media_Outlook_2011.pdf (accessed May 2015).

29. Sevanti Ninan, 2007, *Headlines from the Heartland* (New Delhi: Sage Publications), 83–84.

30. Vanita Kohli-Khandekar, 2013, *The Indian Media Business* (New Delhi: Sage Publications, 4e), 58.

31. Paranjoy Guha Thakurta, 2012, 'Media Ownership in India—An Overview', *The Hoot*, 30 June 2012. Available at http://www.thehoot.org/resources/media-ownership/media-ownership-in-india-an-overview-6048 (accessed June 2016).

32. Robin Jeffrey and Assa Doron, 2013, *Cellphone Nation* (New Delhi: Hachette India), 210.

33. Tapas Tiwari, et al., 2011, 'Mobile Phones Market in India', Study submitted by Department of Commerce, Delhi School of Economics.

34. Source: Digital, Mobile, and Social Media in India, BBH Data Snapshot, April 2011. Available at http://cn.cnstudiodev.com/uploads/document_attachment/attachment/29/india_techdeck.pdf (accessed June 2015).

35. Vamsee Juluri, quoted in Amit Rai, 2009, *Untimely Bollywood Globalization and India's New Media Assemblage* (Durham and London: Duke University Press), 86.

36. 'Indian User Statistics on Facebook', 10 November 2010. Available at http://www.beevolve.com/2010/11/indian-user-statistics-on-facebook/.

37. Srinivas K. Reddy, 2010, 'Facebook to open first Asia office in India', *The Hindu*, 15 March. Available at http://www.thehindu.com/news/cities/Hyderabad/facebook-to-open-first-asia-office-in-india/article245437.ece (accessed June 2016).

38. Vidhu Goel, 2018, 'In India, Facebook's WhatsApp plays Central Role in Elections', *The New York Times*, 14 May. Available at https://www.nytimes.com/2018/05/14/technology/whatsapp-india-elections.html (accessed May 2018).

39. Vandita Mishra, 2011, 'Anger after Ramlila midnight is over Govt, netas and reservation', *The Indian Express*, 21 August.

40. 'The Twitter Generation—Life in 160 characters', *Business India*, 6 May 2010. Available at http://www.slideshare.net/iffort/business-india-may-2010-twitter-cover-story (accessed July 2015).

41. Number quoted by Radha Kumar, one of the Indian government interlocutors on Kashmir, in an interview with the author.

42. Praveen Swamy, 2010, 'The Ugly World of Online Kashmiri Rebels', *The Hindu*, 24 July. Available at http://www.thehindu.com/news/national/other-states/the-ugly-world-of-kashmirs-online-rebels/article530306.ece (accessed June 2016).

43. Navnita Chadha Behera, 2012, 'A Perception Survey of Media Impact on Kashmiri Youth', Institute for Research on India and International Studies.

44. Arjun Sharma, 2013, 'Kashmir separatists using Facebook to revive stone-pelting say intelligence agencies', *India Today*, June. Available at http://indiatoday.intoday.in/story/kashmir-rebels-use-facebook-to-fan-unrest/1/141288.html (accessed June 2016).

45. Varadharajan Sridhar, 2012, *The Telecom Revolution in India: Technology, Regulation and Policy* (New Delhi: Oxford University Press), 288.

46. Ibid. Also see Naughton, *What You Really Need to Know about the Internet*, 153.

47. Sridhar, *The Telecom Revolution in India*, 288–89.

48. Henry Jenkins, 2006, *Convergence Culture: Where Old and New Media Collide* (New York: New York University Press), 282.

49. Manuel Castells, 2013, *Communication Power* (Oxford: Oxford University Press), 135.

50. Andrew Chadwick, 2013, *The Hybrid Media System: Politics and Power*, Oxford Studies in Digital Politics (Oxford: Oxford University Press), 4.

51. Rai, *Untimely Bollywood*, 70.

52. Henry Jenkins and Mark Deuze, 2008, 'Editorial', *Convergence: The International Journal of Research into New Media Technologies* 14 (1), 5–12.

53. Ibid.

54. Robert W. McChesney, 2013, *Digital Disconnect: How Capitalism is Turning the Internet Against Democracy* (New York: The New Press), 130.

55. Megha Bahree, 2014, 'Reliance Takes Over Network 18: Is This The Death Of Media Independence?', *Forbes*, 30 May. Available at https://www.forbes.com/sites/meghabahree/2014/05/30/reliance-takes-over-network18-is-this-the-death-of-media-independence/#496f98b665c1 (accessed March 2017).

56. Thompson, *Ideology and Modern Culture*, 3–4.

57. Robert W. McChesney, 2014, *Blowing the Roof off the 21st Century: Media, Politics, and the Struggle for Post-capitalist Democracy* (New York: NYU Press), 228.

two

Framing Corruption in Today's Times

Media Discourse and the Anna Campaign

The making of corruption as a political cause through the India Against Corruption (IAC) campaign of 2011 was undergirded by networked communication and media convergence on a scale never before deployed in the country for a single-focus crusade. It held significant socio-political consequences for the country, both at the juncture when it took place and in the years that followed. The long back story of the mediatised IAC protests has two aspects that will be unpacked in this chapter. The first concerns the various ideologies and interests that influenced the manner in which the Indian media covered corruption over the years; and the second is the historical moment of its inception and the importance of the year 2011.

Corruption—which includes misuse of public authority and delays in justice delivery as important constituents—had always been an important theme for mainstream media reportage and editorialising in post-independent India. Such coverage was driven by a combination of public interest and self-interest, feeding as it did the everyday conversations of the media-consuming middle classes and buttressing the media's own credibility. This long association with the theme, it could be argued, was one of the major reasons why newspapers and television channels were prepared to invest time and money in the IAC protests of 2011, once they had gained traction with people.

The corrupting nature of power has been commented upon by philosophers and poets over the years. It allows those who were already influential to make 'economic gains over and above what they can make legally', and is a source of growing illegality and the black economy.[1] Gunnar Myrdal, in his 1968 work *Asian Drama*, presciently observed that it would be corruption among the ruling classes, rather than a lack of developmental ideas, that would prove the bane of the newly emerging nations in Asia and Africa. In India, time-honoured practices such as gift giving and the widespread notion that those in authority were entitled to the privileges of their station meant that kleptocracy was embedded in the social fabric of the country and was kept alive through a combination of formal rules and informal practices over the millennia.

Post-independence India's first major financial scandal, the Mundhra scam which broke in 1957, concerned the investments made by the government-run Life Insurance Corporation of India (LIC) in a dodgy Calcutta-based firm at the behest of the finance minister, and was brought to national attention by Feroze Gandhi, a parliamentarian, journalist, and the son-in-law of India's first Prime Minister, Jawaharlal Nehru. What lent the scam sustained national attention was the decision of the person heading the inquiry into it, Justice M. C. Chagla, to throw the inquiry proceedings open to the public through the use of loudspeakers. The move drew large crowds, as testified to by a front page photograph in a prominent newspaper of the day, showing people looking into the Council Hall in Bombay where the hearings were being held.[2] Newspaper coverage of these open proceedings was an early instance of the Indian media treating corruption as a public concern. Chagla himself saw these hearings as an education for the public when he voiced the hope that it would prove a corrective to administrators by making them realise that their actions could come under public scrutiny.

The existence of the dark alleys of the parallel economy—referred to colloquially as 'black economy', 'number two economy', 'hawala economy', and the like—was universally known, but concrete instances of malfeasance had excited sustained media coverage over the years from the days of the Mundhra scam in the 1950s through the late 1950s and 1960s. Tabloids like R. K. Karanjia's *Blitz* took such coverage to the next level. *Blitz,*

> week after week ... exposed truths allegedly buried beneath the surface of random and fragmentary events. The embezzlement of public funds, prostitution rackets, sordid stories of seduction and sex in the name of spiritualism, dark political designs behind high-sounding rhetoric, and the fleecing of the poor by rich industrialists and property developers.[3]

The 1970s began with the Nagarwala scandal, which seemed to suggest that the politically powerful—in this case, Prime Minister Indira Gandhi herself—treated public money as if they owned it, and quickly became a source of much public speculation and even inspired popular novels and films.

In 1981, Maharashtra's Chief Minister A. R. Antulay's predilection to amass wealth in return for discretionary favours, chiefly through the sanctioning of cement, a resource rationed in that era, was the subject of a celebrated investigative series by the editor of *The Indian Express*, Arun Shourie. A magazine report of the time went:

> What has since come to be known as India's Watergate—or Antulay's Trustgate scandal—was the result of no random leak, no subversive hint surreptitiously passed on, nor the sum total of common tittle-tattle gleaned from a bunch of squealers; it was a consciously studied and calculatedly pursued investigation of organised corruption in high places, a meticulously-researched exposure with supporting evidence that ran into 7,500 words and 140 column-inches of blistering copy.[4]

If the Antulay exposes turned the light on corruption as a major theme for reportage, the scandal over the procurement of the Bofors gun, a few years later, led to blistering and sustained newspaper investigations. Broken in 1987 by the Swedish media—in this case the Swedish State Radio—the story was kept alive over the years by the extensive and painstaking sleuthing of Indian reporters, notably by Chitra Subramaniam, who gained access to over 350 documents from a Swedish whistleblower. Subramaniam was to later recall that the 'real breakthrough in the Bofors story came in the spring of 1988 when, during one of my strips to Stockholm, Sting (her source) invited me to help myself to a vast set of documents'.[5] Bofors became synonymous with political malfeasance in the country and destroyed the political future of Rajiv Gandhi, a man who had become prime minister in 1984 with the largest electoral mandate in India's history. It also shored up the credentials of the print media as a crusader against corruption.

At the start of the decade of the 1990s, a scandal that came to be known as the 'hawala scam', involving payments allegedly received by some of the country's leading politicians through the Jain brothers, who were hawala operators, was featured prominently in the media and details of it kept surfacing throughout the rest of the decade. The case led to the resignation in 1996 of prominent BJP leader, L. K. Advani, as Member of Parliament.

Coverage of the Antulay exposes, the Bofors investigations, or the court orders on the Jain hawala scandal was evidence of how the media contributed a great deal to concentrating the mind of the urban, middle-class Indian on the issue of public corruption, which was now framed as the lack of State accountability deepened by a notion of citizens' rights that was slowly gaining currency. The majority of Indians, regardless of their class or location, had experienced the impacts of corruption personally, especially in the form of bribe-giving and taking. A survey conducted by Samuel Paul and Manubhai Shah in 1997 found that 33 per cent of the urban poor in Bangalore needed to pay a bribe to access a public service or solve a problem. In 2005, Transparency International (TI) estimated that at least 50 per cent of Indians had either bribed someone or used their connections to get something done. In 2012, a Centre for Media Studies survey established that three out of every four slum dwellers in Delhi had paid a gratification in order to get their legitimate entitlements.

MEDIA COVERAGE AND THE STATE

The attention the newspapers of the day paid to the issue was undeniably one of the reasons why the newly independent Indian State was under constant pressure to be seen to address the crime. The Prevention of Corruption Act 1947 attempted an expansion of the anti-corruption provisions in the Indian Penal Code (IPC) of 1860, but did not expand upon its list of offences. In 1952, the law was tweaked to allow enhanced punishment. It needed the Bofors scam for the Prevention of Corruption (Amendment) Act to come into force in 1988. The law consolidated the provisions of pre-existing legal instruments into one piece of legislation, broadened the definition of 'public servant', enhanced penalties, and hastened the pace of the trial process.

Meanwhile, in order to put in place more 'practical steps' to make anti-corruption measures more effective, a Committee on the Prevention on Corruption was set up in June 1963 under a former newspaper editor, K. Santhanam. It was at the suggestions of this committee that the country got itself the Central Bureau of Investigation (CBI) and a Central Vigilance Commission (CVC). The latter went on to identify thirty-three distinct modes of corruption, which were classified under two broad categories—the first involved the public and included acts like the giving of bribes or the submission of false tax returns; the second related to the administration, and ranged from relatively minor offences like making false claims for personal allowances to crimes like accepting illegal gratification or profiteering from the selling of government property.

In 1966, the Administrative Reforms Commission headed by Morarji Desai mooted the idea of a Lokpal and Lokayukta, envisaged along the lines of a Scandinavian-style ombudsman, to deal with complaints of corruption against ministers and senior officials. Whether the Lokpal and Lokayukta would indeed have brought down the levels of corruption is of course a matter of conjecture, but it is telling that the suggested measures did not even make it through both Houses of Parliament. It took nearly half a century and the prolonged anti-corruption campaign of 2011 for legislation on this to come into force. Such implicit resistance on the part of legislators to holding themselves accountable remained a symbolic rebuke of the political system, and provided traction for anti-corruption and right to information mobilisations in the years that followed.

The restructuring of the Indian economy in 1991 led the discourse on corruption in India to conform to two broadly contending frameworks, each determined by considerations of class and location.

The first tended to define corruption narrowly. The argument here was not so much in favour of overhauling the structures of society as it was on pressurising the State to deliver better in order to meet the aspirations of its citizens. Corruption, in this reading, was a blot on India as a moral nation and an emerging economic power. For instance, N. Vittal, who was appointed Central Vigilance Commissioner in 1998, maintained in his anti-corruption advocacy through newspaper articles and public speeches that corruption was a national failing that required all sections of society to unite and battle it together. There was also the apprehension that corruption was creating an adverse investor climate and undermining economic progress. In the late 1990s, Pranab Bardhan, defining corruption as 'the abuse of public office for private gain', was among the first to argue that 'corruption has its adverse effects not just on static efficiency but also on investment and growth'.[6] The suggestions offered to stem this tide—amplified by media coverage—included the whittling down of a bloated and mendacious bureaucracy, curbing the discretionary powers of officials, and allowing the markets a free rein in order to create a level playing field. Listing the barriers in the way of the structural transformation of the Indian economy, a 2006 Planning Commission paper pointedly underlined that 'a large proportion of public functionaries (including people's representatives) do not care about the public interest', going on to note that about 80 per cent of them (from the peon upwards) are corrupt.[7]

This perspective rested on the conception of the State as being socially neutral, and therefore non-partisan in its policymaking and in the distribution of the benefits of these policies. It also presumed that all citizens were alike, eschewing the idea that 'common citizenship render invisible the many inequalities that lie concealed beneath the mask of formal equality'.[8] The mainstream media generally adopted this framework in their reports, editorials, and opinion pieces.

The opposing discourse on corruption unpacked both state and citizenship in post-liberalisation India. It regarded the State as structurally biased, arguing that the accrual of the benefits of a liberalised economy was confined to a certain category of people and that this in itself was symbolic of a larger corruption. It held the State to account for its failure to discharge its constitutional responsibility of furthering social equality, and choosing instead to unleash its coercive forces to rob the poor of their access to livelihoods, social services, governmental spending, and common property resources.

Emerging largely from the social movements of the day, the second argument framed corruption as coterminous with the discretionary powers of the State, mobilised in pursuit of a model of neoliberal economic growth. A case in point was the Narmada Bachao Andolan's critique of the politician-engineer-politician nexus and unaccounted public spending in mega-dam projects, which had resulted in the displacement of hundreds of thousands of hapless men, women, and children.

What did change was that the hitherto quiet acceptance of corruption as an unchangeable reality of Indian life came to be replaced by more explicit public expressions of resistance. In Rajasthan, a theoretical understanding of the link between information and corruption emerged with the activism of the Mazdoor Kishan Shakti Sanghathan (MKSS), set up 1990. Working with farmers and workers at the grassroots, the MKSS provided startling evidence of the discrepancies between outlays shown in government records and the money that was actually being spent. This pointed, in turn, to the centrality of ensuring transparency in government functioning, which could only happen if information about governmental decision-making and expenditure was made public.

Aruna Roy, founder of the MKSS and key architect of the right to information movement, reflected in an interview[9] that the malaise of corruption is not just red tape and bureaucratic control, but 'the denial of equality to people outside the system, the denial, in fact, of their right to question'. People's right to articulate their experiences and counter the State was an idea that the MKSS fought for and campaigned on across the country, reconstituting the struggle for the right to resources as a struggle for the right to information. Tamil Nadu and Goa were the first states to enact a Right to Information law in 1997, with Rajasthan following in 2000. In Maharashtra, Anna Hazare had launched a movement for a Right to Information law in 1997. Yielding to his fast-unto-death at Mumbai's Azad Maidan in 2003, the state enacted the law with retrospective effect from 2002. Several other states, including Madhya Pradesh and Assam, followed and the demand for a national law grew stronger. The newspapers of the day supported this movement to varying degrees, with some senior editors becoming RTI activists themselves. Former *Jansatta* editor, Prabhash Joshi, for instance, argued in newspapers articles and at public forums that RTI was a foundational aid to journalism. In October 2005, the national Right to Information Act finally became the law of the land.

One of the consequences of the RTI movement was the understanding among ordinary people that it was incumbent upon the media to monitor governmental functioning and corporate influence. Unassailable evidence that poor, rural voters found corruption extremely disempowering, and wanted the State to address it, emerged in the innumerable *jan sunwai*s (public hearings) that organisations like the MKSS organised, as indeed in numerous academic studies from the field. An election study in Uttar Pradesh, for instance, found that 'all things being equal, allegations of impropriety have a powerful effect on voter preferences'.[10]

It was the mediatised middle class, however, who developed a more intimate feeling of being denied their due entitlements as citizens, consumers, and voters, and were quick to take ownership of anti-corruption activism, spurred by the perception (furthered by mainstream media editorialising) that corruption was an attempt to steal the assets of the tax-paying public. Despite the rural roots of the RTI movement, development scholars like Roy Jenkins and Anne Marie Goetz noted the over-representation of middle-class concerns in RTI applications.[11] In 1995, Common Cause India, a Delhi-based civil society organisation working on what it termed as 'accountability of public institutions and governance reforms', filed a Public Interest Litigation (PIL) in the Supreme Court demanding an effective Lokpal at the Centre, a demand that was to be taken up by the IAC team fifteen years later. Interestingly, it also drew up in a court affidavit a framework to operationalise a Lokpal and Lokayukta—an early forbearer to the IAC's Jan Lokpal Bill.

The existence of a thriving parallel economy and evidence of the country's wealth being channelled to tax havens abroad by unscrupulous politicians and their patrons added to the widespread belief among the articulate middle class that the citizens of the country were being denied the wealth that was rightfully theirs. The Association for Democratic Reform (ADR), set up in 2002, provided evidence of how even a process considered central to democratic functioning—elections to state legislatures and Parliament—was not free of the insidious and corrupting influences of money power. In 2005, a Transparency International survey, widely featured in the media, estimated that the sum paid as bribes every year by ordinary citizens to avail of one or more of eleven public services amounted to Rs 21,068 crore. In 2010, management guru C. K. Prahalad came up with an estimation that corruption was costing the country over Rs 2,50,000 crore.[12]

CHANGING MEDIA

While all this was going on, something intriguing was happening to mainstream media. Globalisation and the subsequent corporatisation of newspaper and television content had by the first decade of the twenty-first century led to a conscious discarding of the normative frameworks that had guided the media thus far. Until this point, they had perceived themselves as reflecting, if not actually doing so, the interests of the country and all its citizens as a whole. With the focus now on the market economy, a discourse based on the idea of rights and citizenship shifted to one based on choice and consumption.

With the media deeply imbricated in the neoliberal project, information itself became a commodity to be traded. At least one prominent media group went so far as to monetise its content by striking open and covert deals with corporate entities. Others chose to set up parallel businesses in sectors like real estate, mining, and entertainment by bending the rules and peddling influence.

The point to note here is that wealth generation, whether through fair means or foul, now gained a new legitimacy among media actors. In the early 2000s, the Government of India allowed 26 per cent and 74 per cent foreign direct investment in the news print media and non-news publications, respectively. By the end of that decade, television software production could be totally funded by foreign entities, subject to certain government stipulations. The need to attract foreign funding pressured many media organisations to undertake structural reform, even if it meant divesting themselves of full operational control of their organisations. They began to project themselves as professionally managed publicly financed companies based on a business model projected as 'transparent'. This change in image was a 'direct result of the inflow of external investments and share capital into the media business, and the subsequent need to cultivate market confidence'.[13] By 2010, foreign direct investment (FDI) in the media and entertainment sector had touched Rs 178.7 billion.[14]

The changing media content blurred the traditional distinction between news and opinion and made more porous the boundaries between editorial and advertisement content. The 2003 announcement of its 'latest innovation', a paid content service called 'Medianet', put out by *The Times of India*, was revealing in its statement of intent: 'The purpose of a newspaper is to act as an information provider ... traditional modes of news-gathering have not been able to keep up with the dynamics of new areas of reader interest, like lifestyle, fashion, entertainment, events, product launches, social personalities and city happenings, to name a few'. It went on to state that the envisioned role of Medianet 'is that of a conscience-keeper, auditor and watchdog, regulating the media's burgeoning interaction with the PR sector'.[15]

Media professionals now had to function as lobbyists, public relations agents, traders in information, and power brokers in order to extend the reach of their respective organisations. In an earlier era, jute mill owners and paper manufacturers had set up newspaper establishments, but post-liberalisation India saw a reversal of this pattern: large industrial houses simply bought up established media units, even as newspaper conglomerates ventured into profitable enterprises of all kinds. Media power, 'or the direct control over the means of media production',[16] has been an important constituent of power in modern societies, and the new patterns of media ownership and control reflected this. A Telecom Regulatory Authority of India (TRAI) paper, commenting on ownership patterns in the Indian media, noted that corporate and political interests exercised an 'overwhelming' and 'high degree' of control over the media, respectively.[17]

Inevitably, the content that mainstream media generated was made to conform to these realities by becoming more market-friendly, with editors justifying the shift as an effort to provide people with the stories they 'wanted'. Analysing this trend, one media scholar writes: markets do not 'give people what they want' as much as 'give the people what they want within the range of what is most profitable to produce and/or in the political interests of the producers'.[18] In the process, the two central and interlinked functions of the media in modern societies—'the credible-informational and the critical-investigative-adversarial'[19]—were considerably undermined. Throughout the 2000s, there was a steady erosion of the credible-informational function of the media, as a large part of their content came to be shaped by advertising conglomerates and public relations behemoths, a development that in turn had an adverse impact on their critical-investigative-adversarial role.

In this new phase, the media valorised those they deemed as 'creators of wealth', and openly took sides in the internecine battles between industrial houses, depending on which side was supporting them. Some even profited from the proliferation of paid news. This pattern was by no means confined to India. In the US, 'bottom-line pressure to turn a profit plus the need to protect the image of corporations as good' pressurised journalists to create media content that was politically safe.[20] British investigative journalist Nick Davies adopted the term 'churnalism' in his 2008 book, *Flat Earth News*, to describe this global collapse of information-gathering and truth telling. The lack of financial incentive to investigate corruption and malpractice was almost built into the system, which brought about a shift in the manner in which stories on corruption were accessed and framed. Notions of the public good were no longer the guiding force, nor was the concept of corruption free from the manipulations of interest groups and patronage networks. The old axiom that news is what somebody, somewhere does not want reported could now be read as: news is something that somebody, somewhere wants reported.

In India, ironically, this was happening precisely at a time when three significant trends had begun to manifest themselves. First was the mushrooming of corrupt practices within the economic and political spheres. The Global Financial Integrity report of 2010 expressly noted that the period of deregulation and trade liberalisation had seen a sharp increase in illicit money flowing into tax havens from India.[21] Second was the rising awareness about the citizen's right to know, buttressed by the new Right to

Information law of 2005, made possible by the activism of civil rights organisations. Third, the digital age had led to the creation of alternative media platforms which, because they were relatively less inhibited by corporate influence, could break stories and prove to be credible competitors to mainstream media.

Mainstream media, consequently, found themselves between a rock and a hard place: ignoring news breaks on corruption would have meant undermining their status as the primary dispensers of public information and creators of public discourse. At the same time, focusing on scams and scandal through investigative due process would have meant exposing interests very close to their own. Many therefore chose the expedient course of reporting on political and bureaucratic wrongdoing rather than corporate crime, with the primary focus on the corrupted than on the corrupters.

Politicians had always been softer targets in the media's drive to appear tough on crime, even if the biggest sources of financial wheeling-dealing lay in the corporate arena. The then editor-in-chief of *Tehelka*, in an interview, pointed out that mainstream media's exposes of corporate wrongdoing were elusive because 'the Indian media constantly focused on soft targets and completely steered clear of hard targets ... if (a TV channel) happens to get a rabbit in its crosshairs, it will run the rabbit down until it is dead. But it will never take on the hound ....'[22]

This was the general pattern throughout the 2000s. Most of the news breaks on corruption in high places became public for reasons that had little to do with the efforts of mainstream media to unearth the facts. The very first major expose of the decade, which provided visible, undeniable evidence of bribe-taking within government and army circles, emerged in 2001. It came not from the mainstream media but from *tehelka.com*, one of India's early web-based media platforms, which had by then already established a reputation for risk-taking by having exposed match-fixing allegations within the Indian cricket team. Termed Operation West End, the story broke the mould of the standard newspaper investigation by deploying digital media tools like hidden cameras in a series of sting operations, a methodology that was to be adopted by social activists a decade later.

For *tehelka.com,* the consequences of running the Operation West End story were immediate and portentous. The Atal Bihari Vajpayee government drove the organisation into bankruptcy. This was yet another signal to the mainstream media that the costs of turning whistleblower could be prohibitively high. Throughout the decade of the 2000s, which saw several episodes of serious political and corporate corruption, the mainstream media was content to play a secondary role, dwelling on the story only after it had become public and could no longer be ignored. If the financial scandal involving India's fourth largest software services enterprise, Satyam Computer Services, for instance, became known, it was only because its chairperson himself confessed in 2009 to having manipulated company accounts to the tune of $1.5 billion.

More evidence of the close business–politics–media nexus emerged towards the end of this eventful decade. In 2009 came direct evidence of a politician paying newspapers to carry news that was favourable to him.[23] A few months later, the existence of the Niira Radia Tapes surfaced. Even after two popular English language magazines, the *Open* magazine and *Outlook,* mustered the courage to carry excerpts from these transcripts, which established a clear nexus between senior media personnel and lobbyists for industrial magnates, silence on the issue was the preferred option for the majority of media houses.

The lack of appetite to uncover corporate wrongdoing and seek punishment for the guilty reflected not only a lack of professionalism, but also a failure to read the public mind. The media projection of an NDA victory in the fourteenth General Election of 2004—the so-called 'Atal Bihari Vajpayee wave'—was a case in point.[24] Several factors could be cited for that election verdict, which brought the Indian National Congress (INC) back to power after nearly a decade. The years of NDA rule from 1998 to 2004 had seen many disturbing developments, including the Kargil war. The Vajpayee government also presided over a string of financial scams like the fraudulent purchase of coffins, Operation West End, and the meltdown of the United Trust of India, which directly affected over twenty million middle-class investors. The inability of the media in general to perceive the negative political fallout of all this could, in part, be attributed to their euphoria over growth and the projection of India as an emerging global player. In 2003, a widely cited paper[25] hailed the Indian economy as one of the world's fastest growing ones that was slated to outstrip that of Japan by the year 2032. A popular formulation of the time—economic growth would lift all boats—was taken as an article of faith by a large number of mainstream media editors and commentators.

It needed the success-hungry Hindi film industry to discern that corruption remained a compelling public concern. The 2000s saw a succession of box office grossers which had corruption as their main theme, whether it was *Ganga Jal* in 2003, which portrayed a police officer taking on a corrupt politician, *Sarkar*, released in 2005, where a don who runs his own fiefdom is laid low, or the 2007 multi-starrer *Guru*, which, while glamorising the life of a tycoon, also portrayed the manner in which he corrupted the system.

The cult status accorded to the 2006 film *Rang De Basanti* (RDB)—released significantly on Republic Day that year—demonstrated conclusively the emotional connect that the urban middle classes had with the issue. The story of the film revolved essentially around the awakening of civic consciousness in a group of youngsters after they learnt that the death of a mutual friend, a fighter pilot, in an air crash was the result of the political corruption that marked the acquisition of the aircraft he was flying. The central message was that people, especially the youth of the country, had to take on the avaricious politician and build a transparent and accountable society—a theme that was to be replayed during the IAC campaign half-a-decade later.

RDB saw a synchrony of media response, with its content finding an echo in other media platforms. Both mainstream media commentators and bloggers used the film as a prism through which to view the political situation prevailing in the country, drawing parallels between the political leaders of the day and the corrupt politicians portrayed in the film. Media scholars have argued, in relation to the mainstream media in the US, that the media generally operate in a manner that encourages 'apathy, cynicism, and quiescence, rather than active citizenship and participation'. But they also point to the possibility that the 'underdetermined nature of media discourse' would allow challengers to 'construct meaning in ways that go beyond media imagery'.[26]

The discourse emanating out of RDB rejected the quiet and pervasive acceptance of a corrupt order. One analysis of the blogs on RDB concludes that 'the consumption of RDB not only helped stimulate people into voicing their citizen-concerns on the public space of the Internet but also motivated and provoked them to think of the ways in which they could become socially conscious and politically informed citizens'.[27] Commentators like Evgeny Morozov have words of caution against an unthinking endorsement of online activism: 'The problem with political activism facilitated by social networking sites is that much of it happens for reasons that have nothing to do with one's commitments to ideas and politics in general, but rather to impress one's friends.'[28] While keeping these cautionary words in mind, it would still appear that the exchange of views in the online and offline media on RDB seemed to go beyond the need to 'impress one's friends', triggering as it did short bursts of citizen activism.

Both the mobilisers and the mobilised in these instances emerged from the universe of the urban, middle-class, upwardly mobile, media savvy, and young, and consequently the issues they articulated were strongly marked by their class and caste backgrounds. One of the first causes taken up by the cohort inspired by the film revolved around allegations of corruption in the acquisition of military hardware. It was an issue that Pune-based Kavita Gadgil, who had lost her son Flight Lieutenant Abhijit Gadgil during a MiG-21 training exercise in 2001, had been championing, and her story had figured in the RDB plotline. Another controversy that sparked protest a couple of months after the film was released was the proposal of the then UPA government to reserve 27 per cent of seats in institutions of higher learning for the Other Backward Classes (OBC). It led to students from the general category in many cities going on strike over what they regarded as a patently unfair move, dictated by the desire to build an OBC vote bank. References to the film kept surfacing during the two months of April and May 2006, over which this agitation ran its course. When students at the prestigious All India Institute of Medical Sciences in Delhi went on a hunger strike on the proposed reservations, RDB was shown at the protest site and there were innumerable references to it in the speeches made. Much like the young protagonists in the film, many of the protesters regarded their actions as a way of cleansing India of the wrong practices perpetrated by cynical politicians who were only interested in protecting their own interests.

It was a similar reading that sparked public anger in Delhi over the acquittal by the courts of the man who had killed model Jessica Lal at a private party, and who happened to be the son of a prominent politician belonging to the ruling party. It may be useful to recall at this point that Delhi had already emerged as the site where the Association of Victims of Uphaar Tragedy (AVUT), comprising the families of those who had perished in the fire that broke out in the Uphaar film theatre in 1997, came together and made visible their grief and anger. Their innovative activism had struck a chord with the media, which in turn helped them take on the Ansal brothers, two politically well-connected property magnates who owned the theatre. Although the AVUT mobilisation certainly inspired the Jessica Lal demonstrations, the difference was that those who rallied over it were not directly related to the affected family, but were random citizens driven by the need 'to do something'. The Lal protests were an early instance of the convergence of mainstream media and social media content. While front page headlines condemned the acquittal, the blogosphere was alive with indignation and prominent television channels captured voices campaigning for a retrial in the case on primetime. One television channel even anchored an SMS campaign demanding

'Justice for Jessica', with viewers being invited to text their outrage over the acquittal of the accused. The candlelight protest against this acquittal, in which around 2,500 Delhiites spontaneously participated on 4 March 2006, was a faithful re-enactment of an epiphanic moment in RDB when the protagonists staged a protest by lighting candles against the backdrop of Delhi's India Gate, which symbolised the nation. A few months later, similar protests were repeated, this time to ensure justice for Priyadarshini Mattoo, whose well-connected rapist and killer had also been acquitted on the grounds of insufficient evidence.

In both cases, public pressure saw a reversal of the earlier verdicts and the conviction of the guilty. Questions, however, lingered about the selective and class-defined nature of such outrage, the media-inspired theatricality of its social action, and the apprehension that media trials could also lead to miscarriages of justice. Scholars have also recognised that such protests are marked by a certain lack of permanence. Ritesh Mehta termed it 'flash activism', observing that the 'best way to explain its uniqueness is that flash activism is by definition not organizational but temporal in scope'.[29]

Such critiques notwithstanding, an unwavering, monochromatic reading of political corruption essentially informed the popular media discourse. Three of the major news breaks and public conversations in the later years of this decade involved politicians directly: profiteering over the Commonwealth Games, the diversion of coal block allocation to profit certain politico-corporate interests, and the 2G scam, or the fraudulent selling of electromagnetic spectrum for second-generation telecommunications services. A fourth scandal concerned the Adarsh Cooperative Housing Society, an illegally constructed multi-storied building on a prime location in the southern tip of Mumbai, which had several senior politicians as beneficiaries.

None of the stories were directly broken by mainstream media and were largely the outcome of leaked reports from the offices of the Comptroller and Auditor General (CAG) or the Chief Vigilance Commissioner, and information gathered by activists through

RTI applications. Yet, once they escaped from files secreted in the corridors of power, they became the stuff of public conversations, steadily building a mass perception that the Congress-led UPA government that was in power was irredeemably corrupt. This was the discursive backdrop for the IAC campaign of 2011. No particular ideological underpinnings could be discerned in the creation of this brand of militancy at that point. The IAC activists stepped on to the public space, motivated by 'affect and emotional narration—stirred by visual media and social media, both of which have played a huge role. The appeal here is to an individual sense of morality, of what is felt to be right, rather than to ideology.'[30]

2011 AS THE YEAR OF PROTESTS

The IAC campaign, it needs to be remembered, took place a year after the Wikileaks revelations re-framed old debates on transparency and offered a tantalising glimpse of the power of networked citizens in countering State power. Transcripts of Wikileaks cables pertaining to India would become public some months thereafter and reveal, among other 'secrets', details of how money was exchanged to help the Manmohan Singh government survive a no-confidence vote over the Indo-US nuclear deal in 2008.[31]

The IAC mobilisations also took place at a time of global ferment. The year 2011 was like no other in terms of the number of people's mobilisations across the world it had witnessed, leading it to be compared with another world-altering year—1968—which saw the Prague Spring in erstwhile Czechoslovakia, student riots in Paris, anti-Vietnam demonstrations in London and New York, civil rights marches in the US, and the unforgettable Black Power salute at the Olympic Games, all of which were captured in newspapers and on television screens of that time.

The first month of 2011 saw the full-throated demand for the overthrow of Hosni Mubarak, a dictator for thirty-three years, raised in Cairo's Tahrir Square, with 25 January demarcated the 'Day of

Rage'. Just a little over a month earlier, a vendor had set himself on fire in Tunis to protest police repression and unaffordable living conditions, leading to widespread demonstration in Tunisia and forcing President Ben Ali, who had ruled Tunisia since 1987, into exile. The term 'Arab Spring' has been used rather loosely, but there can be no denying that the Muslim world, from north Africa and the Arab Peninsula to West Asia, was in the grip of a history altering phenomenon, as protests broke out in cities dotting the region—Sa'ana, Manama, Morocco, Tripoli, and many others—over the first six months of 2011.

When a tsunami hit Japan in March that year, rendering the nuclear power plant in Fukushima into a ticking time bomb, it triggered a series of anti-nuclear demonstrations in that country. Another part of the world was to see the eponymous Occupy Movement. Inspired by the occupation of the Wisconsin State Home to protest the local governor's attack on collective bargaining in February, the Occupy Movement was formally launched with an indefinite sit-in at New York's Zuccotti Park, near the city's financial centre that September. The action was replicated in cities across the US. Spain had already seen the 15M protests in Madrid Square, also known as the Indignados movement, in May of that year, with France simultaneously staging its own version called the Les Indignes. Three months later, the shooting of a young man by the police in the London borough of Tottenham led to riots breaking out in a large swathe of the city.

Although the sources for popular rage varied, the simmering mood reflected economic disempowerment caused by the high cost of living, the tightening grip of cutbacks on local economies, global recession, State repression, as well as corporate greed and corruption. The freshly minted Occupy Movement slogan—'We are 99% and you are the 1%'—spoke for many millions. In February, when the World Social Forum took place in Dakar, Senegal, attended by around 18,000 people, a call was issued for a Global Day of Action Against Capitalism, which saw the participation of people in 951 cities across eighty-two countries.

The role of new communication technologies and social media in enabling such widespread displays of solidarity across the world has drawn the attention of many commentators. Some perceived it as evidence that the world was entering 'the dawn of a third great wave of egalitarianism .... The Information Revolution will be the primary force for change for decades to come.'[32] But the argument that it was social media that created these demonstrations of mass discontent also drew severe criticism. As Evgeny Mozorov scathingly remarks, tools like Twitter and Facebook are not very successful in converting 'awareness into action'.[33]

It may seem contradictory, but it could be argued that the fact that communication technologies had played such a decisive and disproportionate role in these various uprisings only underlined that they were not just about the use of communication technology. This was because the use of such technologies came with very strong markers, including the distinctive demographic profiles of its users. It was a particular moment in world history that demands, in fact, wider frames of reference. In his work on the Arab Spring, Hamid Dabashi sees the events in West Asia in 2011 as a part of the continuum of intensely felt economic disempowerment that was reflected in protests elsewhere in the world. He situates them in a context of 'a multivalent political culture of Islamism, socialism and nationalism', and argues that they reflect a retrieval by people of 'their organic cosmopolitan cultures'.[34] But Dabashi also recognised the production and circulation of knowledge as essential factors in this process of revolt. He acknowledges the catalytic role that the television network Al Jazeera, for instance, played in the Arab protests, recognising that 'defying stabilized governmentality' through these 'transversal revolts' necessitated 'alternative modes of knowledge production'[35] that was opposed to secrecy, disinformation, and State propaganda.

This synergy between power struggles and new knowledge production/communication technologies is what interested Paul Mason when he observed that in the year 2011, there was 'something in the air that defies historical parallels: something new to do with technology, behaviour and popular culture'. For the first time in decades, he notes, 'people are using methods of protest that do not seem archaic or at odds with the modern contemporary world; the protesters seem more in tune with modernity than the methods of their rulers.'[36]

IAC PROTESTS: INFORMATION BUILD-UP

By the time the IAC protests were to sweep over the country in 2011, corruption as a public issue had acquired an almost palpable presence. In India, the CAG had indicated that there were large-scale irregularities in 2G licence allocation in May 2010 and by November that year, its estimation that the country had lost Rs 1,76,000 crore as a result was leaked to the media. Similarly, in July that year, the CVC came up with evidence of a massive fraud in fourteen projects linked to the Commonwealth Games. This drip feed of information, considered credible since it was sourced from the government's own regulatory institutions, allowed the media to successfully project corruption as a national crisis of overwhelming proportions, even as the Congress-led government appeared weak, incompetent, and worse, indifferent, having lost the ability to put out an effective counter-narrative. Aditya Nigam and Nivedita Menon define this phenomenon in terms of a betrayal of democracy: 'the term "corruption" as it plays out in the movement, condenses within it a range of discontents—an accumulating anger over repeated betrayals of democratic expectations over years, but especially over the last decade.'[37]

Once any subject is marked as a legitimate and important theme for public engagement, it tends to attract an informational build-up. This phenomenon has been referred to as 'media issue attention cycle', defined as the 'sudden ascendance of an issue from previous obscurity to a sustained prominence ... that dominates the news for a period of time before once again fading from media attention.'[38] As long as an issue is within the attention cycle, the news desk/editors tend to favour content related to that particular issue, even at the cost of other important themes since they do not happen to be in the limelight to quite the same extent. Similarly, it will be this theme that will tend to dominate chat shows, the blogosphere, Twitter feeds, and Facebook pages by virtue of its attention cycle predominance.

Opinion pieces of this period had a disproportionately larger focus on corruption. A quick glance at the editorial and op-ed columns of *The Hindu* over the second half of 2010, for instance, would reveal the frequency with which corruption figured as the central theme. While Prabhudev Konana worried about the 'slippery slope of corruption' on the editorial page of 4 September 2010, a few weeks later C. P. Chandrasekhar rued 'corruption in the neoliberal era', and two weeks later Jaswant Singh was raising the question of whether Indian parliamentary democracy was in peril because of corruption.

A columnist like Chetan Bhagat, whose new-age novels were much admired in urban youth circles, furthered the prevailing mood even as he drew upon it. Commenting on the scams associated with the Commonwealth Games of 2010 in his unambiguously titled, 'Please don't cheer this lootfest', Bhagat wrote: 'The CWG 2010 is, by far, the biggest and most blatant, exercise in corruption in independent India's history.' He went on to urge readers to use the opportunity that the Games affords to highlight corruption,

> The CWG is an amazing opportunity because all Indians have been robbed at the same time .... the government is desperate to save face. Now is when we can get them. And the way to do it is simply what the father of our nation pioneered in his time—non-cooperation .... do not watch these Games ....[39]

What was striking about this passage was the manner in which Bhagat read the CWG scam as signifying a personal affront to 'Us' (that is, all Indians who 'have been robbed at the same time') by 'Them' (the looting government).

The findings of a small study conducted between January and May 2010 by the Delhi-based Centre for Media Studies, which looked at the coverage accorded to corruption as a theme by seven mainstream newspapers and six major television channels, revealed five significant trends. One, the time given for news stories on corruption in 2010 had increased by over four times from the time accorded to the subject in 2005. Two, the time apportioned to stories on health and education put together was less than that given to corruption coverage. Three, this was a trend that had become even more pronounced since 2008. Four, media exposes tended to focus on State, rather than private-sector, corruption. Five, the perception of citizens that corruption was rising more sharply than ever drew more directly from media coverage than their own experience of it.[40]

This perception of an all-encompassing corruption eating into the vitals of the country, robbing hardworking professionals, was central to the IAC protests. Was this mediatised activism the 'politics of anti-politics', as some analysts have characterised it? Interestingly, Mason, in his study of those who had taken part in the global protests of 2011, also noted a certain detachment that the young protagonists had vis-a-vis mainstream politics, and in fact attributes their eventual lack of success in taking on the establishment to this 'disengagement from ideology and structure'.[41] This 'politics of anti-politics' rose directly out of a perception among the urban middle class that those in power cannot, or will no longer, address the multiple crises of everyday life and that they themselves, through their own capacities and ability to interact through their media networks, could fix the old, flawed political system if they came together.

Corruption became the signifier of that old, flawed system, while ending corruption signified a modernising project, one that was in consonance with the neoliberal concept of 'good governance'. In fact, it can even be argued that the global anti-corruption campaigns should not be seen as a reaction to neoliberalism, but as part and parcel of its agenda.[42]

With all the play that they gave corruption as a theme over the years, mainstream media in post-liberalisation India have actually been critiqued for their silences and general reticence to carry out investigative journalism, with television in particular inviting the greatest censure for its tendency to frame news as discrete bundles of talking points mounted on rhetorical bridges. Much of the early behind-the-scenes action on the IAC mobilisation eluded the attention of the mainstream media precisely because it was non-sensational and did not fit the 'breaking news' format. This meant that the older media and the general public were deprived of a deeper understanding of the IAC in general, and the Jan Lokpal Bill, or a Citizen's Ombudsman Bill, in particular, with consequences for the credibility of both—a point iterated by Jagdeep Chhokar, founder of the Association for Democratic Reforms (ADR), who was part of the discussions in 2010 among activists on an effective anti-corruption intervention.

Chhokar believes that the IAC emerged out of the RTI movement in general, but pointed out that its formal genesis began at a meeting called by the National Campaign for People's Right to Information (NCPRI) in September 2010, which had conceived of a legislative architecture to fight corruption. This included, apart from a Lokpal bill, legal instruments that would protect whistleblowers, as well as a system to ensure public grievance redressal and judicial accountability. Arvind Kejriwal, a former officer with the Indian Revenue Service, working as an RTI activist in Delhi, volunteered, through his organisation Parivartan, to coordinate the drafting of the Whistleblower's Act for NCPRI. Shortly thereafter, he broke away from the NCPRI to initiate a series of consultations independently, a process that eventually led to the setting up of the IAC campaign with its own team of activists. As Chhokar recalls,

> I think Kejriwal met a lot of people and that was when he was persuaded of the need for a larger focus on corruption, which was a major, even fashionable, concern at that point. In this way, the old idea of the Lok Pal led to the resurrecting of the Lok Pal Bill, which gave birth to the IAC movement and in turn to the IAC's Jan Lokpal Bill. The media did not seem very interested in any of these developments and public attention paid to them was minimal.[43]

In the Kejriwal team were senior lawyers Shanti Bhushan and Prashant Bhushan, former Supreme Court judge Santosh Hegde, former police officer Kiran Bedi, and Kejriwal himself. Anna Hazare was inducted into the campaign a few weeks later as the moral face of the campaign. All these personalities were well-known and enjoyed a certain public credibility, with their views having been solicited by the media on a variety of issues of national import much before the IAC campaign was even conceived. The team also consisted of a line-up of subsidiary players, many of whom had been media professionals before becoming social activists. That the IAC team was able to break down the initial media apathy to its project and unleash one of the most interactive and unorthodox media outreach efforts that the country has ever seen under the IAC banner, was primarily because of its strategy to jumpstart public interest by creating its own content, using new communication technology and social media.

Through social media, it reached out to three sets of people: volunteers, participants, and audiences. One IAC volunteer explained in an interview the reasoning behind the move to deploy Facebook and Twitter: 'We figured the solution (to lack of funds) was to open all channels for volunteers and donors via the fastest viral mode, which was social media.'[44] When IAC content started figuring in social media, it attracted mainstream media attention. In that sense, social media acted as a catalyst to achieve the impressive convergence of media presence that marked the IAC protests.

The IAC protests eventually turned out to be the biggest story of 2011 for legacy media, but a closer examination of the reportage reveals the self-interest that marked it. Focusing on a campaign that had already been invested with so much public attention made great business sense, because it meant tapping 'into the mood of a brewing revolt by the elite, which sees its material security and privileges threatened by economic uncertainties and is impatient with a political system that is much too messy, noisy and disorderly'.[45]

In addition, the campaign also presented mainstream media with an opportunity to respond to, and perhaps even co-opt, a popular protest to shore up their own image and redeem some of the credibility that had been badly undermined by the revelations in the Radia tapes. The rich irony of the corruption-tainted mainstream media taking up the anti-corruption crusade was not lost on commentators, one of whom remarked, 'the corruption of civil society is best indicated in an ethically challenged but extremely powerful media campaigning for a less corrupt state and public sphere with no sense of self-reflection'.[46]

Complementing the IAC's online activities was its offline strategy to organise a series of events, ranging from rallies, press conferences, and meetings, starting from early 2011. They also fed off the non-stop and insistent international media coverage of the events playing out in Cairo's Tahrir Square and other theatres of dissent. While the proximate reasons for the anger may have varied from country to country, media images transmitted and re-transmitted through various media nodes from the theatres of protest created a 'shared sense of disempowerment'.[47]

In India, it was the IAC campaign that was best placed to benefit from this sense of disempowerment among ordinary people. Persuaded by their personal experiences and what they had read and seen in the media, they came to invest IAC's anti-corruption activism with a certain moral authority. Feeling oppressed and victimised by the varied manifestations of a corrupt system, they were now willing to valorise those individuals and campaigns that embraced the cause.

The moral authority steadily accruing to the campaign made any association with it a useful and attractive proposition for individuals and groups, including media organisations looking to enhance their public profile. If newspaper houses and television channels wished to add to their credibility by projecting themselves through the IAC campaign, individual members of the film industry seized it as an additional platform to promote themselves and their cinema. Aamir Khan, much to the delight of the crowds that participated in IAC events, kept tweeting in support of Hazare and even shared the stage with the fasting icon; Shah Rukh Khan, during a promotional tour for his film *Don 2*, urged all Indians to support the IAC cause in order to make sure no corruption remains in the country. Several other film stars were also conspicuous by their tweets and statements of support.

For the major opposition parties, the protests were something of a mixed blessing. The BJP, sensitive to the imminence of a crucial Uttar Pradesh state election slated for early 2012 and a general election two years away, adopted divergent stances as the situation warranted. Most of the time it saw the campaign as a convenient stick with which to beat its political rival, the ruling Congress. However, a consciousness of its own vulnerability to corruption charges prevented it from offering Anna and his team unqualified support. There were occasions when the party distanced itself from some of the demands made by the campaign, most notably during the parliamentary debate on the Lokpal Bill in the Winter Session of 2011. For the most part, however, going by its statements to the media and parliamentary speeches, the BJP made good use of the opportunity presented by the anti-corruption mood in the country to present itself as the moral arbiter of the country's politics. BJP leader Arun Jaitley's speech in Parliament as the Ramlila fast was underway was a good example of the latter approach. He characterised the protests as a 'wake-up call' for the country's politicians and urged them to put their house in order.

Individual politicians, including many who were in the political wilderness, also watched the campaign unfold closely. Among their number was former Andhra Pradesh Chief Minister Chandrababu Naidu, who, in a bid to regain power, launched what he termed as his war against corruption through a foundation he had set up, and joined a rally of opposition leaders in August 2011.[48] Gujarat Chief Minister Narendra Modi, who was to become the country's prime minister in 2014 and was among the first Indian politicians to connect on Twitter, also tweeted on the issue. One of the tweets he sent out to his three lakh followers during Hazare's Ramlila Maidan fast read: 'Nation is concerned about Anna's health. Congress talks of democracy and parliament but uses anti-democratic means to wipe out Anna's movement.'

Spiritual leaders like Shri Shri Ravi Shankar and Baba Ramdev, who were initially sought by the organisers of the IAC campaign because of the crowds they could commandeer for the cause, allied themselves with the anti-corruption mobilisations for their own purposes. Ramdev, whose trusts and businesses were valued at around Rs 1,100 crore in 2011[49] and whose television yoga show shown in India and around the world, Om Yog Sadhana, was watched by millions, organised two major public meetings in Delhi that year, demanding the return of *'kala dhan'* (black money, or funds sent out of the country through corrupt means). Ramdev's rallies, which took place around the same time as the IAC events, attracted a great deal of attention from newspapers and television channels. This was partly because of his personal clout with media owners, but also reflected the mass popularity of mega events built around his persona as yoga guru.

Unlikely additions to this list of supporters were representatives of corporate India. An 'open letter' widely circulated in the media in mid-January 2011 and signed by industrialists like Keshub Mahindra, Jamshyd Godrej, Anu Aga, and Azim Premji, noted that corruption was 'possibly the biggest issue corroding the fabric of our nation' and needed to be tackled on a 'war footing'.[50] Prominent personalities like Rahul Bajaj, Uday Kotak, and Kiran Mazumdar Shaw were to later offer their personal backing to the IAC campaign, and some corporates like Jindal Aluminium provided funds to keep it going.[51] Anand Mahindra sent out the following tweet when Hazare launched his second fast on 16 August: 'Democracy means no voice, however small, must go unheard. The anti-corruption sentiment is not a whisper—it's a scream. Grave error to ignore it.'

These interventions from sections of Indian big business were aimed at claiming the moral high ground. It afforded these tycoons a chance to define the nature of the popular discourse on corruption and deflect any anger and criticism that may have come their way. In their anxiety to distance themselves from their tainted business counterparts, who were facing serious allegations of corruption, they were prepared to join forces with a campaign that was regarded as 'safe', since it was essentially apolitical and not necessarily anti-corporate.

JANTAR MANTAR: LIVE

All these various streams of support for Hazare coalesced into what could be called a grand media narrative on corruption, which the IAC campaign seized, unified, amplified, and purported to address through the legal instrument of the Jan Lokpal Bill.

The active solicitation of mainstream media support had begun by early 2011. All the interactions the IAC team had with the Government of India were made public through timely press conferences or the deliberate leaking of correspondence. Just after the Jantar Mantar fast commenced on 5 April, a letter Hazare had written to Prime Minister Manmohan Singh was widely circulated in the media and helped immensely to build a cache of empathy within the media and the public. The letter ended with the words:

> It is being said that the government wants to talk to us and we are not talking to them. This is utterly false. Tell me a single meeting when you called us and we did not come. We strongly believe in dialogue and engagement. Kindly do not mislead the country by saying that we are shunning dialogue.

Meanwhile, the venue of the fast began to exercise a magnetic effect on the crowds. An idea of how both the crowds and the media were kept engaged at this juncture emerges from a media report: 'From the dais, Hazare entertained the crowd with patriotic songs and irreverent jokes about politicians. Backstage, Kejriwal guided the campaign: feeding stories and tips to reporters, comparing his protest with Tahrir Square, drafting press releases ....'[52]

Initially, it was television coverage that was the most effective because the scenes emanating from the venue made for compelling visuals and arresting soundbites. Newspapers, in contrast, had to grapple with technicalities like the differences between the Lokpal bill of the Government of India and the Jan Lokpal Bill of the IAC, which lay at the centre of the controversy. The prominent English language channel Times Now, anxious to emerge as the undisputed news channel in its class, presented an instance of how riding a popular mood did yield rich dividends in terms of television rating points (TRPs). According to insiders, the channel's Editor-in-Chief, Arnab Goswami, had just a month earlier found little news value in the story of an elderly social activist threatening to go on a hunger strike to end corruption. But by the first week of April, after realising the popular impact of the Hazare campaign, he personally ensured that it was made the sole focus of Times Now's news programming. The channel was among the first to devote attention to Anna Hazare when he began his fast on 5 April. Over the next three days, its coverage rose from two hours a day to six hours, finally becoming the only story that featured on the screen. In his News Hour debate of 7 April, Goswami hinted at why he was upping the ante on the IAC protests—they had reached a 'tipping point'.[53] As the participating crowds swelled, as he anticipated they would, the content on it would also go viral.

Coverage of such proportions had a domino effect. 'By the second day, a television channel like Headlines Today had five crews on rotation at Jantar Mantar. By the third day over 42 OB (outdoor broadcast) vans were milling around the Jantar Mantar site according to some reports.'[54] IndiaTV, a popular Hindi news channel, was beaming headlines that claimed that 'everyone' was with Anna. The channel had young, excitable students claiming to have come from distant suburbs of the Capital with the sole intent of wiping corruption from the face of the country, even as professors gravely averred on screen that this was the 'second freedom struggle'. The highly charged language used by interviewers and interviewees also adopted the 'Us, the people, versus Them, the corrupt government' framing.

Two aspects need to be noted here. Jantar Mantar's location close to Parliament House in the Capital made it an easy prime time site. As senior television anchor Rajdeep Sardesai observed in another context, 'Most news channels have dozens of reporters in Delhi but just one for the entire seven states of the Northeast .... Naturally, news becomes metro-centric.'[55] The other is the difference in tone adopted by the Hindi and English language media. While the former generally displayed a greater empathy towards the protests, some sections of the latter mounted a critique of the protest on the grounds that the tactics of Team Anna was marginalising electoral democracy in India.[56]

Such differences apart, there was no stopping the 'accumulation of pious vox-pop soundbites "against corruption"', which led to a 'tsunami of "sentiment" that brooks no dissent'.[57] Even news veterans were swept away in this tide of emotion. Sardesai confessed in hindsight to having 'overplayed' the protests. He remembered anchoring a show from Jantar Mantar surrounded by Anna supporters, towards the end of which he found himself having become one of them.[58] Anchors thus became the voice by proxy of those sections of society that supported the campaign. 'The stance adopted by anchors and commentators signalled the moral-political agency of the emergent middle classes.'[59] Ashutosh, founder-editor of IBN7, took his deep engagement as a television professional with Hazare's fasts to the next level: he joined AAP, the political party that was to be set up by Kejriwal, in 2014. As he explained later, it was the lure of its projected credibility that had moved him: 'They were honest people, committed to changing the very fabric of politics.'[60]

When Hazare ended his fast after the government capitulated to his demands on 10 April, it was time to count the gains. Times Now's 'News Hour' had the claim '84 hours continuous coverage' emblazoned on the screen, along with the words 'Victory for India'. Its print counterpart, *The Times of India*, had a similar spin: 'India Wins, Again'. If such headlines recalled the euphoric coverage that had greeted India's win over Sri Lanka in the cricket World Cup Final that had taken place just a week earlier, it may not have been entirely coincidental. By constantly casting the face-off between the

IAC campaigners and the government as a cricketing encounter, drawing liberally from the terminology associated with the game, the media was deliberately using the drawing power of cricket to keep the public engaged with the campaign and their coverage of it.

Between print and television, it was the visual media that had overwhelmingly rallied to the IAC cause. A television monitoring intelligence report revealed that between 3–11 April 2011, there were 655 hours of coverage. Of the 5,657 news clips reviewed, only sixty-five were found to be negative. The other significant conclusion reached was that this empathetic coverage, which was in sync with the public mood, was a profitable enterprise, gleaning an estimated Rs 175.86 crore for the various channels. At their height—on 8 April—the protests translated into 167 hours of news coverage, bringing in Rs 38 crore worth of advertisements.[61]

RAMLILA MAIDAN: LIVE

Such handsome returns were certainly one reason why the swell of media presence witnessed during the four-day Hazare fast at Jantar Mantar in April had turned into a flood by August, when he undertook a thirteen-day fast at the Ramlila Maidan in Delhi. None of this would have been possible without the hard work that Kejriwal put in, through tireless micromanagement, to leverage the moral authority of Hazare, in order to ensure that the IAC protests kept gaining public traction. The scale of the second event was much larger—if Jantar Mantar had seen a peak crowd of 25,000, estimations of the number at the Ramlila at its peak ranged from 50,000 to 100,000. This exponential rise required the consolidation of popular sentiment on view at Jantar Mantar. 'The spectacle of popular mobilisation was seen to be a thing of virtue, the greater the mobilization, the more virtuous civil society was assumed to be.'[62] Added to this was what one political scientist termed as 'a carnivalesque celebration of the pure ideals of democracy—of the idea that "we the people" are sovereign, that politicians are the servants of the people, that laws must originate in the needs and demands of the people'.[63]

The manner in which the government tried to prevent the fast, by initially remanding Anna Hazare to judicial custody, only lent an added appeal to his activism. He had, in the eyes of his thronging supporters, become a man who could do no wrong. When Congress spokesperson Manish Tewari made an uncharitable remark about Anna being corrupt from 'head to toe', the backlash was so swift that Tewari had to apologise almost immediately; such was the moral stature that had come to be attributed to Anna at this point.

The parallels between the original mahatma and the man now invested with the aura of the original figure were striking. Hazare and his team constantly strove to deepen that comparison. An impromptu decision of Hazare's to visit Rajghat on the morning of Independence Day made for stunning visuals as he sat on the green grass of Rajghat in deep meditation, even as supporters spoke into television microphones about how they perceived him as '*aaj ki Gandhi*'. When he was whisked to jail the next morning amidst a swirl of slogan chanting crowds and television cameras, once again it strongly recalled the incarceration of freedom fighters. Supporters raised angry slogans, tonsured their heads, and courted arrest in different parts of the country, most of it on live television. In a pre-recorded address to his supporters, Hazare spoke of the IAC campaign as a second national movement. Once he emerged from Tihar jail, the '*aaj ki Gandhi*' metaphor was sought to be reinforced at the Ramlila Maidan. Most significantly, the Bharat Mata/Mother India iconography that had marked the backdrop of the Jantar Mantar fast was now replaced by an enormous portrait of Gandhi, which drew an immediate parallel between the Father of the Nation and the elderly man now on fast before the crowds thronging the venue.

The Hazare arrest was the only news on television on 16 August, the day of the arrest. Many newspapers, which were generally more restrained than television during the Jantar Mantar days, now began to display a new appetite for projecting the story in a manner that mimicked television coverage. It was a clear example of how the battle for ratings pushed even traditional media entities to imitate the competition and experience the power of 'being on the side of the middle class'.[64] The front page of *The Times of India* of 17 August 2011, for instance, was completely devoted to the Hazare story, with a banner headline that read, 'Govt Can't Stop August Kranti'. *Kranti*, or revolution, is a loaded term, which usually invites severe censure from mainstream media when Maoists or Kashmiri militants use it, but the approval granted to Hazare's *'kranti'* was unqualified. The newspaper also carried a poll on whether the government's handling of Hazare was democratic, with 92 per cent of respondents believing that it was not. Another story on the same page, reporting on protests in other parts of the country, had the rather florid headline, 'Anna Hazare arrest: A million mutinies erupt across India'.

The major Hindi newspaper, *Dainik Bhaskar*, encouraged a totalising view of an India uniting to fight corruption. Its poll of 17 August, inviting readers to vote on whether they were with Anna or not, drew responses like, *'Anna, tum great ho. Bharstachar dimak ki tarah desh ko kha raha hai tum ise khatam karo. Pura Hindusthan tumhare* (Anna, you are great. Corruption is like termites eating into the country. Put an end to it. The whole of India will be with you).' *Navbharat Times*, another mainstream Hindi newspaper, even enjoined its readers to give their time to this 'national movement': *'Ek saptha desh ke naam, Anna ke saath utariyae'* (one week for the nation's cause, rise with Anna). As the days went by and Hazare grew visibly frailer, the media consciously heightened public feelings of anxiety over his health. Television anchors talked about how the 'nation is in a sense on tenterhooks, anxious about when Anna Hazare will call off his fast', and how 'India unites with Anna'.

Real life and media representation came to mirror each other. Not only was the popular emotion on display at the Ramlila Maidan reflective of 'the frenzy on TV news shows',[65] but it was also obvious that the crowds that poured into the venue were following the media coverage of the fast very closely. There were instances when journalists and television teams were targeted for putting out less than totally supportive content. On 25 August, there was the case of someone in a crowd accusing the NDTV team of biased reporting. Within seconds, an angry group shouted slogans against the young representatives of the news channel who were filming the proceedings, and the situation almost threatened to get out of hand. The 'with-us-or-against-us' tone of the public discourse that emanated from Ramlila Maidan had a corrosive edge to it, which could have intimidated reporters into adopting a more supportive coverage than they would have otherwise done. In that sense, such coverage compromised the status of the media as a 'live document of contemporary history and as the arbiter of truth'.[66]

By mid-August, Hazare's moral authority as a Gandhian figure ill-treated by the State was at its height, and favourable coverage only grew across all sections of the media. Media academic Arvind Rajagopal argues that this was perhaps the first mass campaign in India after 1947 where English and vernacular media had come together so visibly.[67] The coverage certainly reflected the expansion of support for Hazare across large sections of society, geographically and demographically, with even the 'dabbawallahs' of Mumbai coming out in support. A few intellectuals were the only exception to this near universal endorsement. One Dalit intellectual put it this way, 'The language, symbols used by the movement clearly reflects its upper caste Hindu nature, a very rightwing Hindu patriotism is being used to get the entire country against corruption. And as a dalit, I have a problem with it.'[68] But critiques of this kind were either talked down in television chat shows or underplayed on news pages at this point.

A review of the content put out by two Hindi channels, Star News and Aaj Tak, during prime time between 16 and 28 August indicated that they had devoted 97 per cent and 92.2 per cent, respectively, to the Hazare fast, with the English language channels NDTV 24×7 and CNN-IBN notching slightly lower figures of 85 per cent and 81 per cent, respectively. Some of this coverage consisted solely of footage of the crowds, with only their slogans providing the audio support; but clearly, even such bare-bones content drew viewers. TAM data for the week ending 20 August saw increases of 87 per cent and 74 per cent in viewerships for Hindi and English language news channels, respectively. The data suggested that not only did more people view the news channels, they also watched for longer spans of time.[69] By now, Hazare had emerged as a brand in his own right, in the language of the market. By August-end, he was among the ten top brands, placed higher than even the iconic Amitabh Bachchan, according to his Klout score based on the influence he was wielding.

MMRDA GROUNDS: LIVE

If the Jantar Mantar fast proved the springboard for increased media engagement with the IAC campaign, the Ramlila Maidan saw its climactic moment. The question then arises: Why did Hazare's third fast, staged at the Mumbai Metropolitan Region Development Authority (MMRDA) Grounds in Mumbai at the end of the year, witness such a dramatic reversal of the tide? While tens of thousands had flocked to the Ramlila Maidan during the thirteen-day fast in Delhi, and large crowds had risen in protest against Hazare's arrest on 16 August in Mumbai itself, there were just a few hundred who turned up at the MMRDA Grounds this time, and a fast slated for three days was prematurely concluded a day earlier. The reasons cited for this sharp decline have varied. Some analysts pointed to poor timing because the fast took place at that very point when the Lokpal Bill was being discussed in Parliament; others spoke of the interpersonal tensions that had arisen within Team Anna. But there could be no denying the growing disillusionment with the Hazare movement among the very section that had championed him at the beginning of the year—and most notably within the media.

Such disillusionment went beyond local factors like excessive policing and poor connectivity in Mumbai, because even the crowds congregating at the fasts held simultaneously in other cities like Delhi and Bengaluru were also markedly smaller than earlier.

Some saw this as evidence of a 'fundamental disconnect' between Hazare and his middle-class supporters: 'for the former, corruption is a black-and-white moral issue, to be fought like absolute evil. For the mass supporters, corruption is a nuisance, an inconvenience that needed to be fixed or sidelined.'[70]

Discerning whether it was media disillusionment that led to the tepid public response or the other way around is of course the classic chicken-and-egg conundrum. But it is also a fact that even as the Ramlila Maidan event was reaching its crescendo, the narrative of the 'Anna movement' being a second freedom struggle was beginning to wear thin. There was already the criticism that was often featured in media commentary and furthered by the UPA government that Team Anna and its Jan Lokpal Bill bore strong elements of autocracy; that it constituted unelected individuals seeking to impose their will on the elected. The claim that the Jan Lokpal Bill would prove a panacea for all the ills visiting the nation, that a single law would wipe out all corruption in the country, was always strongly critiqued. Comment pieces argued that 'any claim that a particular law can eradicate corruption is a dishonest claim far removed from the truth' and that it was the 'ineptitude of mainstream political parties in addressing various pressing issues of the polity, particularly corruption', rather than coherent and collective thinking within the IAC collective that had imparted it with the public credibility that it had enjoyed thus far.[71]

In his popular television show, Devil's Advocate, of 21 August, Karan Thapar aggressively questioned the two stalwarts of the IAC campaign, Arvind Kejriwal and Prashant Bhushan, suggesting that the media had showcased the IAC campaign without a deeper understanding of the issues at hand.[72] This particular stance on a major English-language platform at a moment when the Anna Hazare mystique was its height seemed to point to an imminent shift in the media narrative.

There were at least four major developments between August and December 2011 which cast the IAC campaign in poor light as far as media coverage went. The first of these were the serious disagreements between IAC members over participating on an aggressive anti-Congress platform in the Lok Sabha Hisar by-polls. The second flashpoint was the sharp differences over the Prashant Bhushan view favouring a plebiscite in Kashmir, a stance from which Hazare publicly distanced himself. Allegations of personal impropriety against senior members Kiran Bedi and Arvind Kejriwal constituted the third factor. Bedi was publicly accused of passing on the benefits from inflated travel bills to her NGO and Kejriwal was said to have transferred Rs 80 lakh of public donations to the Public Cause Research Foundation, an organisation set up by him. The fourth, and perhaps most damaging development because it concerned Anna Hazare directly, were revelations made in the Hindi daily, *Nai Duniya*, about Hazare's strong association with the Rashtriya Swayamsevak Sangh (RSS), which were carried with an old photograph of him with RSS ideologue Nanaji Deshmukh, taken in 1983. The estranged IAC member, Swami Agnivesh, had already publicly attacked Team Anna for conducting itself in an anti-democratic and casteist manner, and this revelation only seemed to emphasise these attributes. Picked up by large Hindi channels like Aaj Tak and Zee News, the story attracted a lot of media attention. Hazare and IAC members vigorously denied the charge, but this controversy, along with the others, went some way in diminishing the aura that had once surrounded the campaign. The sensational headlines and text that had supported Hazare in an unambiguous fashion were now replaced by more considered, even critical, reportage.

Evidence of this shift was obvious in the front page report of *The Times of India* after the first day of the third fast: 'Notwithstanding the media hype over the fast, there were hardly around 200 people from the public at the ground which has the capacity of 40,000.' TV channel coverage now juxtaposed scenes of the jam-packed Ramlila Maidan with the desultory audience at the MMRDA Grounds, with headlines that went: 'Low turnout at Anna fast venue'. Nothing reflected this lost aura more eloquently than the manner in which Hazare ended the press conference that had been arranged at the

MMRDA Grounds, after he had ended his fast prematurely. Riled by the hostile questioning, he chose to walk out, even as media persons kept requesting him to answer their questions. That evening, for perhaps the first time since the 5 April fast at Jantar Mantar, the mainstream media's coverage was distinctly critical. One television banner read: 'Is Team Anna taking the right line?'

A blogging site, annahazare.blogspot.in, had a critic berating Hazare for damaging his own cause by sticking to his 'my way or the highway' stance, and there was implied criticism over the expenses incurred in the hiring of the MMRDA Grounds, which were estimated to have set the campaign back by several lakhs. It was not long before the inevitable question was being raised: Had 'Anna fatigue' set in? The days that followed indicated that this was emphatically the case. Hazare would never again be able to revive the hope he seemed to project in April in Jantar Mantar, let alone the euphoria he inspired at the Ramlila Maidan in August.

There could be many reasons for this change in the media's stance. The credibility of the IAC campaign to deliver on their well-packaged and promoted promise of a corruption-free India had been badly undermined in the days after the Ramlila Maidan euphoria. There could also have been a realisation among those who control the media that this campaign, if promoted beyond a point, could have seriously detrimental impacts on the economy. Sukumar Muralidharan identifies the UPA government's notification in November 2011 allowing foreign direct investment into the retail sector as a key turning point in media response.[73] He cites as proof the tone *The Times of India* adopted in an editorial that appeared shortly after this move, in which the government was commended for its 'first big ticket reform initiative in a long time'.

Whether market-driven media disenchantment with the Anna project led in turn to a decline in the public's engagement with it, or whether the media, ever sensitive to its user base, sensed a growing popular disillusionment and withdrew its patronage of it, is an intriguing question and difficult to answer, but the unravelling of the Anna mystique and 'movement' was decisive and irreversible.

Within nine months of the MMRDA fast in Mumbai, Hazare had dissolved Team Anna.

Did mainstream media kill the IAC campaign? That newspaper and television channels helped to build ownership of the IAC campaign among urban, middle-class India cannot be disputed, but did they also ensure its demise? An IAC supporter in fact termed the relationship between the media and the IAC campaign as the kiss of death:

> Support from television channels like *Times Now* and *CNN-IBN* was the worst thing that could have happened to the fledgling movement. These channels have distinguished themselves, over the years, by presenting themselves as the self-appointed guardians of 'probity' in public life. Shrill in the rhetoric they deploy against politicians and intellectuals, they (and their noisy anchors) have reduced public debate in India to a farce. No wonder the moment they stepped in, in support of Anna Hazare and the anti-corruption movement, a certain polarization of debate was bound to occur.[74]

The IAC leaders, however, were more circumspect in their assessment. Anna Hazare formally acknowledged the role of big media when a prominent television house recognised him as the Indian of the Year 2011: 'If your cameras had not followed me everywhere, who would know me?'[75] As the driving force behind the IAC campaign, Kejriwal too knew the value of mainstream media support, as evident in the speech he made on 28 August 2011 to mark the end of Hazare's fast at the Ramlila Maidan, where he thanked the media profusely and observed that they had now become a part of the struggle ('*yeh log ab andolan ka hissa hain*').

The Role of Social Media

Kejriwal was canny enough, however, to realise very early on in the campaign that mainstream media cannot be depended upon to take the IAC's voice to people at all times. In a newspaper interview given in 2011, Kejriwal pointed out that while television helped to bring in the crowds during the fasts at Jantar Mantar and

Ramlila Maidan, it could not have created the 'moment';[76] for that to happen, the IAC literally had to fashion its own media system, which was why new communication technologies and social media were so important.

Manuel Castells, who developed the idea of the 'network society', argues that the arrival of mobile telephony and digital communication constituted a turning point in the creation of this network society. He sees mediated communication as constituting 'the symbolic environment in which people receive, process and send the signals that produce meaning in their lives'.[77] This leads to a shift from mass communication to mass self-communication, 'where the production of the message is self-generated, the retrieval of the message is self-directed, and the reception and remixing of content from electronic networks is self-selected'.[78] What interests Castells is the way this diffusion of horizontal communication alters the exercise of power and counter-power, and he argues that the growth of mass self-communication 'has supported an unexpected, extraordinary broadening of the ability of individuals and social actors to challenge the power of the state'. While recognising that technology by itself cannot determine everything, he concludes that it did maximise 'the chances for the expansion for the expression and mobilization of alternative projects that have emerged from society to challenge the powers that be'.[79]

Unpacking the many ways the IAC protests achieved 'mass self-communication' is striking.

Team Anna found a ready resource in mobile telephony and social media—SMSes, missed calls, Facebook, MySpace, YouTube, BlackBerry Messaging Service, and the now defunct platform, Orkut, were all pressed into service. A technology like mobile phone messaging, for instance, had been used to solicit votes even in the 2004 general election. An early form of Twitter had made its presence felt in the country on a mass scale during the Mumbai terrorist attacks of 2008. Over the next couple of years, civil society organisations, especially those with an urban, middle-class appeal, had begun to use social media more consistently. In September 2008, for example, Tata Tea partnered various civil society organisations to get people to become more involved in civic activism through its 'Jaago Re! One Billion Votes Campaign'. The ipaidabribe.com campaign, initiated by the Bengaluru-based Janaagraha Centre for Citizenship and Democracy in August 2010, can be cited as another instance of social media being used to further a moral crusade.

Yet the IAC team could take the process a step forward. The first indication of progress was when the IAC campaign organised a large rally on 30 January 2011. The rally had initially been envisaged as a single event against corruption, to be held on Martyr's Day, but the IAC managed to successfully conduct similar rallies simultaneously in sixty-four cities through its Facebook network.[80] This provided a model on how to reach out to large numbers spread out over a vast geographical space in a cost-effective manner, using internet connectivity and a range of social media tools, but always in sync with mainstream media in a constant feedback loop—the first evidence of media convergence in the country at a mass level.

The attempt was to send messages to every connected citizen of India through the internet and mobile phones, with the intention of connecting the streets and squares where people came out to protest with 'a web of satellite television, the internet, round-the-clock circulation and movement of images, sounds, and affective experiences'.[81] The founder of Juvenis Technologies—himself a volunteer in the campaign—came up with an application that allowed participants to demonstrate their solidarity by communicating with IAC through missed calls. Millions of such calls were received. Other software concerns like Netcore Company also came in to help. Netcore used IBM technology to send bulk SMSes to 100,000 recipients at a time. The receipt of missed calls and the dispatch of bulk messages neatly supplemented each other. With an estimated five million calls coming in from unique numbers, the IAC campaign could, over time, build itself a data base of supporters to whom it could send information.

Not only were the mainstream media according blanket coverage to Hazare and social media sites like Facebook and Twitter registering unprecedented activity, but online activist groups were also making their presence felt, requesting people to fax or electronically petition the government on the issue. The most notable of these interventions was that of the international platform Avaaz. org, which self-defines itself as an online campaigning community. Its petition in support of a strong Jan Lokpal Bill during the Jantar Mantar fast drew a lot of attention, but its greatest impact was felt when it put out a second petition on 18 August to the government:

> We call on you to immediately release Anna Hazare, and all of those arrested. We urge you to ensure the police uphold the constitutional right of all Indians to peacefully protest and demand an end to corruption. We stand with Anna Hazare in his urgent call for a Jan Lokpal. Free Anna and Free India of Corruption Now!

Within two-and-a-half hours of the petition being sent out, 33,000 signatures were received.

Kejriwal revealed later that he had strong reservations against the use of social media at the start of the campaign because he believed it would connect only with a limited section of the urban elite. The emphasis initially was on circulating drafts of the Lokpal bill, filing of RTIs, following up on cases of corruption, and staging rallies. But the need to achieve something that had a bigger, more immediate impact was constantly being felt. By early 2011, as the idea of deploying the moral authority of Anna Hazare to promote the movement was taking shape, the campaign got itself a name—India Against Corruption—as well as an exclusive Facebook page in that name, even as its backroom boys, youth volunteers, and infotech professionals were working out a media strategy.

Some of these volunteers were political activists before they joined up. Sundeep Narwani, who had started as a Communist Party of India (Marxist) cadre, was one of them. He found that the Left party was failing to strike a chord with people; the IAC campaign, in contrast, seemed to promise an instant connect.

> When we went for door to door in Mumbai, we found that corruption was an issue that touched people across classes, from the elite to the lowest strata. In fact, it was among the poorest that we found the

greatest response. The rich would say things like, 'We should leave the country', but the poor of course understood they could not run away from the reality of corruption. The middle classes were also enthusiastic. I remember standing near Regal Cinema in Mumbai, waiting for the lights to turn red so that I could go from car to car to approach motorists on the issue. People were surprisingly receptive, perhaps because of the anti-establishment mood among the public created by the innumerable citizens' groups that had sprung up after the Mumbai blasts of November 2008.[82]

A Lot of Facebook, A Little Twitter

Although the IAC campaign used a medley of communication technologies and media platforms, Facebook remained the principal platform for several reasons. According to Narwani, Twitter was important to the campaign and it was perhaps for the first time that a public mobilisation had used a Twitter handle. It was still relatively unfamiliar and certainly did not have the heft it was to have during the Delhi gang rape protests of December 2012, but Twitter came into its own during the events leading to the Ramlila Maidan fast. On 16 and 17 August, when Anna Hazare was incarcerated by the Delhi Police, hashtag #isupportannahazare unleashed 8,000 tweets and hashtag #Janlokpal another 9,000 tweets. About 15,000 tweets with the mention of Anna Hazare were published on Twitter over those two days. The Klout score, which measures the influence of a Twitter handle, indicated that #janlokpal went up from sixty-eight on 15 August to seventy-four by 17 August, indicating that the campaign was now enjoying an influence on Twitter comparable to personalities like Shah Rukh Khan and the Dalai Lama, whose Twitter presence had been built over a period of time.[83] There was also a Twitter app made available 'to take India's fight against corruption to the next level', which tweeted on the subject's behalf, with one message sent to more than 126 on an average.

Yet, all said and done, Twitter was considered to be elitist.

> In those days not many used it. Besides it offered fewer options. It was only later that apps like Twitpic and Dubsmash were available on this platform. Since we relied a lot on visuals, we much preferred Facebook which allowed us the space to be creative. Some of us worked almost 24 hours on Facebook posts for the campaign.[84]

The setting up of the IAC Facebook page had a history. It played a fundamental role in helping to invest the IAC campaign with an identity distinct from that of the NCPRI, which was working for a draft Lokpal Bill in September 2011. Once Kejriwal broke away from the NCPRI to create his own team and organisation, which also had as its core objective the institution of a Jan Lokpal, the need to build a distinct character for the IAC began to be felt. He undertook several steps towards the end of 2010 and early 2011 to achieve this, including the staging of an anti-corruption rally in the Capital in concert with crowd pullers like Ramdev and Sri Sri Ravi Shankar, publicly dispatching a draft Lokpal Bill to Prime Minister Manmohan Singh, and inducting Anna Hazare as the figurehead of the IAC campaign. Crucially, he and his team also simultaneously set up the IAC website and Facebook account, having intuitively understood the importance of mass self-communication.

More than the website, it was the IAC Facebook page that came to be the mothership of the campaign. Its content was an admixture of careful strategising and spontaneous response to changing situations. The languages used were largely English and Hindi and its appeal was directed at young adults, given that it was this cohort that was most likely to use this platform.

> We felt we were sowing the seeds of a new future, the idea was to create a buzz especially among youth. The information that figured on our page ranged from cultural events to data from Janaagraha's Ipaidabribe campaign. When Aamir Khan decided to support us, the information was first put out on Facebook; when Manish Tewari made that atrocious comment about Anna being corrupt, our page carried the ripple of outrage that followed.[85]

There were also lighter offshoots like the 'Mera Neta Chor Hai' (my leader is a crook) pages on Facebook that created a sub-culture of its own, spawning tattoos and haircuts bearing those words.

Revisiting the IAC's Facebook discourse would reveal how early experiments in communication acquired both depth and focus as time went by—both creating the campaign and being created by it. In the initial weeks, the emphasis was on building an identity for the campaign and a sense of ownership among those associated with it. A post put out on 30 November 2010 went: 'Dear IAC-ians. All of us are equal stakeholders in this campaign and I urge you all to help build it.' Corruption as a concern was constantly highlighted, in ways ranging from the serious to the frivolous and comic. Often, cartoons that appeared in mainstream newspapers made their way on to the IAC Facebook wall, as did celebrity tweets and quotes from sources ranging from Rabindranath Tagore to Udham Singh.

Gaining a substantial volunteer base was clearly seen as one of the main objectives of the IAC Facebook page, and there were posts instructing all those who wished to volunteer to come on board. All they had to do was message back. According to one estimate, activists from about 350 cities and towns in India and around 100 cities outside the country used this platform to keep abreast of the campaign, and plan their own activities in tandem with Team Anna's plans.[86]

But a campaign comprising such disparate supporters spread over a vast geographical area needed to achieve a certain unity and cohesiveness. Here again, Facebook proved useful. There was a fair degree of interactive strategising that went on. The idea of tricolour flag-bearers on bikes winding their way through the city as a form of protest was tested on Facebook; designs of logos, banners, and other material, including Gandhi caps, could be downloaded from a common URL source (http://iacbranding.org) and customised for local needs. Similarly, slogans were also posted, so that all protesters everywhere were on the same page in terms of how they projected themselves to the public.

While various cities and regions came up with their own IAC Facebook pages, reports of IAC actions across the country were faithfully carried on the main Facebook page, whether it was taking place in small towns like Barabanki and Thiruchirapalli, or in Bengaluru's Freedom Park and Mumbai's Azad Maidan. IAC supporters were also constantly being urged to send petitions to the government, light candles, join rallies. Zany, out-of-the-box ideas were showcased. One striking instance of this was the initiative shown by a group of volunteers in Nagpur, who wanted to use the venue of the World Cup match between India and South Africa to display a poster emblazoned with the words, 'India Against Corruption/Cricket Against Corruption'.

Besides providing mundane details about venues for meetings and the number of people who turned up for them, content from mainstream media that was sympathetic to the campaign or reported instances of corruption were also put out. In fact, the Facebook page soon became the preferred platform for those fighting corruption across India to share their experiences and record their victories and reversals; and to keep their Facebook friends engaged, the campaign's tech team tried to introduce a strong element of interactivity to the content in order to foster feelings of ownership and involvement.

A post of 19 May, for instance, asked: 'Should the Prime Minister be under the jurisdiction of the Jan Lokpal?' Interestingly, as if in sync with the thinking of Team Anna, an overwhelming number of respondents ticked the 'Yes' box. An opinion poll, put out on 26 June, posed another interesting question: 'How far are you willing to go to get the Jan Lokpal?' The choices were (*a*) I am ready to face bullets/lathi charge/court arrest; (*b*) I can only comment on Facebook/Twitter; (*c*) I will do whatever Anna Hazare asks us to do; (*d*) I can observe fast at home/office. Once again, most of the respondents opted for the first option.

The careful construction of personality cults through the IAC Facebook page was also very evident. On 7 March, the day Hazare announced his fast unto death at Jantar Mantar, a message was posted that was headlined, 'A Mahatma announces fast unto death', with the injunction, 'Please copy and email to all friends!!!' The Mahatma iconisation continued in subsequent posts with one particular image—of Hazare and Gandhi, both looking out of the frame in identical fashion—being posted and reposted several times. Arvind Kerjiwal's tireless activism also found constant references on the Facebook page, along with images of him interacting with volunteers in various cities. Despite the occasional sighting of Kiran Bedi or Manish Sisodia, or a reference to Kumar Viswas, it was Kejriwal who came across as the real power behind the IAC campaign.

The IAC Facebook page was at its most 'liked' and 'shared' when Hazare was on fast, constantly focusing on the man at the centre of it all and building support for him. A post of 7 April during the Jantar Mantar fast reported that 'Anna was too weak to make an appearance on the stage'. Another post the next day announced that he would be ending his fast at 10 am. It got 2,937 likes.

By the time the Ramlila Maidan fast took place in August, the IAC campaign had carved for itself a significant presence on social media, with more than 150 Facebook pages related to it having been set up over the course of a few months, some of which had thousands of followers. The climactic point in Facebook activism was reached in the seven hours between 1 pm and 8 pm on 23 August, as the second Anna fast at Ramlila Maidan was reaching its crescendo, with the official India Against Corruption page—which had nearly half a million Friends by now—received over 5,000 comments, with at least ten times that number hitting the 'like' button.[87] On 27 August, a new post described the scene at the end of the second fast, reporting how Hazare had asked those who had assembled at the Ramlila Maidan whether he had their permission to break his fast, as if he was surrendering his body to the will of the people. It resonated with hundreds of thousands who pleaded with Anna to give up his fast, and Facebook was one of the platforms they used.

This untiring effort to build popular empathy for Hazare did contribute to keeping the momentum going for a full year. But by December 2011, fatigue had clearly set in and the Facebook space also reflected it. If the crowd that had turned up to watch him break his fast on 28 December was markedly smaller, so too were the likes and shares on the post announcing this. Nothing reflected the new mood of pessimism that had gripped Team Anna more than the last post of 2011: 'Yes it is a difficult task to end corruption and get a strong Lokpal ... but WE are up to the challenge! Hum honge kamiyaab ek din! (We will overcome one day).'

IAC CAMPAIGN MELTDOWN

'It was amply clear that the movement had lived its life.'[88] That was the verdict pronounced by CNN7 anchor Ashutosh, after observing the dwindling of public support in Mumbai. Here again, mainstream media's jettisoning of the Anna project was evidence that even the faint democratic possibilities inherent in such activism were constantly moderated and even undone by the mainstream media, which, dictated as always by their own commercial interests, pull back when they perceive that the narrative could go out of hand and hurt their core interests.

The mainstream media coverage of the IAC protests could then be seen, at one level, as the culmination of half-a-century of close journalistic focus on public corruption. The manner in which such corruption had played out over these five decades was driven also by the media's own self-interest, which in turn was influenced—as we saw—by political pressures, corporate influence, and careful assessments of the public mood. What is interesting to observe is that while social media was instrumental in getting mainstream media to take note of the IAC campaign, it was also true that social media coverage suffered a meltdown once mainstream media turned indifferent to this story.

In this context, it may be useful to revisit the polemical arguments between those who suggest that Web 2.0, because of its potential for horizontal communication, is by its very nature a platform for activism, resistance, and social change, and those who disagreed with such a proposition. An early theorist of the internet, Clay Shirky, points out that the new communication network through the internet and mobile phone has made group forming 'ridiculously easy'.[89] He traces the four rungs of association these media achieve—the sharing of information within a group, conversation within the group, collaboration among members of the group, and ultimately, collective action launched by those in the group. Shirky recognises that the last is the hardest to get going, but maintains that the potential of social media to usher in transformation within society is considerable. Others like Malcolm Gladwell disagree, and point out that social media are built around weak ties, which have their uses in terms of the exchange of ideas and information and the creation of interdisciplinary collaborations, but seldom lead to high-risk activism.[90] Evgeny Mozorov takes Gladwell's critique a step further and argues that social media potentially undermines social movements, precisely because they promoted 'slacktivism', or 'feel-good online activism that has zero political or social impact. It gives those who participate in "slacktivist" campaigns an illusion of having a meaningful impact on the world without demanding anything more than joining a Facebook group'.[91]

Bellamy Foster and Robert McChesney, while acknowledging that peer-to-peer activities like Open Source movement and WikiLeaks are important reminders of how the internet could be different, believe that such models inevitably wilt under the 'pressure of capital to consolidate monopoly power, create artificial scarcity and erect fences wherever possible', and point out that 'at nearly every turn, industries connected to the Internet have transitioned from competitive to oligopolistic in short order'.[92]

The IAC campaign of 2011 reflected both the strengths and the weaknesses of media activism, especially that of social media: disruptive impacts; middle-class appeal; low threshold of participation, which allowed large numbers to participate; and the inherent limitations of a 'slacktivist' campaign that had its moments of history-making, disillusion, and disintegration. There can also be no doubting that it was social media that led the media charge initially by helping the IAC campaign to quietly build its presence, beginning from November 2010 right up to March 2011. By early April, this changed dramatically, with legacy media assuming the dominant role, albeit in concert with social media. For the corporate mainstream media, the Anna mobilisation came to be a sign of their own success, in that it 'proved that the media could help move people onto the streets for a cause'.[93] It also afforded them yet another opportunity to re-visit a theme that had always helped shore up their visibility and 'moral' authority—that of political corruption.

But did the IAC campaign's audacious activism realise its anti-corruption vision, if not in its entirety, then at least in part? It certainly set in motion a chain of political developments that impacted Indian politics in innumerable and radical ways. In the immediate term, it pushed the political establishment to table the Lokpal and Lokayukta Bills in the Winter Session of Parliament of 2011. It is another matter that it took another two years for the law to come into force. The ruling Indian National Congress finally ensured that it was passed into law in the run-up to the General Election of 2014, driven undoubtedly by expectations of political dividends. Despite such last-ditch efforts, the party could not fully recover from the body blow dealt it by the IAC campaign, as testified in the consecutive state elections that followed and the debacle that came with the 2014 general election. Zoya Hasan has argued that the 'success of the Anna Hazare movement was the way in which it was able to pin it (corruption) on politicians and on Congress in particular'.[94]

The Congress Party, held to be corrupt both by the courts of law and the general public, was the singular reference point of IAC activism and its direct casualty. Inevitably, the biggest beneficiary of this brand of activism was the BJP. By being the principal opposition party, it was obviously best placed to draw political mileage from the agitation. But there were also striking commonalities between the symbols, vocabulary, and idiom used by the IAC activists and those employed by the BJP and its parent organisation, the RSS, as also the spiritual figures who acted as bridges between Hazare and his team and the Sangh Parivar, notably godmen like Baba Ramdev and Sri Sri Ravi Shankar. Media coverage of the protests, which rarely interrogated their ideological underpinnings, actually contributed to the valorisation of religio-cultural politics. It could even be argued that the campaign laid the ideological foundation for the spectacular return of the BJP to power in 2014.

When it first began, the IAC protests were projected as a social movement that was strongly apolitical and non-partisan in orientation. But in fact they never evolved from being a campaign to a movement. This dissipation led to a breakdown of consensus on what was to be its role in the future. While Hazare persisted in seeing it as a civil society 'movement' exerting moral authority on the State, Kejriwal now nursed ambitions to test the model against the grain of electoral politics. As the year progressed, he increasingly gave up on the anonymity of being the backroom boy and began to share in some of the moral iconisation that had hitherto been strictly reserved for Hazare. Symptomatic of this shift was a telling image put out on the IAC Facebook page of 29 August 2011, showing Kejriwal and his close associate, Manish Sisodia, sleeping on the floor of a railway station along with other passengers. The text extolled their 'simple living HIGH thinking' and insisted that: 'Only ordinary people like them can understand the pain of "Aam Aadmi"'. This was a clear signalling of political intent.

The divergent stances of Hazare and Kejriwal on participating in formal politics reflected the age difference of over three decades between the two men, and the way they perceived the future. More fundamentally, this disagreement reflected their respective styles of activism. Hazare saw himself more as an icon for a patriotic, nationalist India that is morally 'clean', and he did not want to sully that image by entering what he was to later describe as 'dirty politics'. Kejriwal would later claim that, although initially opposed to the idea of forming a political party, he was forced by circumstances and the pressure from supporters to reconsider that stance. 'We never wanted to fight elections, never in my dreams I wanted to form a political party. It was after so many movements, when nothing worked we were left with no option, every leader would mock us "go make your party and fight election," we revisited our decision.'[95]

An IAC Facebook post of 25 September 2012 claimed that a referendum conducted through social media involving 700,000 people had indicated that 76 per cent had supported the idea of setting up a political party. Subsequent events proved that the idea of a political party did hold a certain resonance with people. While Hazare and the IAC campaign sank into relative obscurity, Kejriwal and those IAC activists who sided with him launched an urban-based, non-legacy political force called the Aam Aadmi Party (AAP) in November 2012. The party, projecting itself as speaking up for the '*aam aadmi*' or ordinary citizen, went on to take a bow on the national political stage, helped in no small measure by the efficacious management of the media that utilised many of the insights into political communication gained during the IAC campaign. How this was achieved will be examined in subsequent chapters.

The millenarian dream of the protests to clean the country's public life remained unrealised. 'Corruption-free' politics remained a chimera. Even a rough blueprint on how to achieve it had failed to emerge. On the contrary, the IAC team's focus on the corruption of the State and the conscious overlooking of corporate wrongdoing laid it open to the charge that its agenda was essentially neoliberal, in that by 'weakening the state's grip on the polity, it served the purposes of neoliberal capital to privatise every aspect of social life.'[96]

The meltdown of the IAC campaign in 2011–12 at a pace far faster than that which had marked its building would suggest that the media can act as a force multiplier to build public support for a campaign, but can just as easily contribute to its dissipation. They may be able to expedite agenda setting on a national scale, but cannot alter the relations of power within society, partly because they emerge from those very same structures of power.

NOTES AND REFERENCES

1. Arun Kumar, 2002, *The Black Economy in India* (New Delhi: Penguin Books), 11.

2. *The Indian Express* (Bombay edition), 22 January 1958.

3. Gyan Prakash, 2003, 'Blitz's Bombay', *Seminar*. Available at http://www.india-seminar.com/2003/528/528%20gyan%20prakash.htm (accessed May 2015).

4. 'Arun Shourie: From the barrel of a pen', *India Today*, 15 October 1981.

5. Chitra Subramaniam, 2003, 'Sting and Stink in the Tale', in B. G. Verghese (ed.), *Breaking the Big Story* (New Delhi: Viking), 103.

6. Pranab Bardhan, 1997, 'Corruption and Development: A Review of Issues', *Journal of Economic Literature* XXXV (September).

7. Arvind Virmani, 2006, 'Sustaining Employment and Equitable Growth: Polices for Structural Transformation of the Indian Economy', Planning Commission Working Paper No. 3/2006-PC.

8. Niraja Gopal Jayal, 2013, *Citizens and its Discontents: An Indian History* (Boston: Harvard University Press), 200.

9. Pamela Philipose, 2011, 'Aruna Roy speaks of Keeping Intact RTI Law, explains Approach to Jan Lokpal', *Mainstream* XLIX (44), 22 October.

10. Abhijeet Banerjee, Donald P. Green, Jeffery McManus, and Rohini Pande, 2012, 'Are Poor Voters Indifferent to Whether Elected Leaders are Criminal or Corrupt? A Vignette Experiment in Rural India'. Available at http://www.hks.harvard.edu/fs/rpande/papers/UP%20Vignette_2012-10-22_final_wfig1.pdf (17 April 2015).

11. Roy Jenkins and Anne Marie Goetz, 1999, 'Constraints of Civil-Society's Capacity to Curb Corruption: Lessons from the Indian Experience', *IDS Bulletin* 30 (4), October. Available at http://onlinelibrary.wiley.com/doi/10.1111/j.1759-5436.1999.mp30004006.x/abstract (accessed May 2015).

12. 'Corruption costs India Rs 2.5 lakh cr, says Prahalad', *Business Standard* news report, 15 January 2010.

13. Adrian Athique, 2012, *Indian Media* (Cambridge: Polity Press), 140.

14. *Indian Entertainment and Media Outlook, 2011*, PwC.

15. 'Medianet: Innovative Content, Integrated Offering'. Available at http://timesofindia.indiatimes.com/india/Medianet-Innovative-content-integrated-offering/articleshow/39286961.cms (accessed April 2015).

16. Nick Couldry and James Curran (eds), 2003, *Alternative Media in a Networked World* (Lanham, MD: Rowman & Littlefield).

17. 'Recommendations on Issues Relating to Media Ownership', Telecom Regulatory Authority of India, 12 August 2014. Available at www.trai.gov.in.

18. Robert W. McChesney, 1996, 'The Global Struggle for Democratic Communication', *Monthly Review* July–August.

19. N. Ram, 2011, 'The Changing Role of the News Media in Contemporary India', Paper presented at the 72nd Session of the Indian History Conference, December.

20. William A. Gamson, David Croteau, William Hoynes, and Theodore Sasson, 1992, 'Media Images and the Social Construction of Reality', *Annual Review of Sociology* 18, 379.

21. 'The Drivers and Dynamics of Illicit Financial Flows from India: 1948–2008', Global Financial Integrity. Available at http://www.gfintegrity.org/report/country-case-study-india/ (accessed 15 April 2015).

22. Pamela Philipose, 2009, 'Media and Civil Society', *Infochange*. Available at http://infochangeindia.org/downloads/agenda_17.pdf (accessed April 2015).

23. P. Sainath, 2009, 'Is the "Era of Ashok" a new era for "news"?', *The Hindu*, 29 November.

24. 'Atal Wave', *India Today*, 9 February 2004. Available at http://indiatoday.intoday.in/story/vajpayee-bjp-set-for-landslide-win-in-forthcoming-2004-elections/1/197000.html (accessed April 2015).

25. 'Dreaming With Brics: The Path to 2050', Goldman Sachs, 2003.

26. Gamson, et al., 'Media Images and the Social Construction of Reality', 373.

27. Dilip Meghana, 2008, *Rang de Basanti—Consumption, Citizenship and the Public Sphere* (Amherst: University of Massachusetts). Available at http://scholarworks.umass.edu/cgi/viewcontent.cgi?article=1116&context=theses (accessed March 2015).

28. Evgeny Morozov, 2011, *The New Delusion: How Not to Liberate the World* (New York: Penguin Books), 186.

29. Ritesh Mehta, 2012, 'Flash Activism: How a Bollywood Film Catalyzed Civic Justice toward a Murder Trial', in Henry Jenkins and

Sangita Shresthova (eds), *Transformative Works and Fan Activism*. Special issue, *Transformative Works and Cultures* 10. Available at http://journal.transformativeworks.org/index.php/twc/article/view/345/271 (accessed 27 April 2015).

30. Richa Singh, 2014, *New Citizens' Activism in India: Moments, Movements, and Mobilisation—An Exploratory Study* (New Delhi: Centre for Democracy and Social Action), 11.

31. Varadarajan, 'Satish Sharma aide showed U.S. Embassy employee cash to be used as "pay-offs" in confidence vote'.

32. David Hoffman, 2013, *Citizens Rising: Independent Journalism and the Spread of Democracy* (New York: CUNY Journalism Press), 14.

33. Morozov, *The New Delusion*, 191.

34. Hamid Dabashi, 2012, *The Arab Spring: The End of Postcolonialism* (London: Zed Books), 114–15.

35. Ibid., 214–15.

36. Paul Mason, 2013, *Why it's Still Kicking off Everywhere: The New Global Revolutions* (London: Verso), 65.

37. Aditya Nigam and Nivedita Menon, 2011, 'Anti-Corruption Movement and the Left', *Economic and Political Weekly* XLVI (37), 10 September.

38. John D. McCarthy, Clark McPhail, and Jackie Smith, 1996, 'Images of Protest: Dimensions of Selection Bias in Media Coverage of Washington Demonstrations, 1982 and 1991', *American Sociology Review* 61 (3), 481. Available at http://www.sscnet.ucla.edu/polisci/faculty/chwe/ps269/mccarthymcphailsmith.pdf (accessed May 2015).

39. Chetan Bhagat, 2010, 'Please don't cheer this loot-fest', *The Times of India*, 29 August.

40. CMS MediaLab Report, 2010, 'Face of Corruption in News Media—A Report of their coverage'. Available at http://www.cmsindia.org/publications/Face-of-Corruption-in-News-Media-Report-2010.pdf (accessed 26 May 2015).

41. Mason, *Why it's Still Kicking off* Everywhere, 269.

42. Cited in Marc Saxer, *Fighting Corruption in Transformation Societies* (Bangkok: Friedrich Ebert Stiftung, 2014).

43. Interview with transparency activist Jagdeep Chokkar, 10 December 2015.

44. Abhinandan Sekhri, quoted in Shaili Chopra, 2014, *The Big Connect* (New Delhi: Random House India), 145.

45. Sukumar Muralidharan, 2011, 'Hazare and his children', *Economic and Political Weekly* XLVI (16), 16 April.

46. Subarno Chattarji, 2014, 'Culture(s) of Corruption', in Nalini Rajan (ed.), *Covering and Explaining Conflict in Civil Society* (New Delhi: Orient BlackSwan), 98.

47. Hoffman, *Citizens Rising*, 195.

48. 'Opposition parties to hold protests on August 23 on Corruption', PTI/NDTV, 19 August 2011. Available at https://www.ndtv.com/india-news/opposition-parties-to-hold-protests-on-august-23-on-corruption-464914 (accessed June 2015).

49. 'Baba Ramdev's business empire worth Rs 1,100 crore', Press Trust of India, 10 June 2011.

50. 'An Open Letter to our Leaders', *Hindustan Times*, 17 January 2011. Available at http://www.hindustantimes.com/newdelhi/an-open-letter-to-our-leaders/article1-651546.aspx (accessed 9 June 2015).

51. 'Jindal Aluminium contributed 20 lakh, says India Against Corruption', *The Times of India*, 15 April 2011, cited in 'A Lokpal for India'. Available at https://lokpaldissent.wordpress.com/2011/08/22/jindal-aluminium-contributed-20-lakh-says-india-against-corruption/ (accessed July 2015).

52. Mehboob Jeelani, 2011, 'The Insurgent', *The Caravan*, 1 September.

53. https://www.youtube.com/watch?v=ZcNWIi3vl-Y.

54. Rahul Bhatia, 2012, 'Fast and Furious: The Turbulent Reign of Arnab Goswami', *The Caravan*, 1 December.

55. Rajdeep Sardesai, 2014, *2014: The Election That Changed India* (New Delhi: Penguin Viking), 194.

56. Anup Kumar, 2014, 'Jan Lokpal Andolan and Alternative Politics', in Taberez Ahmedi Neyazi, Akio Tanabe, and Shinya Ishikzaka (eds), *Democratic Transformation of the Vernacular Public Arena in India* (New Delhi: Routledge).

57. Shuddabhrata Sengupta, 2011, 'At the Risk of Heresy: Why I am not celebrating with Anna Hazare', *Kafila*, 9 April. Available at http://kafila.org/2011/04/09/at-the-risk-of-heresy-why-i-am-not-celebrating-with-anna-hazare/ (accessed June 2015).

58. Sardesai, *2014*, 82.

59. Biswarup Sen and Abhijit Roy, 2014, 'Introduction', in Biswarup Sen and Abhijit Roy (eds), *Channeling Cultures: Television Studies from India* (New Delhi: Oxford University Press), 1.

60. Ashutosh, 2015, *The Crown Prince: The Gladiator and The Hope* (New Delhi: HarperCollins), 119.

61. 'Why TV Channels love Anna Hazare', *The Hoot*, 19 August 2011. Available at http://thehoot.org/web/Why-TV-channels-love-Anna-Hazare/5448-1-1-4-true.html (accessed June 2015).

62. Arvind Rajagopal, 2011, 'Am I Still Anna When Nobody is Watching?', *The Hindu*, 12 September.

63. Nivedita Menon, 2011, 'We should be there. The Left and the Anna Movement', *Kafila*, 20 August. Available at http://kafila.org/2011/08/20/we-should-be-there-the-left-and-the-anna-moment/ (accessed June 2015).

64. Usha M. Rodrigues, 2015, 'Anna's Movement: Social Media Sets Traditional Media's Agenda', in Usha M. Rodrigues and Maya Ranganathan (eds), *Indian News Media: From Observer to Participant* (New Delhi: Sage Publications), 167.

65. Archana Venkat, 2011, 'For Anna or Against Him. Do I have a choice?', *The Hoot*, August. Available at http://thehoot.org/web/ForAnnaoragainsthimDoIhaveachoice/5459-1-1-14-true.html (accessed June 2015).

66. Sen and Roy, 'Introduction', 1.

67. Rajagopal, 'Am I still Anna ...?'

68. Avijit Ghosh, 2011, 'Anna Hazare's movement is anti-social justice, manuwadi', *The Times of India*, 19 August. Available at http://timesofindia.indiatimes.com/india/Anna-Hazares-movement-is-anti-social-justice-manuwadi/articleshow/9664784.cms (accessed June 2015).

69. 'Anna obsession boosts TV news channels', *Indian Television.com*, 27 August 2011. Available at http://www.indiantelevision.com/television/broadcasting/tv-channels/news/anna-obsession-boosts-tv-news-channels (accessed June 2015).

70. R. Jagannathan, 2011, 'Lokpal Fiasco: Post-mortem on a flawed beginning', *Firstpost*, 30 December.

71. Venkitesh Ramakrishnan, 2011, 'Crusaders in the dock', *Frontline* 28 (23), 5–18 November.

72. Venkat, 'For Anna or Against Him ...'.

73. Sukumar Muralidharan, 2014, 'Civil Society, Media and the Politics of Anti-Politics', in Nalini Rajan (ed.), *Covering and Explaining Conflict in Civil Society'* (New Delhi: Orient BlackSwan).

74. Aditya Nigam, 2011, 'Democracy, Populism and the "Middle Class": The Return of Anna Hazare', *Kafila*, 5 August. Available at http://kafila.org/2011/08/05/democracy-populism-and-the-%E2%80%98middle-class%E2%80%99-the-return-of-anna-hazare/ (accessed June 2015).

75. Rajdeep Sardesai, 2011, 'Media, a double-edged sword for Anna, Govt', *CNN-IBN Live*, 30 December. Available at http://www.ibnlive.com/blogs/india/rajdeep-sardesai/media-a-double-edged-sword-for-anna-govt-11095-746353.html (accessed July 2015).

76. Vidya Subrahmaniam, 2011, 'It's a long journey: Kejriwal', *The Hindu*, 12 September.

77. Manuel Castells, 2013, *Communication Power* (Oxford: Oxford University Press), xix.

78. Ibid., xxiv.

79. Ibid., xxv.

80. 'It is a long journey ahead: Kejriwal', *The Hindu*, 31 August 2011.

81. Singh, 'New Citizens' Activism ...', 28.

82. Interview with Sundeep Narwani, 1 October 2015.

83. Kapil Ohri, 2011, 'How powerful is Anna Hazare on Facebook and Twitter?', *afaqs*, 18 August. Available at http://www.afaqs.com/news/story/31413_How-powerful-is-Anna-Hazare-on-Facebook-and-Twitter (accessed June 2015).

84. Interview with Sundeep Narwani, 1 October 2015.

85. Ibid.

86. Rajeev M. V. Gowda and Purnima Prakash, 2014, 'The India Against Corruption Movement', in Ashu M. G. Solu (ed.), *Handbook of Research on Political Activism in the Information Age* (Maverich Technologies America Inc.), 249.

87. J. Kattayam, 2011, 'Social Networking Sites Helping Team Anna', *The Hindu*, 30 August.

88. Ashutosh, *The Crown Prince*, 70.

89. Clay Shirky, 2008, *Here Comes Everybody: The Power of Organizing Without Organizations* (London: Allen Lane), 54.

90. Malcolm Gladwell, 2010, 'Small Change: Why the revolution will not be tweeted', *The New Yorker*, 4 October. Available at http://www.newyorker.com/magazine/2010/10/04/small-change-malcolm-gladwell (accessed August 2015).

91. Evgeny Morozov, 2009, 'Foreign Policy: Brave New World of Slacktivism', 19 May. Available at http://www.npr.org/templates/story/story.php?storyId=104302141 (accessed August 2015).

92. John Bellamy Foster and Robert W. McChesney, 2011, 'The Internet's Unholy Marriage to Capitalism', *Monthly Review* 62 (10).

93. Arvind Rajagopal, 2011, 'Visibility as a Trap in the Anna Hazare Campaign', *Economic and Political Weekly* 46 (47), 19 November.

94. Quoted in Lance Price, 2015, *The Modi Effect: Inside Narendra Modi's Campaign To Transform India* (London: Hodder & Stoughton), 76.

95. 'Why Arvind Kejriwal is sure of winning 47 seats in Delhi', interview by Nishtha Grover, *First Post*, 28 October 2013.

96. Biswarup Sen, 2016, *Digital Politics and Culture in Contemporary India: The Making of an Info-Nation* (New York: Routledge), 111.

three

Reverberations in the City

Delhi Gang Rape Protests and Media Convergence

The gang rape of 23-year-old physiotherapy student, Jyoti Singh Pandey, in a bus in south Delhi on 16 December 2012, gave rise to an unprecedented display of public outrage and while it played out in Delhi, it echoed across the country.[1] Unlike the India Against Corruption mobilisation, there were no charismatic leaders, civil society organisations, or political parties setting the stage or issuing clarion calls to persuade the crowds to participate. Men, women, and children appeared to spontaneously throng the heart of India's Capital as if they perceived themselves as representing the city's collective conscience. That moment came to be recognised as a key marker in terms of public articulation, social mobilisation, and sociality within an urban Indian setting and the incident continued to resonate in public memory long after it had taken place, with media-bestowed appellations like 'Nirbhaya', 'Damini', 'Braveheart', and 'India's daughter' coming to identify the assaulted woman.

The story of the gang rape did not remain confined to the site of its occurrence, but breached intra national and international boundaries within a remarkably short span of time. News of the incident reached not only the Indian diaspora, but also the general public in countries across the world. This, in itself, was a reflection of 'the paradigmatic changes in creating, delivering, and consuming content'.[2] The widespread and unprecedented media coverage accorded to it by international media included editorials in prominent newspapers like the *New York Times* and *The Washington Post*. According to one estimate, over 1,515 articles appeared in the US media during the period when it occurred and for a couple of months thereafter.[3] Such intensive attention led to a deepening of the impression that sexual crimes were proliferating in a rapidly globalising India and that its society was remarkably tolerant of such behaviour, as implied in a statement issued by UN Secretary-General Ban Ki-Moon, urging the Indian government to take 'further steps and reforms to deter such crimes and bring perpetrators to justice'.

In early 2015, over two years after the incident, *India's Daughter*, a BBC documentary made on it by British filmmaker Leslee Udwin, once again focused public interest on the incident. Some saw the film as an international endorsement for the 'commodification of "Nirbhaya"'[4] and argued that India had become 'the rape nation in the Western imagination'.[5] The ultra-nationalist NDA government, which came to power a year and a half after the gang rape, perceived the film as an 'international conspiracy to defame India', as one senior Indian minister had put it, and obtained a restraining order from the court against the disseminating of the contents of the film. This attempt at censorship to protect the country's image was widely condemned. Even feminists who had critiqued *India's Daughter* made it clear that it was not the film that 'hurts the image of India', but the 'pervasive violence against women' that exists in the country.[6]

One of the major reasons for this deep, wide-ranging, and geographically spread out public scrutiny of this particular incident is directly linked to the manner in which the national media had treated it, in terms of duration and the emotional energy they accorded to it. Despite the exceptional articulation of gender activists and academics on the central issue of violence against women over the years, the issue had never been met with commensurate attention in the media, which had traditionally deemed the subject as 'soft news'. The attack on Jyoti Singh marked an emphatic departure from this norm, as the issue became mainstreamed on front pages, featured in prime-time television studio discussions, and became the stuff of personal blogs, tweets, and posts in a consistent way for the first time in the country's history.

The fallout of this unprecedented engagement was also significant in terms of changes in the law and policymaking, much like what happened after the country-wide protests over the Supreme Court verdict on the Mathura rape case in 1979. For the first time in the country's history, a government-appointed body recognised serious gender-centric lacunae in existing law, even as it argued for putting in place a criminal justice regime driven not by revenge and retribution, but one that seeks to be comprehensively fair and gender equal. The Justice J. S. Verma Committee, set up in late December 2012 even as the protests were taking place, was mandated to inquire into gender justice and the efficacy of the existing legal framework. It received around 80,000 responses on how the existing criminal justice system could be reformed. As committee member Justice Leila Seth later recalled,

> We received advice from experts and academics from abroad, and heard the apprehensions and fears voiced by women's groups, feminists, the lesbian-gay-bisexual-transgender (LGBT) community and many others .... Even though our deadline was long past, the suggestions kept pouring in, and we felt it was important to examine all of them.[7]

The Verma Committee Report, completed in a record span of twenty-nine days in sharp contrast to other reports of its kind, suggested changes in the administration of criminal justice that were so radical that they had never been envisaged in the history of Indian officialdom.[8] The Criminal Law (Amendment) Act passed in 2013, drawing from the Verma Committee report, radically redefined the act of rape to include any act of penetration, not just by the penis, but by any object or any part of the body to any extent in any orifice. It examined the intimate links between sexual violence and dominant patterns of socialisation and situated sexualised violence not only in the domain of law and order, but also within the framework of constitutional rights. The act of rape was seen as an assault on a person's right to free movement, bodily integrity, and sexual autonomy. The Committee discarded the framework of shame, loss of honour, the loss of virginity, and therefore the loss of the possibility of making a 'good marriage' and the prospect of life as a 'living corpse', through which the courts and notables in society had routinely viewed rape survivors. It also drew a new red line against hitherto unacknowledged crimes like stripping, stalking, and acid attacks, and recommended that assaults on women perpetrated by the armed forces, as well as marital rape be brought within the legal ambit.[9]

Violence against women in fact became an important electoral issue for the first time in the country's history, both during the run up to the Delhi assembly polls in 2013 and 2015, as well as the General Election of 2014. The Congress party, which was governing both the state of Delhi and the country at that point, was severely punished for its abject inability to respond in any meaningful way to this crisis in subsequent hustings at both the State and federal levels, despite some desperate measures it undertook to correct its image—for example, the setting up of the Nirbhaya Fund with an outlay of Rs 1,000 crore in the Budget of 2013.

Women's safety was one of the core concerns of voters in the General Election of 2014, figuring fourth in the list of priorities, just below 'corruption', 'lack of livelihood', and 'inflation'.[10] That such violence was seen largely through the prism of rape indicated the strong link between the 2012 Delhi gang rape protests and voter perceptions. Rainuka Dagar argues that 'it was the imagery of the cruel rape that captured the electoral pitches in 2014'.[11] In the 2015 Delhi elections, the Aam Aadmi Party adopted a Charter of Women's Rights and came up with a law that sought to ensure the physical, social, religious, cultural, psychological, and economic safety and well-being of women in the National Capital Territory of Delhi, based on the recommendations of the Justice Verma Committee Report. It was for the first time that any government in the country, at the state or national level, had thought of embarking upon such a process.

There were consequences for student politics too, with many student-centric struggles using the online and offline strategies that had gained ground during the rape protests. In early 2013, the demand for the rollback of the controversial Four-Year Undergraduate Programme (FYUP) that had been introduced in Delhi University played out. Over the next few years, student activism of the kind not seen in the country since the 1970s made itself felt. They included the Film and Television Institute of India protests of 2015, the agitation over the suicide of Dalit student Rohith Vemula in the University of Hyderabad in 2016, and a series of protests mounted by the students and faculty of Jawaharlal Nehru University (JNU), New Delhi, from 2016 onwards. JNU students, incidentally, were the first to come out on the streets in protest when news of the Delhi gang rape broke, indicating what could be seen as an organic link between student agitations and the Jyoti Singh gang rape protests.

At a more individual level, if there is a lasting positive that emerged from those mediatised two weeks that shook Delhi, it was the promise to an emerging generation of the possibilities of achieving, through shared knowledge and activism, a better understanding of their society. In addition, it gave rise to innumerable verbal and visual forms of cultural expression, ranging from the sensitive to the crass, some that even fetishised the gang rape.[12] The ubiquitous nature of rape culture—understood as comprising not only the acts of rapists, but also a social climate that allows such crimes to take place and provides justifications for them—came under the scanner.

Large networks of individuals and discrete groups across the country sought to clarify their own understanding of gender inequality, especially with regard to the right to life and free movement. Discussions on what equal access to a city meant and how the quality of urban life could be defined in terms of class, caste, gender, and socio-economic location now began to take place more widely. An interesting example of such an attempt was the Facebook group set up six months after the gang rape, 'Hyderabad for Feminism' (HfF). Comprising of university students and faculty, it operated mostly through social media, hoping to extend its activism beyond spatial and temporal constraints to collapse the separation between people and enhance 'personal access to information and communities'.[13] As a self-formed, self-funded group, it could survive without external funding and could still grow in terms of membership and ideas into a vibrant dialogic resource. Activism of this kind brought a new momentum to the acknowledgement of feminist concerns, although it remained largely limited to intellectual and university circles.

The many articulations on the theme appeared to have encouraged an increase in the reporting of such crimes. Vasundhara Sirnate and Nithya Nagarathinam found that there had been a 131.73 per cent jump in the reporting of rape in Delhi between 2012 and 2013—the earlier highest recorded jump had been 23.54 per cent (between 2011 and 2012)—and they attributed this, among other reasons, to rape carrying less of a stigma after the protests.[14]

Justice Leila Seth perceived these changes in approach and perception as constituting a turning point: 'The 631-page report that we prepared in just twenty-nine days has led to some changes that I believe will, in time, lead to far-reaching improvements in the lives of the women of this country.'[15] Time will tell whether the optimism she had voiced proves to be valid, but it was also the case that many obscurantist statements were made by public personalities, and several retrogressive government policies justified, by citing the Jyoti Singh gang rape.

All these developments, taken together, both fed off and fed into media content. In the absence of a central figure or organisation leading these protests, the media did come to play a unifying role by pulling together the various elements that constituted them. Raymond Williams had iterated that while nothing either way is determined by (communication) technology, it does offer opportunities for new cultural relationships in ways the old systems could not,[16] and this is what seems to have happened in the last two weeks of December 2012. New communication technologies and social media platforms converged in both direct and convoluted ways with traditional media, whether print or television, to create a meta-narrative of citizen anger and discontent. But while such convergence of media did unleash social energy and social chaos in equal measure, they could not achieve a systematic redefining of the power relations between the sexes or end—or even undermine—the rape culture that had come to mark Delhi's social landscape, as we shall see over the subsequent pages.

INDIAN MEDIA IN 2012

What was the profile of the Indian media in 2012? A high level of mediatisation had already come to mark urban Indian society at this point, with networked forms of communication having achieved a certain critical mass within India's neoliberal economic order. The manner in which a country, which had 45 million phone connections in 2002, ended up with 900 million of them by 2012, is a saga of *laissez faire* practices gaining currency. The increasing pace of economic liberalisation allowed assorted corporate and political forces to take extreme liberties with the law, as the numerous scams involving telecommunications of the previous two decades have flagged. But it was also the case that for a country as hierarchical and unequal as India, where privilege defined the extent of access to systems of communication, the permeation of mobile telephony into the very pores of society held transformative possibilities. In India, the advent of the cheap mobile phone 'proved even more disruptive than elsewhere',[17] and the stone pelting episodes in the Kashmir Valley in 2010 and the India Against Corruption rallies in 2011 had already revealed the extent of its disruptive powers, as dealt with in Chapter 1.

By 2012, smartphone ownership was no longer rare, with a July 2012 report claiming that there were 27 million smartphone owners in urban India,[18] the great majority of whom were young, male adults living in metros. The device not only enabled internet searches and the downloading of mail but, most importantly, expedited social networking, leading to a marked rise in the use of Facebook, Twitter, and other social media.

The homogenising impacts of such devices on behavioural patterns, especially among the young—India was estimated to have one of the youngest online communities in the world—came through in two surveys conducted in 2012. The first was titled 'The Tethered World', and studied the mobile habits of college students in eight countries; the other, Gen Y Survey 2011–12, covered 12,000 high-school students in India aged between 12–18 in twelve cities, including Delhi. Both revealed that not only was the mobile phone the favoured device of communication, but the great majority of users were also dependent on Facebook and Twitter for all their information-seeking and communication activities.

The two major social media-fuelled mobilisations the country witnessed—the 2011 India Against Corruption and the Delhi gang rape of 2012—had clearly contributed to the phenomenal rise in the number of Facebook accounts in India. By the time the Delhi gang rape mobilisations had ended on 31 December 2012, the number of Indian Facebook users had touched 71 million,[19] and one out of every four minutes spent online involving accessing social networking sites.[20] It needs to be reiterated, therefore, that if networked communications had not acquired the proportions they did by the end of 2012, leading in turn to media convergence, the surge in popular participation that Delhi witnessed post-16 December 2012 would not have become the largest mass mobilisation on the issue of sexual violence in the country's history.

At the same time, India continued to buck the trend seen in some other parts of the world, where the rise in the use of social media had led to a decline of older media. Mainstream media, despite the challenge from new communication technologies, remained paramount, both in presence and influence. As social media gained heft with the advent of Web 2.0 in the first decade of the twenty-first century, allowing for greater interactivity and dialoguing between users, media commentators had anticipated that digital media would directly compete with traditional media and then go on to displace them over time. In large swathes of the globe, such a projection did indeed prove prophetic. India, in contrast, had a more complex media ecology, with traditional media still on the growth path even as the newer media were making gains.

In 2012, there were at least 82,237 publications officially registered in India,[21] with readership recording a steady growth of around 13 per cent from the previous year. The television scene, too, was far from dormant. By 2012, the Union Ministry of Information and Broadcasting had permitted 848 TV channels to operate in India, and around 300 of the 650 channels in actual operation were telecasting news and current affairs.[22] In order to guard their own turf against the growing clout of digital media, newspapers and television houses were now hosting websites of their own. Between August 2012 and August 2013, there was a 15 per cent jump in unique visitors for news websites, with numbers rising from 40 million to 45.9 million. What is interesting is that figuring prominently among the top twenty websites of this kind were major players from 'older' media, like *The Times of India*, *Hindustan Times*, India.com, NDTV, the Jagran Group, the India Today Group, and IBN Live.[23]

BREAKING NEWS OF THE GANG RAPE

The news of Jyoti Singh remained in prime focus for two weeks, from 17–31 December 2012. In order to get a better idea of the telling of this story, let us consider how mainstream and digital media covered three major conjunctures in this protest: first, the moment when the story broke on 17 December; second, the mobilisations at New Delhi's India Gate on 22 and 23 December; and finally, the death and cremation of Jyoti Singh from 29–31 December.

The incident occurred around 9.30 pm on 16 December 2012. By the morning of 17 December—at 8.38 am, to be exact, in the case of the Delhi edition of *Hindustan Times*—a small report appeared in the metro page of its online edition with the heading, 'Girl gangraped in moving bus in Delhi'. The story soon began to appear in the web editions of other newspapers as well, some of them embellished with sketches of a terrorised female figure—a symbol that would soon become a fixture in the media over the next few weeks. This visual stereotyping of the raped woman as someone whose life has been destroyed has been commented upon.

> The images associated with the broadcasting of such stories included grainy images of a woman sitting in a corner with her face covered or blurred (CNN-IBN), a woman draped in a white cloth, often associated with widowhood (Aaj Tak), or a woman sitting on a hospital bed with her face covered with a dupatta or scarf (India TV). Writing about coverage of rape in Indian newspapers, Timmons (2012) observed that 'almost inevitably, the art to go with a story about rape depicts a shamed woman'.[24]

In the pre-digital age, a piece of news of this kind would have, at best, made it to the next day's evening television bulletins and the local sections of the newspapers of the following morning. Instead, what we had here was that within a few minutes of the story appearing on newspaper web editions, it was being tweeted and commented upon in multiples of hundred. The sentiments in these responses coming in thick and fast proved to be early portents of the public discourse that was to take place later, and included rants against government incompetence, impatience with the existing criminal justice system, demands for tough, exemplary punishment, and the claiming of the raped woman as sister or daughter.

To take one example, Sanghamitra Sama from Berhampur, Odisha, one of the first digital respondents to a newspaper report, commented on the morning of 17 December: 'time 2 quicky action ... wake-up shila jii' [*sic*]—the reference being to Sheila Dikshit, the chief minister of Delhi at that time. Aksha Acharya, also from Odisha, posted these words: 'Hang till death that dogs in front of our sister.' While 'Man from Delhi' demanded, 'Just KILL them when you arrest them. Do not wait for the police or courts since they are impotent just like the current UPA government', Kumar from UAE wanted the rapists 'shot ... on street after cut their p....s', again an early intimation of the sexually crude language that would soon inundate social media.

When did the mainstream media begin to chase the story? Almost immediately, if we are to go by an eye-witness account, of a youth activist who had decided to go to the hospital where the injured woman had been taken after reading the news in the web edition of a newspaper.

> My day generally begins with going online to catch the news. On the morning of December 17 my attention was immediately attracted to this case given the social media coverage. I and my colleagues from a women's resource centre where I worked were the first ones to go to Safdarjung Hospital in south Delhi. The woman had been admitted the night before and the police were just beginning to assemble in the hospital. We reached by mid-day but were not allowed to enter the ward, so we handed over some material about the organisation to the woman's family and left. I remember seeing OB vans at that point, which meant that the mainstream media had got wind of the story.[25]

By lunchtime, television bulletins were putting out the story, and they included the regional telecasts of TV9, operating in Kannada, Marathi, and Telugu. Since arresting visuals could not be provided apart from shots of the precincts of police stations, many channels chose to telecast lurid sketches of the attack, accompanied by shock-inducing headlines. The 2 pm news bulletin of NDTV 24×7 described the incident as 'horrific', while India TV headlined its story 'Rape Capital', and had its reporter stationed inside a private bus with curtained windows to provide viewers with a more vivid sense of the actual crime scene.

While reporting important stories, the competition for public attention and the pressurised newsroom leads mainstream media houses to adopt radically unconventional treatment. News reports on Indian television, particularly in local language variants, are often cast in a manner that resembles television serials, with sensational headlines, musical accompaniments, shaky camera work, repeat shots, and the climactic build-up. One television anchor even termed the phenomenon 'pulp television' which, like pulp fiction, is directed at the lowest common denominator.[26] A lot of the coverage of this gang rape in the visual media bore strong elements of 'pulp television'.

The creative use of extraneous aids to tell this story could also have been prompted by television reporters being pressed to find arresting visuals for this story. The incident, after all, had occurred away from the camera; the woman, when she was in hospital, was out of bounds; her family was incommunicado; the alleged rapists were in police custody. A patent lack of authentic footage seemed only to encourage the use of studio-created special effects and high-pitched reporting.

Television got into campaign mode from day one, and this could have been a factor in prompting the mass anger that followed.[27] From the very beginning, news channels attempted to reach out directly to their audiences, including web audiences, by introducing interactive elements in their programming. Times Now, in its 5 pm bulletin of 17 December, telecast CCTV images of the bus in which the gang rape had occurred, with the headline: 'Have you seen this vehicle?' News X ran the story in its 6 pm bulletin and exhorted readers to call in and share their views. The responses from viewers were along predictable lines. As we saw earlier in the case of responses to the first reports on the web, here too callers seemed to vie with each other in demanding the most severe punishment possible for the alleged rapists, including placing them in 'burning oil in the middle of the road', as one caller suggested. As such comments came in, the News X anchor kept egging the viewers on by commenting, 'Emotions running high ... something needs to be done.'

Those first reports and television footage were shared widely on Facebook, providing early hints of the sustained media convergence that would follow. In fact, apart from their websites that helped to expand their non-stop coverage, television channels set up their own Facebook pages to capture committed audiences. By the night of 17 December, NDTV had already begun to put out graphic details of the injuries suffered by the gang raped woman on its Facebook page: 'Doctors say there are blunt injuries on her face and abdomen and that the iron rod used to beat her has caused irreparable damage to her abdomen ... (Doctors) described the injuries to her intestines and private parts as "extremely serious".'

In an earlier era, details of this kind would have been edited out before being made public, but the competition between peers fuelled a tidal wave of information that washed away such compliances as had been observed in public interest. The explicit reportage on the condition of the woman's body based on eye-witness accounts also contributed towards the creation of an atavistic desire for retribution that marked the crowd response.[28]

Right through 17 December, the social media space reflected the intensity of public engagement. Apart from a welter of new Facebook pages focused exclusively on the gang rape, there was the very active Twittersphere. Twitter as a tool of mass protest was used in a limited way during the IAC protests. This time it was used far more widely, leading social media researchers Saifuddin Ahmed and Kokil Jaidka to argue that it proved to be a game changer, constituting 'a challenge in the face of the "elite hold" of traditional media',[29] relaying information on events linked to the protest in real time. They estimated that 1,939 tweets and retweets related to this case were put out on 17 December alone. One particular tweet that was widely retweeted came from Pune and had a strongly political message: 'Dear #Delhi, don't limit yourself to outrage on twitter. Protest on Road. And, yes, vote wisely next time. #Gangrape'

While newspapers frontpaged the gang rape story and constantly put out editorialised comment over the two weeks of Jyoti Singh's hospitalisation, television carried wall-to-wall coverage and continuously telecast studio discussions on it. A media organisation surveyed six top English and Hindi television channels—Aaj Tak, DD News, Star News, Zee News, CNN-IBN, and NDTV 24×7—and found that together, they had devoted 546 news stories and 194 special programmes to the incident between 17–31 December during prime time (7–11 pm). This amounted to an unprecedented 125 hours of prime time telecasting on a single incident of gang rape.[30] Television news coverage was complemented by 'news reconstructions', which re-enacted the crime in dramatic ways while taking extreme liberties with facts. Such a format found favour with audiences who had been fed on a steady stream of high voltage television drama serials over the years. It imparted a voyeuristic thrill to the gang rape coverage, blurring the boundaries between truth and fiction as well as between information and entertainment.

As mainstream media products made their way seamlessly into new media, whether through YouTube, Facebook, or Twitter, online content percolated into mainstream platforms. While opinion columns were posted on Facebook pages, television anchors of prime-time chat shows kept urging viewers to tweet in their thoughts. While older media put out messages from one source to many—whether they were readers or viewers—newer media simultaneously connected multiple sources with multiple others. If newer media brought the crowds on the streets, older media drew continually from their experiences through interviews, talk shows, and articles. The ensuing content was then given a further lease of life through tweets and posts, adding to the circularity of media content. What was also striking about this continuous relaying of news was the manner in which information from the crowds made its way back to the crowds in media-enabled feedback loops.

There were also periods when the older media consciously adopted, for the first time ever, the working style and format of social media, with television anchors and newspaper reporters immersing themselves in the crowds—mikes on, cameras rolling, pens at the ready. As the spatial-temporal distance between event and telecast/publication narrowed, with the news scenario taking on the proportions of a giant Twittersphere, the norms that had typically guided mainstream media were discarded. Old-fashioned fact-finding and the deferring to editorial interpretation and judgement were replaced by the unmediated and uninterrupted broadcasting of viewpoints straight from the ground in real time.[31]

A week of this intensive coverage meant that most Delhiites were familiar with every aspect of this story. But it was with the mobilisations at India Gate on 22 December, however, that the media were able to directly influence developments on the ground. The crowds' rejection of the severely constricted Jantar Mantar as the site of protest and its deliberate claiming of the India Gate lawns adjoining Raisina Hill's North and South Blocks, which housed the offices of the Central government, was in itself a highly symbolic assertion. A couple of days after the incident, small groups of protesters had begun to congregate in scattered corners of these lawns, but now it was a visible takeover of the entire stretch from India Gate to Vijay Chowk.

On the surface, it appeared that thousands of angry men, women, and children, many of them clad in their school uniforms, had converged of their own volition on to a space which, by law, was open to the public only for purposes of recreation and not protest. They were driven by what many protesters described to me as 'a need to do something' to end the rising tide of violence against women.

Most participants in the 22 December demonstrations did not, of course, consciously register the fact that a significant factor that prompted their presence at India Gate was the siren call of the media. It is only by analysing the media messaging at that point that we begin to perceive the push and pull impacts that media convergence was having on Delhi's citizens. Facebook posts, for instance, invited people to come to India Gate and shamed those who stayed away. One message posted on 22 December read: 'Be the change you want to see: If you are really protesting with a genuine heart, you need to make a move ...'. As a young college student explained,

> I had seen myself as an observer, not an activist, but the intensity of the exhortations on social media really egged me on and I too wanted to make a difference. It also brought a lump to my throat to see so many people getting together on an issue that did not concern them directly.[32]

Several others expressed similar sentiments.

Protesters we spoke to found it difficult to distinguish the stimuli of social media from that of mainstream media because their messages and impacts seemed to collapse in on each other. The experiences of a young software professional, Himanshu Chawla, could be said to epitomise the response of the average protester. He did not see himself as an activist to begin with, but felt driven to join in the protests by what he read and saw in the media. Not only did he go to the protest site at India Gate, but he also made sure to photograph himself 'protesting' in a very deliberate way, an image he then shared with the mainstream television channel NDTV, and posted on his Facebook page. He also launched a Facebook campaign on the issue and took to blogging. His blog of 20 December explained what drove him to do all this:

> When I read about this shocking incident, I decided to do something .... [W]e launched Night Walkers, ... that would hold protests at different places in the city ... gather messages for the girl and educate people .... Currently, we are stationed outside the Safdarjung Hospital where we are writing messages .... we want to show the family of the girl that the whole country is with them in this difficult time .... Our representatives ... met Home Minister Sushil Kumar Shinde who told them that the government is taking some steps ... I think this is not enough.[33]

Activists participating in these protests realised that they too needed to adapt to the news communication technologies available and for many, this proved to be a process of trial and error. Kavita Krishnan, a politbureau member of the Communist Party of India (Marxist-Leninist) and a secretary of its women's wing, the All India Progressive Women's Association (AIPWA), for instance, began to use Twitter for the first time in her many years of activism. She said she found it more effective than, say, Facebook, because 'it was more open and its reach was immediate'. Yet she also made it a point not to discriminate between the various media platforms available, posting on Facebook even as she gave newspaper interviews and appeared on television talk shows throughout this period. As she recalled, 'Our organisation began two Facebook pages—Freedom against Fear as well as Justice for Women—both of which were popular sites for sharing information on the protests and were regularly visited for at least three months after the protest had ended.'[34]

What is obvious from these developments is that the Delhi gang rape mobilisations were predominantly an urban, middle-class phenomenon, and they glamourised the notion of protest for an apolitical generation, sometimes characterised as 'Manmohan Singh's children', since it is they who stood to benefit the most from the economic liberalisation of the 1990s. People who had never engaged with gender issues now came to perceive themselves, at least during the duration of the protests, as champions of women. As we saw from Chawla's post, there was a strong performative dimension to their actions. Not only did one have to be at the protest site, but one also had to be seen to be there—and a distinctive pattern of sociality emerged, with absolute strangers bonding over lighted candles. Theirs was a widespread drive to use all the various media platforms available in innovative and experimental ways in order to express their thoughts and feelings, with participants transiting from being media consumers to becoming media producers, and vice versa.

Also to be noted was the fact that the protests had several political strands, including the active participation of Left and feminist groups. For the latter category, there was the intuitive realisation that online activism in itself was limiting and needed to be buttressed by offline activity, but that both forms of activism were necessarily ephemeral and did not signify long-term struggle.

On 22 December, live telecasting of the ever-swelling crowds at India Gate set the stage for a violent confrontation between the State and protesters. At 10.19 am that day, NDTV, for instance, telecast the following Twitter message, hashtagged '#Delhi gang-rape: Huge crowds protest at India Gate, Raisina Hill'. In Egypt in 2011, the influence of the mainstream media, particularly the Qatar-headquartered television channel Al Jazeera, in creating the 'synergy in the air' when 25 January was declared 'The Day of Rage', has been commented upon.[35] In Delhi, almost a year later, something similar happened when television channels beamed into homes never-before-seen images of protesters attempting to break police cordons at Raisina Hill and storm into Rashtrapati Bhavan.

Broadcast in real time were scenes of the Delhi Police trying to push back protesters by brutally wielding lathis, tear gas shells, and water cannons in an unconscionable display of repression. These were juxtaposed, sometimes within the same frame, with visuals of the courageous resistance of young activists taking on the might of the State at great personal discomfort. The optics, accompanied by impressionistic, sometimes breathless, on-the-spot reporting, imparted to news television the emotional traction of reality TV. The almost staccato running commentary kept viewers in a constant state of suspense. Something tragic seemed about to occur: 'Protestors are breaking the barricades. Police action is only increasing the anger of the protestors .... They are crossing the area. Police are being pushed back .... Anger is high .... Anything can happen ....' The glamourisation of the protests and the idealisation of scenes from the protest venue proved a powerful magnet for greater public participation. A feeling was created in those watching from the safe space of their homes that they had failed to demonstrate solidarity to the cause by not being present at India Gate, and many were prompted into rushing to join in the action, despite having to negotiate formidable hurdles to reach the cordoned-off site of protest.[36]

The pressure of media platforms competing with each other to gain an edge in this cacophony of words and images resulted in remarkably similar coverage across media platforms, conforming to Pierre Bordieu's observation that journalists subjected to identical pressures and opinion polls made for a homogeneity of reportage.[37] This time, there was similar content not just across rival channels and newspapers, but across all forms of media. Almost every Delhi newspaper on the following morning of 23 December mimicked the television coverage of the day before by choosing to blow up the photograph of the stand-off between the protesters and the police—that single image even occupying half the front page in some newspapers—to earmark it as historically unprecedented. This included conservative newspapers like *Jansatta* and *The Hindu*, not usually known for such exuberant front page displays.

The accompanying headlines, too, had a copycat ring. If Aaj Tak had carried the headline 'India Mange Insaaf' (India demands justice) in its coverage of 22 December, the *Jansatta* headline of 23 December read, 'Rajpath par janta ne chedhi insaaf ki jung' (People on Rajpath launch war for justice), while *Dainik Jagran* went with 'Rajpath Par Jan Hunkar' (People's roar on Rajpath). Short videos bearing images from the protests set to catchy music and uploaded on YouTube did the rounds, as did the observations of celebrities like filmmaker Shekhar Kapur, whose tweet of 22 December read: 'Delhi looks more like India's Tahrir Square'.

Particularly heady was the capacity that social media gave their users to create their own news through Twitter handles like Anonymous@YourAnonNews. Ahmed and Jaidka note that the tweeters of that period worked as a 'virtual army of activists acting as citizen journalists ready to tweet about every action from the ground'. Going by the over one lakh tweets they collected, the language of choice was overwhelmingly English, with Hindi accounting for the lion's share of the 7 per cent tweets in other languages.[38]

Interestingly, some of these tweets were also reactions to the coverage of other media. Some excoriated the mainstream media's reporting on events: 'S---W THE MEDIA!!!!! People were bloody PEACEFUL!!! Sitting down and protesting when POLICE shot Water canons'; others sought to expose the government's repression: 'Instead of punishing the culprits, the government is lathi charging us.' Such words resonated with the young crowd, many of whom were students from schools and colleges located not just in Delhi's NCR region, but in surrounding cities as well. There was a palpable sense of injury, which in turn encouraged more people to join in:

'Don't wait people. We have to be on our way to Rajpath', went one tweeted call.

Social media activity the next day, Sunday, 23 December, reached a new high, according to the Ahmed–Jaidka study. If the average was 5,781 tweets per day during the period of the protests, it touched 15,421 on 23 December. Apart from exhorting people, tweets were generated strategically to inform protesters of the situation on the ground. Arvind Kejriwal and Baba Ramdev, for instance, used Twitter to convey their intention to come to India Gate. Information on the shutdown of the metro was also being conveyed through the microblogging site. A tweet sent out at 11.15 am on 23 December went: 'Public spontaneously pours to protest the Delhi#Gangrape—and, gues what?! Govt gangrapes Delhi by Section 144, No Metro, Brutality!' A Twitpic from Tajinder Pal S. Bagga, who later became a spokesperson for the BJP, attempted to counter the police claims of violence through the words accompanying the photograph: 'Is this 70 Year Old Aunty & A Youth Girl are anti social element??' Bagga's tweet was retweeted seventy-eight times that day.[39]

Some tweets, which spread like wildfire, had unverifiable information. Ahmed and Jaidka cited the instance of a tweet claiming that the police were offering bribes to protesters to stay away: 'The Police offering money to the protesters. F..... #IndiaGate #peaceprotestmarch #Delhi'. The accusation, although serious, was never investigated or confirmed, and the story disappeared without a trace.

What changed the dynamic of the protest was the death of a constable. As news of it became widely known, public sympathy for the protesters—which was essentially the fuel that kept the protests alive—waned dramatically. The Delhi Police, sensing this shift in messaging, moved in to assert their authority. Not only was the India Gate area sealed off and metro stations shut, but the police now also went on a media counter-offensive with a series of press briefings from senior officials. *The Indian Express*'s headline of 24 December read: 'Delhi protests take violent turn, 150 injured, policeman critical'. On 25 December, the *Hindustan Times* front page headline went, 'Controversy surrounds death of cop in post-rape protests'. The Delhi Police's argument that the constable had been felled by the protesters created a discernible disquiet in the social media space; but also obvious was anger over police attempts to frame random protesters as those responsible for this death. A pseudonymous Facebook post on 25 December by 'The Frustrated Indian' pointed out that while the protesters were painted as murderers and barbarians, the truth was entirely different and that the constable had died of a heart condition.

Despite such attempts by demonstrators to put their side of the story across, it was clear that the protest narrative that had thus far galvanised the crowd had broken down. It was not long before what was possibly the most flamboyant and most mediatised protest that India had ever seen up to that point wound down, even as the story of Jyoti Singh was reaching its climactic point.

The policeman's unfortunate death was the turning point, but there were other developments also that contributed to this waning of interest. These included the Gujarat and Himachal Pradesh assembly elections. In addition, on 26 December, the authorities moved to transport Jyoti Singh to Singapore from the public hospital in the heart of Delhi where she was being treated. It was a decision made ostensibly to ensure that she received better medical treatment, but was really a last-minute attempt to tamp down the public attention being paid to the case.

It was not until news of her demise came in a couple of days later that the story once again returned to the media centre-stage. Jyoti Singh died in Singapore at 2.15 am (Indian time) on 29 December, and although the morning newspapers could not catch the story, Twitter was in full flow. The Ahmed–Jaika study traced a secondary spike in Twitter activity coinciding with news of her death, after the first spike of the previous weekend caused by the India Gate protests of 22–23 December. Over 12,000 tweets were generated in a few hours, some of them driven by considerations other than protest. They indicated that the dead woman was now invested with the status of an icon. The tweets made to her memory now served an assortment of purposes, including the shoring up of the public profiles of their senders. Superstar Amitabh Bachchan put out the following words: 'Amanat, Damini just a name now ... her body has passed away, but her soul shall forever stir our hearts!!!' Shah Rukh Khan sent out no less than three tweets: '1. We couldn't save u but wot a big voice u have, u brave little girl. That voice is telling us that rape is not an aberration, not a mistake; 2. Rape embodies sexuality as our culture & society has defined it. i am so sorry that i am a part of this society and culture; 3. I am so sorry that I am a man. I promise I will fight with ur voice. I will respect women, so that I gain my daughter's respect.'

If tweets from film stars now crowded the Twittersphere, so too did those from politicians. Prime Minister Manmohan Singh, who had been badly outpaced in the image war over Jyoti Singh's gang rape, had broken his silence on it a full week after it had occurred through a televised statement. Unfortunately, a blooper that occurred during its telecasting—when his question to the TV crew, 'Theek hain?', also went on air—undermined whatever public relations benefit he had hoped to gain from the effort, and a lashing on social media ensued, with the trending hashtag #TheekHai questioning Singh's ability to lead the nation. On 29 December, he chose Twitter to put out the news of the woman's death through a series of tweets, but his words seemed pedestrian and pro forma:

> I pray for the peace of the departed soul and hope that her family will have the strength to bear this grievous loss. While she may have lost her battle for life, it is up to us all to ensure that her death will not have been in vain. I join the nation in conveying to her family and friends my deepest condolences at this terrible loss.

Narendra Modi, who was to succeed Singh as prime minister and was making the first forays into his extremely mediatised campaign for the General Election of 2014, chose a more direct way to connect: 'Deeply saddened & distressed by the news of India's braveheart daughter passing away.' Modi's immediate rival for BJP's prime ministerial candidacy, Sushma Swaraj, also tweeted:

'Her death has shaken the conscience of the nation. We must wake up and make India safe for daughters.' Many of these tweets had afterlives in newspapers and television screens, giving their sender an extended visibility. Taken together, they indicated how the Delhi gang rape had now transmogrified into a major political issue that would linger in the country's political discourse in the months and years to follow.

Digital petitions like Change.org's 'President, CJI: Stop Rape Now!', undertaken by senior journalist Namita Bhandare, received over 100,000 endorsements within a matter of a few days, and were then handed over to the Justice J. S. Verma Commission in January 2013. A rash of Facebook pages also emerged between 29 December and 1 January, some of them gaining wide support. For example, 'RIP Damini—Delhi Gang Raped Girl', had 6,249 'friends'. As if to remind people of the unfinished task of ensuring death to the rapists, the Facebook account, 'Death Penalty for Rapists in India', carried the following words: 'She is no more .... She was murdered, just her spirit took long to leave her. RIP brave woman ... You fought hard, now we will fight for you ....' Impromptu social media campaigns like 'The Black Dot of Shame' urged Facebook users to adopt the black dot as their profile image. One of its posts on 30 December cast the protest as a second freedom struggle:

> India mourns the Brave One ... Salute to the Brave Girl. We will always remember your Pain, Struggle and Courage. You taught us how to fight back for our Rights and Justice. May our Hero rest in peace and may God give her family strength. We will not rest until we have our country back in our hands.

Mainstream media's coverage was no less fraught. The morning after the death (29 December) saw television breaking the news with emotionally charged headlines. In its telecast of 7.36 am that morning, the channel Headlines Today had the banner: 'Life Ends, Spirit Lives'. The text of the accompanying bulletin, too, was marked by distraught language. Hindi channel Aaj Tak announced the death by stating that the woman had 'lost her battle with death (zindagi ka jung haar chukhi hain)'. Later, it had the word 'Alvida' (farewell) flowing across the screen with a close-up of a woman's cheek with a tear trickling down it. Responses from viewers and readers to these programmes were similarly impassioned: '*Mai mard hone par sharminda hoo*' (being a man, I am ashamed) was one such response.

The intrusive nature of media coverage on this case had resulted in some attempts at self-correction. The News Broadcasters Association issued instructions that television cameras be kept away from recording the funeral in order to give the family their privacy. However, the newspapers of the following morning—30 December—as if to make up for lost time, took the coverage to a whole new level. Social media had already created a semiotics of memorialisation through emotion-charged words accompanied by images like candles, tear drops, teddy bears, and floral sprigs. Legacy media, hitherto more formal in its responses, also succumbed to the lure of the 'touchy feely' approach adopted by other media platforms. *The Times of India* carried the banner headline: 'Rest In Peace Nirbhaya. We Won't'. Once again, the interactivity offered by the internet was resorted to, with readers encouraged to register a pledge to fight violence against women on a specially created webpage. Over 4,500 did so. The cover headline of the Hindi newspaper, *Dainik Jagran*, similarly attempted to tug at the heartstrings: 'Desh ko jaghakar so gayi woh (awakening the country, she went to sleep)', with a follow-up headline slamming the message home: 'Nahi rahi bahadur yuvati, seesak uta saara desh (the courageous young woman has gone, the entire country sobs)'. *The Hindu*, which very rarely carries an editorial on the front page, did so on 30 December, with its editor-in-chief justifying the decision on the basis that it represented a 'teachable' moment.[40]

Hindustan Times devoted its front page flap, a space sometimes reserved for high-paying advertisements, to the dead woman. The text, bordering on the hyperbolic, read: '... The prayers of a nation proved in vain as the 23-year-old victim of a savage gang rape on a moving bus lost her long-odds battle to survive at 2.15 am IST in Singapore ... ' The inner flap recalled the last few days in images, while the main headline read, 'Wake up India. She is dead'. A re-examination of this text, removed from the context of the times, would reveal its lack of coherence and logic. Striking, for instance, among the words used, are 'those who knew her'. In actual fact, Jyoti Singh in real life was not known outside a small circle of family and friends. The intimacy with which she was now referred to, the way she was constructed as someone the whole 'nation' knew, would not have been possible without the massive ceremony of iconisation conducted by the media over the two weeks that the story ran. She had become 'the property of the nation'[41]—and possibly the world—with big internet giants gaining immense public profile from the frenetic public engagement with this story. Google paid its homage by having an animated candle flickering on its India home page.

In the days that followed, the story continued to play out, although in a more muted fashion. On 1 January 2013, one newspaper had a boxed item in the middle of the front page with the words, 'Keep the flame burning', and an image from a candlelight demonstration at Jantar Mantar from the previous night. Another newspaper, in its annual summing up of the events of the year that had just gone by, focused on incidents of violence against women. Yet another pronounced: 'Let 2013 be Year of the Woman'.

Throughout 2013, news reports related to the gang rape kept surfacing. There was also some coverage of how Jyoti Singh's family was coping with the aftermath. When one of the accused in the case, Ram Singh, committed suicide in Tihar jail on 11 March that year, the media described him as a man prone to violent behaviour and mood swings, and that he had suicidal tendencies. Significantly, the entire media missed out on an opportunity to understand more deeply the social forces that had created men like him.

WHY DID THIS CASE RECEIVE ATTENTION?

It is against this background of the two weeks that followed Jyoti Singh's gang rape that we need to consider the proximate reasons for why this particular incident, and no other, came to occupy a polar position in the national consciousness. The National Criminal Records Bureau data indicated that 706 women were reportedly raped in Delhi in 2012, so why was it that all but one—the case of Jyoti Singh—sank from public view without a trace? Five framing contexts can be identified to arrive at a plausible assessment of why this turned out to be the case.

The first was that the class and location of the protesters broadly reflected Jyoti Singh's own class and location and gave the story an urban, middle-class appeal. The media—television in particular—has consistently privileged the sexual violence faced by middle and upper classes and castes, tending to ignore that experienced by their poorer and lower-caste counterparts.[42] The structural reasons for such bias ranged from the business model of media organisations that encouraged focus on core audiences, to contingent factors like the social profile of those reporting on the story. The domination of the newsrooms by upper-caste journalists has been well-established. The often-cited Centre for the Study of Developing Societies (CSDS) survey in 2006 found that no Dalit or tribal figured among the 300 most highly influential journalists in the country.[43] The upper-caste domination of newsrooms across India tended to influence both the choice of the story and its focus. Social media, although potentially capable of overturning the pyramid, were unlikely to do so, given the metropolitan background and preoccupations of their users: in 2012, 70 per cent of social media users were located in urban India.[44]

Dalit activist and author Anand Teltumbde, after comparing the indifference with which the mainstream media reacted to the case involving Surekha and Priyanka Bhotmange, members of a Dalit family, who were attacked, stripped, gang raped, and killed in Khairlanji, Maharashtra, in 2007, with the totalising engagement demonstrated on the Jyoti Singh gang rape, suggests that biases dictated by caste, class, and location were at play here.[45] Jyoti Singh's caste may not have been known, but her identity as a young urban woman who was attacked while returning at night with her male friend after seeing a film in a mall was part of the media narrative from almost the very beginning. As more details came out, she ticked all the boxes for the average middle-class Delhi reader, viewer, Facebook user, or tweeter—she was a student of a 'respectable' discipline like physiotherapy; doing 'normal' things like catching a popular English-language movie in a downtown mall; someone who had taken the precaution to go to the movies at a 'decent' hour with a companion who was an engineering graduate.

Jyoti's Singh's desire to change her life for the better resonated with those of her generation, who were making a 'fundamental political demand: *the right to social mobility*, both (a) in the literal sense of being able to be on the streets irrespective of the time of day or gender, and (b) in the social sense of being able to change the circumstances of their lives'.[46] It could therefore be argued that the story worked for the media because it was a compelling saga of a young woman, a product of 'aspirational urban India' which, like a television serial, had a compelling unpredictability. Would Jyoti Singh survive? Will her rapists face exemplary punishment? How long will the protests carry on? The questions kept opening up new story possibilities, while whetting the appetite of media audiences for more information, thus making the story an 'ideal' source of 'breaking news' for the media.

The second framing context was the way in which Jyoti Singh emerged as someone whom everyone knew closely. She was invested with a heroic quality, ranging from her 'extraordinarily courageous' attempt to fend off the attackers in order to protect her 'honour', to the dogged way she fought to survive. Sentences attributed to her, like '*mujhe jeena hain*, I want to live', projected a person of extraordinary resilience. Family members and hospital spokespersons, acting as intermediaries between the woman and the public, contributed to the shaping of this media narrative. Personal details like her 'friend' having visited her in hospital on 22 December were also leaked to the media, with her brother reporting that 'she was very concerned about him .... He didn't go close, but saw her from a distance. There were tears in her eyes.'[47] Then there was her mother's grief, which got tremendous play in newspaper columns, with the older woman's initially reported words, 'we want our daughter back', rife with pathos.

Coverage of the regular medical updates on the woman's condition underlined the great public investment in this case, with the doctors attending on her emerging like the chorus in a Greek tragedy, underlining the exceptional nature of the case. Every detail seemed to be made available to the public: whether the patient was on the ventilator or off it; whether she was being fed through a tube or not; whether she was drinking orange or apple juice; whether the infection in her body could be controlled by antibiotics or not; whether she would be going in for an organ transplant. Each tidbit of news was eagerly consumed by the public and became topics of everyday conversations. There was more to this than the mere relaying of facts—it was about creating a mega spectacle which served to fixate attention on events that 'distract people from the pressing issues of everyday life'.[48]

Social media circulated the material put out by mainstream media even while taking the narrative to a level that newspapers and television coverage dared not attempt. Although their coverage too had systematically catered to the morbid curiosity of readers and viewers—even the gathering of evidence from the crime scene on the bus by the police was conducted under the glare of TV cameras—there were certain well-established conventions of privacy with regard to an individual's health that the mainstream media found difficult to breach. Facebook posts, however, suffered from no such constraint. This was a comment that appeared on a Facebook page of 19 December and attracted innumerable likes and shares:

> The 23 year old girl gangraped on a bus in Delhi was brutalised so badly that she had only 5% of her INTESTINE left inside her when she was brought to Hospital .... On Wednesday Doctors removed the remaining 15 inches of Intestine in a bid to stop the spread of life-threatening infection .... The Girl is in a critical condition & she is never being able to eat a meal in her Life if she Survives but

> Doctors said she was fighting on & her brother told that she had written "Mother, I want to LIVE" on a piece of paper .... The Rod being inserted into her vagina was pulled out with so much force that it brought her INTESTINES along ... OMG this thing has caused severe damage to her Intestines .... One of d accused persons who were brought to d hospital for a medical examination confessed to havin seen a Rope like object (her intestines) being pulled out of d girl's vagina by other assailants on d bus. The girl had bite marks on her body there was a permanent damage to her intestines & she will have to feed through fluids all her life ... How can somebody be so brutal?? Omg! how much she has suffered just wanna say 'Death Penalty' for those b------ds .... Please forward it as much as you can ....

The tone adopted may appear to reflect a deep concern for Jyoti Singh, but ended up treating her as an object for public voyeurism.

Conversations with protesters confirmed their awareness of every detail conveyed by the media of Jyoti Singh's health status, as if she were a family member. The sister/daughter framing betrayed a remarkable fixity. One student, in an interview, revealed how she and some friends had asked male protesters, between the ages of twenty and sixty, why they perceived the woman in the familial terms of sister or daughter and found that while a clear answer was not forthcoming, most respondents felt that Jyoti Singh's story touched them because she was a middle-class girl who only wanted to get ahead in her life like any 'normal person'. While protesters may have perceived her in their distinct ways, going by the words they spoke and the posters they created, there was intense personal connect laced with feelings of pity. The emphasis was on her innocence and 'purity'; paintings that came up at protest sites showed her as a bleeding virginal figure poised on a lotus, or a female form encased within the map of India.[49] These images also circulated widely as memes within the virtual community of protesters, and prompted similar depictions in turn.

The mediatised empathy also created a desire in ordinary people to contribute in some way towards alleviating the assaulted woman's trauma. A protester–social activist recalled that many of those who joined in the protests had never participated in public demonstrations earlier. She remembered how a group of elderly women, after finishing a bhajan session in a temple, agreed to take part in a march and kept going enthusiastically for a long while. On another occasion, when demonstrators ran out of candles, they found that local shopkeepers were more than willing to hand over the item without charge. This protester herself felt so personally involved in the Jyoti Singh story that she undertook the responsibility of collating the messages that the public wanted to convey to Jyoti while she was at Safdarjung Hospital, and handed them over to her family. The Facebook page she started for this purpose received 785 uniformly supportive messages, with one woman writing in: 'You are my daughter, get well soon.'[50]

Coming to the third framing context, the incident took place at an important juncture in the country's politics. Such pressure on people to participate in public action and discussion around a gang rape would have been impossible to imagine even a decade earlier. But there was something about this interregnum that had created the conditions for deep dissatisfaction with the ruling political establishment among the middle class. Corruption, which had emerged as the rallying factor for the IAC protests in 2011, seemed endemic, with court verdicts and clearer information on various scams under the UPA government emerging as the year 2012 wore on. In February 2012, the Supreme Court had ruled that the allotment of 2G spectrum was 'unconstitutional and arbitrary'. Over the next few months, the full facts of the Commonwealth Games scam involving a Union minister and a chief minister, both from the ruling Congress party, as well as government officials, became public knowledge. The year also witnessed a slowdown in the economy, with India's GDP growth rate having declined from 7.8 per cent in 2010–11 to 6.9 per cent in 2011–12,[51] and public disquiet over recessionary trends was palpable.

The political opposition led by the BJP, a party that was impatient to come to power after having spent two parliamentary terms in the political wilderness, focused on converting the widely prevalent public despair into power-building exercises, something they were dramatically successful at doing. As the year wound down, matters came to a head. The last two weeks of December 2012 that saw the gang rape, hospitalisation, and death of Jyoti Singh coincided with the Winter Session of Parliament, even as the results of the state assembly elections in Gujarat and Himachal Pradesh were coming in and the emotionally charged issue of Telangana was playing out. The BJP's emphatic victory in Gujarat for the third consecutive time brightened Narendra Modi's prime ministerial prospects considerably, with party workers who supported him now openly expressing their confidence that the party would be able to sweep the General Election of 2014. The old UPA order appeared to be in terminal decline, faced as it was with multiple political challenges.

Meanwhile, on 26 November, three weeks prior to the incident, the Aam Aadmi Party (AAP) had been instituted, with its leaders indicating their intention to fight and win the Delhi elections that were to take place a year later in December 2013. The tweets of the man behind the party, Arvind Kejriwal—who was to become the chief minister of Delhi a year later—were striking in this context. His tweet on Jyoti Singh's death on 29 December 2012 was the first indication of how he planned to draw political relevance from the incident: 'Aren't we all responsible for her death? Can we all now do something so that half of humanity starts feeling safe amongst us?' The hint that he personally planned to do 'something' became clearer in the run up to the Delhi election of 2013, as we shall see in subsequent chapters, with the Delhi gang rape being a major theme in his electioneering.

The shadow of impending elections to the Delhi assembly added to an incipient jostling for power, which was being played out even as the grievously injured woman was battling for life in a Delhi hospital. The media coverage of the period reflected these parallel developments, creating, in the process, an overlap between them. Jyoti Singh soon came to embody the failure of the incumbent government to protect the lives of ordinary people. Every sentiment expressed by political leaders drew on this trope. Party workers of Kejriwal's AAP claimed the incident as an image-building exercise by distributing and wearing black bandannas with 'December 16' emblazoned on them. With Parliament in session, women MPs staged a protest outside the headquarters of the Delhi Police and Sushma Swaraj's loaded words uttered in the Lok Sabha two days after the incident reverberated beyond the walls of the Parliament building: 'You tell me, don't people who have reduced a girl to a "jeevit lash" (living corpse)—if she survives she will survive as a "zinda lash"—don't they deserve to be hanged?' Uploaded on YouTube, the speech elicited many approving responses, with one person stating: 'BJP any day rocks over Congress'. Politicians from the opposition and figures with political ambitions like the former chief of army staff, General V. K. Singh, sensed in the gang rape an opportunity to enter the corridors of power, and utilised it to the fullest.

As for the Congress Party and its governments at the Centre and state, they had never appeared as disoriented as they did at that point. A moment that needed an assertive political leadership saw uneasy silence instead. Even crass, sexist statements made by the likes of President Pranab Mukherjee's son, Abhijit Mukherjee, went uncontested by the political party in power. It took a full week for Prime Minister Manmohan Singh to issue a formal statement on the gang rape, and it was not until the woman had died that a statement of sorrow and regret on behalf of the Government of India was issued.

In fact, the government's first response to the emerging situation was a media advisory, issued on 24 December, which held out the veiled threat of punitive action. It read:

> It has been observed that some private satellite news TV channels in their 24×7 coverage have not been showing due responsibility and maturity in telecasting the events relating the said demonstration and such a telecast is likely to cause deterioration in the law & order situation, hindering the efforts of the law enforcing authorities .... Now, therefore, all private satellite television channels are advised to scrupulously follow the Programme Code laid down in the Cable Television Networks Rules, 1994 and to ensure to telecast the matter

> in a responsible manner with due care, maturity and restraint. Any violation of the Programme Code will invite such action as provided for in the Cable Television (Regulation) Act, 1995 and the Rules framed there under as well as the terms & conditions stipulated in Uplinking & Downlinking Guidelines.

If any evidence was required that the UPA government had misread the popular mood and was clueless about how it should confront this unprecedented and extremely critical response from the media, these words provided it. A senior member of the Union Cabinet allowed his irritation to show at a press conference when he observed that his government was confronting the new phenomenon of the 'flash mob'. He complained, 'Sometimes they gather to dance and sing, but sometimes they can gather to protest also ... we need to take note of it ... I don't think we are fully prepared to deal with it ... we need to device SOPs (standard operating procedures).'[52]

The frustration of the ruling elite was clearly evident. The Congress Party gave its newly-installed Information & Broadcasting Minister the responsibility to work on ways to simultaneously use new media and counter their effects. During its Jaipur '*chintan shivir*' (meeting for reflection) held in January 2013, the party, for the first time in its history, actually discussed the impacts of social media and decided to set aside Rs 100 crore to deploy new communication technology in the lead up to the 2014 general election.[53] It was as if all that was required to make up for the monumental blunders perpetrated by an apathetic and tone deaf government was to set up a digital war room.

The fourth facet we need to consider was the site of the attack. The centrality that Jyoti Singh's gang rape came to possess was also driven by the fact that it took place in the national capital. Delhi, a city viewed as the country in a microcosm and one that has a disproportionately larger media presence, has always been the cynosure of all eyes, and every major incident or event that takes place on its soil immediately assumes national importance.

Delhi and the National Capital Region (NCR) constituted one of the most networked of Indian urban conglomerations.

Census 2011 reported that 91 per cent of Delhi households owned a phone connection, 68 per cent of which were mobile phones, which meant that Delhi had a phone connectivity that was even higher than its television penetration. Delhi may not have made the complete transition from an industrial city to an informational city, but Debal K. Singharoy's research on the metropolis conducted in 2010–11 reveals that only 14 per cent of respondents here fell in the category of 'labour and other activities', only 1 per cent of its population were involved in cultivation, even as 85 per cent were in business and services.[54] Delhi therefore displays several features of Manuel Castells' 'informational city', which he defined as a space of flows or 'system of exchanges of information, capital, and power that structures the basic processes of societies, economies and state'.[55]

Despite its informational connect, however, hierarchies and inequalities were very much a feature of Delhi's society. The elite and the mainstream media promote a vision of Delhi as a world-class city, while consciously overlooking the large number of working poor who contribute to its existence. Dhunu Roy has cited the fact that between 1994 and 2002, there were thirty writs filed in the Delhi High Court for the removal of slums, while at the same time there were only thirty-six petitions from slum associations and individuals asking for adequate housing. There is a 'vast discontent brewing within the army of the dispossessed' as they 'hear the voices of arrogance that claim the city for their own'.[56] Slogans like 'Delhi's Shame', which surfaced during the protest, reflected the widely held perception that the city, as the site of the assault, was itself culpable in this violence.

Sociologist Deepak Mehta, who has studied crowd formations in urban areas in India, argues that the specificity of Delhi is striking because of what he terms its 'wound culture'. In an interview given to me, Mehta observed the 'peculiar brutality' that marked a city, with its vast underclass finding the task of keeping life going even more difficult. Everyday life is more fiercely contested here, he argues, than in most other cities, breeding cynicism and corruption in its citizens; turning them into honey badgers, a raccoon species known to eat up to 20 per cent of its body weight.[57]

Related to this was the manner in which a culture of impunity had come to be associated with masculinity among young male adults in the Capital, a 'hyper-masculine bravado' that lead them to perceive women as 'goods' (*mal*) that exist for their ultimate delectation. Dreze and Sen termed this trend of gender violence as Delhi's 'special problem', while pointing out that the level of rapes in the city were estimated to be nine times higher than that of Kolkata.[58]

The fifth framing context was arguably the most important: media coverage. The question of what came first, media coverage or public opinion, is difficult to answer and will, in a profound sense, remain unknowable. But what was beyond doubt was that the media invested this moment with engaged and continuous attention. Jean Dreze and Amartya Sen have observed how, in this instance, women's insecurity and vulnerability became national issues overnight, with newspapers reinventing themselves as 'rape-reporting vehicles'.[59]

The protests saw traditional and social media content combining to make common impact. In order to understand it better, Henry Jenkins' formulation of a convergence media culture, where he argues that content flows across multiple platforms, new and old,[60] could be useful. It was a pattern that played out during the Delhi gang rape protests. Ahmed and Jaidka point out how social media users constantly accessed traditional media in order to authenticate their own news.[61] The finding led them to support a 'media complementarity framework' based on the argument that there is congruence between the way online and mainstream media are used.[62]

Mainstream media do not generally threaten the status quo and, in fact, contribute to the social reproduction of order and stability by acting on the behalf of elites. They tend to favour those in power and perceive their own survival as being crucially hinged on the stability of the existing status quo. This perception is directly related to the business model of legacy media, whose primary source of financial sustainability is corporate advertising. Unless the ruling class is actually undermining what is perceived as the ruling order, and thereby the media's own interests, they do not frontally attack it. Combative they may be on occasion, but this is a combat carried out in the comfort zone of overlapping spheres of power and influence, where debate and criticism are conducted 'within the system of presuppositions and principles that constitute an elite consensus'.[63] The primary rule of engagement, it is understood, is never to push the coverage to the point where it could lead to anarchy. Media academics focusing on India have observed, especially in the context of the print media in states like Uttar Pradesh, that while a general pretence is maintained that politicians and journalists inhabit separate spheres and provide checks and balances on each others' functioning, there is in fact a lot of mutually beneficial interaction and secret deals that take place, and this has almost become the norm.[64]

What was distinctive about media coverage during the Delhi gang rape protests, however, was the manner in which both television and print never fought shy of criticising the Congress-led federal government. In that sense, this mobilisation can be seen as a continuation of the anti-government mood that had marked the IAC protests of the earlier year. Influenced by the outrage on the streets and the edgy and high-pitched voices on digital media, older media made strenuous efforts throughout these two weeks to connect not just with their own committed readers and viewers, but with social media users in general and street crowds in particular by constantly soliciting their responses. They also laid claim to the story in order to make it their own. *The Times of India*, for instance, branded the Delhi gang rape story by bestowing a pseudonym on the assaulted woman, who had to remain unnamed because the law mandated it. A few days after the story broke, the newspaper issued the following statement: 'She has come to symbolise rare courage, an inspiration for a movement demanding respect for women and much more. Such a symbol deserves a name. We will henceforth call her Nirbhaya (the Fearless One).' Although other publications followed suit, some calling her 'Braveheart', others 'Damini', a title borrowed from a 1993 Hindi film by Rajkumar Santoshi that had as its theme a woman seeking justice for rape, the appellation 'Nirbhaya', perhaps because it was the first, proved the most popular, remaining as a signifier of the tragedy years after Jyoti Singh's demise.

The visceral edge that reporting on this case came to acquire could be directly linked to the raw sentiments in favour of savage revenge and retribution expressed on the street, allowing them a legitimacy they may not have otherwise come to possess. A gender activist who was present at the protests found some of the content of the discourse very problematic, with the potential to trigger violence at any point. According to him, while social media by and large were not dwelling on substantive issues like women's right to public spaces, mainstream media failed to focus sufficiently on them.[65]

> Mainstream media in fact went along with the public sentiment without asking any of the mandatory questions required of them, much like the users of social media who were, in any case, not accountable to anyone for their content. This soon shaped into a trial by the media based on mass feelings of revenge and retribution.[66]

There could also have been other pragmatic considerations driving these mutual dependencies. An editor-in-chief of a national newspaper explained that both mainstream media and social media needed each other at that point. While print media in this particular case brought perspective to the public, the online media made the public present; while social media was successful in mobilising and creating a community of protesters and networks of solidarity from around the country and the world, mainstream media on their part could keep in touch with what the protesters were thinking and planning through the social media, and could speak to individual protesters. In this way, Facebook, Twitter, and other digital platforms emerged as a major source of news for mainstream journalism.[67]

Beyond considerations of professional efficiency was an intuitive sense among professionals and users in both the digital and mainstream media spheres that if they worked in unison, they could actually set the public agenda in the vacuum left by a fumbling government. It was this unfamiliar sense of power and leverage that encouraged representatives of mainstream media to join social media users in assuming the role of 'social activists' and discard the norms of 'balanced' reportage and standard operating procedures. This crusading zeal seemed to be driven by the need to remain relevant in a highly charged news scenario, rather than any real commitment towards ending violence against women. The manner in which the cameras and reporters quickly moved away shortly after the death of Jyoti Singh, rather than persist with the broader issues thrown up by the tragedy, would seem to indicate that it was the pressure to retain readership and eyeballs that was the driving force.

Shifts in focus of this kind are perhaps inevitable, given the media's preoccupation with what is framed as 'breaking news'. Mainstream editors have to contend with both push and pull factors. Competition from peers could force attention on a particular event, even as readers complain about the manner in which the news is being interpreted. In the case of the Delhi gang rape, some readers and viewers did raise searching questions as to why rape was suddenly being awarded front page status, and in the process creating a climate of fear.

In hindsight, it appeared that the mainstream media had to struggle between two contradictory impulses: to gain visibility and profile by echoing public sentiment, on the one hand, and to provide a much-needed perspective on rapidly unfolding developments, on the other. Social media users, in contrast, did not have to worry about such concerns. Being a self-driven model, the dividing line between the producers and consumers of information were often blurred, with the relative homogeneity of social background and preoccupations of both sets of users making for a certain similitude of response. This allowed social media users the possibility of being more lightfooted in their reaction to an ever-changing scenario, and they often gained the upper hand in setting the terms of the narrative and seeming more 'in tune with modernity than the methods of their rulers'.[68] Yet, it also needs to be remembered that communication technologies develop in a social, political, and economic context,[69] and to overlook that could be to over-emphasise their impact. Miriyam Aouragh, a scholar of the Arab movements and social media, even while agreeing that the internet was an important means to disseminate 'counter-hegemonic' content, cautions against a tendency to perceive these technologies as liberatory in and of themselves. According to her, 'many forms of online politics are rendered meaningless—unless organically related to offline street politics'.[70]

Two years after the Jyoti Singh gang rape, Justice Leila Seth expressed her dismay at the fact that women in India continued to be raped almost daily, and that 'the great swell of outrage that accompanied the tragic death of a brave young woman would seem to have achieved almost nothing at all'.[71] The question arises whether media coverage of the Jyoti Singh gang rape made adequate use of the power of journalism to understand a brutal criminal act and interpret it for large and diverse audiences in a manner that meaningfully confronts endemic sexual violence.

The answer is unequivocal: it did not. Without doubt, these protests had the immediate effect of persuading the mainstream media to display a greater alacrity in reporting gender-related violence, as evidenced by the hectic ground reportage accorded to the Badaun incident, which had occurred shortly thereafter. The incident, involving two sisters who were allegedly raped and then hanged on a tree in rural Uttar Pradesh, meant a long, bumpy car ride of several hours. This would have deterred Delhi journalists from following up on the story just a month earlier. Now, however, large numbers of journalists converged on Badaun. There was similar aggregated media attention paid to the gang rape of a photojournalist in Mumbai in 2013 and the rape of a woman in a taxi in Delhi in 2014. In 2015 a case of murder-rape in the

Haryana town of Rohtak once again saw extremely sensationalised reportage with headlines that screamed, 'Another Nirbhaya'. With the Jyoti Singh case emerging as the benchmark, a real concern was that both the public and the media would become desensitised to rapes in general, resulting in only those incidents marked by the most brutal violence being deemed worthy of public attention and media coverage.

A body of research conducted four years after the Jyoti Singh gang rape unearthed a curious paradox. It was found that although the English-language press in India was covering incidents of rape more than they had done earlier, sexual violence was failing to generate sustained media attention. In these four years, no case had resonated with the public in quite the same way as Jyoti Singh's had done. There was also something of a backlash against empathetic reportage of rape, with a small but significant rise in news reports of 'false rapes'.[72] Equally disturbing was a return to the old, familiar tendency to blame the assaulted persons for the crimes perpetrated against them—the why-were-they-there brand of journalism.

TWO COMPETING TROPES: CONTROL VS. FREEDOM

Two competing tropes had marked the protests, both of which were articulated in loud and passionate terms. One was the cry for the rapists to be given the death penalty; the other was in favour of greater equality and freedom for women and young people. Although both conversations had their origins in a demand for justice, they represented sharply differing approaches and ideological viewpoints. The media's failure in its coverage of the Delhi gang rape stems from their having provided salience to the first at the cost of the second, indicating the extent to which they themselves were imbricated in systems of power.

If we were to unpack the demand for the death sentence, its strongly patriarchal aspect would soon be discernable. Delhi's 'wound culture', to use Deepak Mehta's terminology, implied the existence of an inchoate sense of rage, especially among male residents, over the failure of the system to deliver a decent quality of life and a modicum of justice, and this could have been an underlying factor for the full-throated demand that the harshest of retributive punishment be meted out to the rapist-murderers. If Jyoti Singh could be framed as a symbol of a new and globalised India, her rapists were just as easily portrayed as representing an 'old and backward' India; criminalised migrants living in urban ghettoes, for whom sexual assault was second nature.[73]

Mainstream media as well as social media systematically amplified an already widespread perception that such criminals were a threat to society, and they invariably escaped retribution because of a slow and unresponsive criminal justice system. The feeling that the time had come to ensure that bestial criminals like these would 'pay for their sins', 'that enough was enough' was ubiquitous. The hanging just a month earlier of 'Kasab', the Pakistani who was one of the perpetrators of the November 2008 assault on Mumbai, had occasioned much publicly expressed approval, even celebrations; and the demand that Afzal Guru be hanged forthwith for the attack on the Indian Parliament a decade earlier had continued to be forcefully articulated in the media over the years. This sentiment may have been one of the precipitating factors for Afzal Guru's secret hanging in February 2013.

The mainstream media have, in any case, always adopted a tough stance on terror and crime, and the refrain voiced in both editorials and news reports was that an emerging global power like India cannot afford to be 'soft' when it came to issues of this kind. Such an editorial position also made business sense for them because it was a reflection of general opinion, both on the street and in business and political circles. The argument was to now segue seamlessly into the narrative for women's safety and the demand that Jyoti Singh's rapists be promptly put to death.

The Times of India coverage of 19 December 2012 illustrated this eloquently. 'Times View', a quasi-editorial, appeared on the front page, under the facile title, 'Here's How It Can Be Done':

> Every time there is a rape in the city we cringe at the reports in shame, wring our hands in frustration, and often cower in fear because our daughters, sisters and wives go out for work taking the very same routes stalked by depraved men who think nothing of violating, maiming and torturing women.

The expressions used in the piece, like 'enough is enough', were the very words used by protesters, and went on to be repeated ad infinitum in television studio arguments justifying capital punishment. Adjoining this editorial was a boxed item headlined 'Enough talk, let's make women safe', which laid out a six-point action plan. The first point of this action plan was a call for harsher punishment, and one of the possible solutions casually put forward was chemical castration. There was also an 'online poll' carried in the same space, asking readers to choose the most appropriate punishment for the rapists. The choices ranged from life imprisonment and death sentence to 'bobbitisation' and chemical castration.

Memories of Delhi's many brushes with kidnappers, rapists, and murderers over the years were resurrected in newspaper reports throughout this period to lend additional weight to the ongoing demand for capital punishment. *Jansatta* of 31 December, to take one example, tapped into the city's collective memory of the notorious Billa and Ranga case and how the killers were promptly hanged, while *Hindustan Times* drew a similar parallel in a piece that appeared a few days later.[74]

Television was no less restrained. As soon as the story broke, television reporters with live mikes roamed among the crowds, eliciting opinions and posing questions. Almost everybody was asked how the rapists should be treated, and each respondent was inevitably led into taking a maximalist position on punishment through skilful questioning. Some of these discussions were conducted against a backdrop of protesters holding up banners bearing an image of the noose, which had become ubiquitous during this period because it was freely distributed and widely used by the protesters. Television studio debates picked up the theme almost immediately. On 19 December, NDTV's Sonia Singh posed a leading question: Can Capital Punishment Be a Deterrent? It carried responses, not only from studio guests but also from protesters on the street, who echoed the general view that unless real fear is put into potential trangressors, offences of this kind will continue.

NDTV's rival channel, Times Now, carried a marathon, three-hour Newshour debate that projected the idea even more frontally, with the anchor, Arnab Goswami, making no effort to hide his own passionate endorsement of the death penalty. Through the entire discussion, the anchor kept encouraging his viewers to keep tweeting. The channel also created Facebook pages for the cause, which attracted comments like: 'Hang the culprits .... dont delay like kasaab' to '*aisa ghinona kaam karne wale ko Munirka ke chauraahe per hi ulta latka kar, inke sir kaat dena chaiye jaise pehle zamaane mein hota tha*!! (People who do such things should be strung up at the Munirka crossroads and decapitated, as in medieval times)'. The impatience with the normal course of justice was very evident in all these instances. Times Now's Facebook page even carried a letter from '3 Disturbed young Delhi Women' to the prime minister, urging him to make rape laws 'tough and strictly non-bailable' and ensure that the culprit was awarded capital punishment. Many Facebook pages came up on the theme of the death penalty, bearing names like 'Delhi gangrape even death penalty would be less' and 'Delhi rape.case penalty to death'. Each of them created their own ever-expanding circles of consensus favouring the death penalty.

A trial by media thus took shape, with capital punishment as the main discussion point. What seemed to exercise many people inordinately was the possibility of the juvenile involved in the gang rape escaping capital punishment because he happened to be underage for such punishment under the existing law. Here, too, the media spared no effort to highlight his alleged culpability. *Hindustan Times* carried a report about how the juvenile was said to be among 'three of the four who had most demonically assaulted the victim during her 45-minute-long ordeal on the fateful evening', without evidence being cited. A related story in the same newspaper highlighted the rising number of juvenile delinquents, with police sources claiming that the number of juveniles committing criminal acts had risen from fifty to over ninety-six between 2011 and 2012, and adding that many of these youth were now turning towards 'unnatural sex'—all this information cited without supporting evidence.

When news came of the chargesheets being filed against the rapists, there were queries as to why the juvenile had been kept out. Sushma Swaraj, speaking at a condolence meeting called by the Delhi wing of the BJP for Jyoti Singh, pointedly drew attention once again to the reported conduct of the juvenile, and how he had lured the woman by calling her 'sister'. This, in fact, was later proved to be untrue, but Swaraj was consciously reflecting the popular demand of the hour that the juvenile should also be hanged, despite the existing legal provision that children and adolescents below eighteen could not be tried as adults. As observed earlier, this was also a factor in getting the law amended subsequently.

The coarseness of the media and public response in the wake of this eye-for-an-eye articulation from the street was difficult to miss. Even the despicable treatment, including beatings and abuse, meted out to Jyoti Singh's rapists in Tihar Jail was met with public approval. A rash of songs and docu-dramas in support of the most bestial forms of punishment for her attackers were uploaded on YouTube, purveying high levels of misinformation and marked by a perverse voyeurism. In some of them, a photoshopped image of a woman with a tonsured head on a ventilator, ostensibly that of Jyoti Singh, went viral, making its way into the music videos and other media content.

Many of the videos have since been removed, but at the time they had drawn widespread response. Daood Hussain and Gaurav Pandey's music video 'Delhi Rape Story', was posted three days after the incident (20 December), and was largely a pastiche of media images from the incident slapped on to bhangra rap lyrics. Later, as news of Jyoti Singh's death came in, several 'musical tributes' to her emerged on YouTube, some of them marked by the crassest of visuals. A Telugu offering from 'Siddhu' entitled, 'Bad News for all Indians, Damini died today', posted on 28 December 2012, had visuals of her attackers being fed to rats. On 30 December Pradeep Dhaniya, in his 'Delhi Gang Rape Ke Doshi Song', urged listeners not to protest by going to Jantar Mantar, but to instead kill the rapists in full public view. Plumbing new depths of depravity, it urged that rods be rammed into them. That particular song received over 65,000 views with innumerable congratulatory comments, including one that said: 'Every word is true in this song. It's a great effort to wake up Indians. Wish to hear more songs like this.'

One particularly crass video, entitled 'Delhi Rapists', made by a Telugu studio and published on YouTube shortly after the death, depicted a large, muscular character, introduced as a software engineer, who takes upon himself the task of delivering instant justice. A series of monstrously sadistic acts are then picturised, reflecting some of the demands for vigilante punishment that had been voiced during the protests. The hero, after accomplishing his mission, then strides away triumphantly, declaring that he had done this for the honour of *'amma, akka, cheli, bharaya'* (mother, elder sister, younger sister, wife). The film attracted over 2.7 million views on YouTube over the next couple of years.

In September 2013, nine months after the incident, when the fast track court in Delhi appointed to adjudicate on the case handed the death sentence to all the four men involved in the Delhi gang rape, the campaign of the death penalty seekers received a fresh lease of life. In scenes reminiscent of December 2012, protesters, largely male, who had gathered outside the courtroom in great numbers, held placards bearing the familiar images of the noose with words like, 'Hang all the culprits'. They lustily cheered the verdict, demanding that the juvenile, too, be hanged. Celebrities like Kiran Bedi, who went on to become the Governor of Puducherry, joined in by tweeting, 'Justice Done! Thanku Judiciary! You keep the faith in rule of law alive! Jai hind.' A regressive new imaginary of justice was thus allowed free play on the media centre-stage.

The argument for capital punishment arose from an ideology that constructed rape as the worst thing that could happen to a 'proper' woman and demanded a protectionist framework to keep women 'safe', even as it iconised Jyoti Singh as the eternally virginal victim. What was distinctive about the capital punishment narrative was the seamlessly circular manner in which it made its way from media to the public and from the public to the media, to finally emerge as the commonsense of the faceless crowds. What provided it added legitimacy was the stamp of approval that Jyoti Singh's family accorded it. One of the first statements that figured widely in the media was a quotation from her brother indicating that the family wanted the culprits to be hanged as early as possible. It was a demand that was to be reiterated several times by the family in the days ahead, lending it a uniquely emotional justification for the public.

Pitted against this cry for retribution to avenge the violation of the 'good' woman was the parallel articulation by concerned citizens, notably women activists, for justice for all women survivors of violence and greater freedoms. As legal academic Pratiksha Baxi wrote,

> There has been the emergence of a public in solidarity, which has inspired, provoked and supported each one of us in our determined fight against sexual violence anywhere in the country. We have experienced Delhi differently perhaps for the first time in our lives. We have made affective connections with each other, grown from collective strength and learnt from each other.[75]

In media coverage, unfortunately, the significance of this 'public solidarity' was hardly captured.

This section of protesters publicly opposed the call for capital punishment. One feminist activist recalled how the Bhanwari Devi gang rape had also seen protests in the early 1990s in Jaipur, but they had been remarkably free of the crude sloganeering that marked the Delhi gang rape. 'For us, these slogans seemed to rise from regressive and ignorant attitudes and they needed to be defeated. The call for the death penalty needed to be firmly opposed not just from a human rights perspective, but because it came from an ideology of patriarchal control and protectionism.'[76]

Many instances of such counter-mobilisations surfaced during the Delhi gang rape protests, but they were either ignored by the mainstream media or treated cursorily. A powerful instance of this was the protest speech made outside the residence of Delhi Chief Minister Sheila Dikshit on 19 December by Kavita Krishnan. Responding to an observation made by Dikshit that women courted trouble because they were 'adventurous', Krishnan declaimed:

> We will be adventurous. We will be reckless. We will be rash. We will do nothing for our safety. Don't you dare tell us how to dress, when to go out at night, in the day, or how to walk or how many escorts we need! .... Even if women walk out on the streets alone, even if it is late at night, why should justifications need to be provided .... Freedom without fear is what we need to protect, to guard and respect.

The speech, recorded by an amateur filmmaker and put out on YouTube, went viral within a few hours and Krishnan's Facebook inbox was overflowing with messages of thanks that young girls from across the country had sent in. Krishnan recalled, 'I then realised that I had struck a chord and that there were hundreds of women in the country who longed for someone to speak up for their freedoms.'[77]

Such expressions of independence were apparent in digital campaigns that had been mounted to challenge patriarchal assumptions even earlier. The 'Pink Chaddi' protest of 2009, or the 'Besharmi Morcha' of 2011, although largely metropolitan, found support in smaller cities and towns as well. What was being attempted was a systematic countering of the socially constructed image of the Indian woman—the so-called 'Bharatiya nari' weighted down by tradition—by deliberately adopting stances designed to outrage conservative sentiments and iterate the right to sexual freedom and desire. The women behind the 'Pink Chaddi' intervention, for instance, called themselves the 'Consortium of Pub Going, Loose and Forward Women' in their bid to challenge the Ram Sene members who had physically attacked women visiting a Mangalore pub. The Besharmi Morcha which followed, according to Baxi, was the emerging generation's response to the manner in which women in the country had been confined and regulated, even as they were 'routinely stigmatised, medicalised, sexualised, maimed, stalked, harassed, raped, burnt or killed', and argued that women have to reclaim their rights, even if it meant inviting the charge of being deemed 'shameless' by a strongly patriarchal society.[78]

The gang rape protests also witnessed similar innovative and creative forms of cultural expression that attempted to dismantle the shame-honour paradigm that invariably marked public responses to assaults on women, and instead asserted that they were violations of a person's right to free movement, bodily integrity, and sexual autonomy. Facebook pages and Twitter feeds were harnessed to convey information that ranged from advice on how to negotiate the city safely, to incisive, even humorous, critiques of the hypocritical stances of religious leaders and politicians. The active participation of men in large numbers in such counter-mobilisation was seen as a 'turning point ... wherein, women's issues have transitioned into gender issues'.[79]

The theme was revisited in new and compelling ways, through photo exhibitions, song, dance, poetry, and theatre. The Ravinder Randhawa–Swara Bhaskar song, '*Maa ni meri*' (Look Mother! Look how I fought. I was one, they were six. But afraid I was not ... Mother, I will not become you ...) was one such attempt. Juxtaposing powerful dialogues and lyrics in Hindustani and Punjabi, the song celebrated the spirit of a girl who would not remain silent, who would rather drown than swim obediently in the tide of patriarchal norms. It became an overnight success on platforms like YouTube, liked and shared by thousands across the country and the world.

These discrete initiatives and campaigns were to become the progenitors of new youth and feminist activism. It was in response to such initiatives that the Justice Verma Committee had commended in its report the 'youth of India' who, through their 'extraordinary protest have reinforced reason and have attempted to confront the state and political elite, to what is modern reality in the context of the Constitution'.[80]

In subsequent years, the online space became the site of a new protean feminist militancy. The international #MeToo campaign, triggered by the egregious sexual harassment conduct of influential Hollywood producer Harvey Weinstein in 2017, which had its resonances in India among young, educated, urbanised feminists, was a case in point. Its failure, however, to connect with marginalised categories like Dalit women and those of the hinterland living off the internet grid was conspicuous, and flagged the limitations of online activism. A positive, if tangential, outcome was the emergence and flourishing of feminist cyber portals, like Feminism in India, which self-defined itself as 'an intersectional feminist platform that amplifies voices of women & the marginalised using art, media, culture, tech & community', and Ladies Finger, an 'online women's magazine delivering fresh and witty perspectives on politics, culture, health, sex, work and everything in between ...'.

By underplaying the feminist creativity embedded in some of the protests, the mainstream media demonstrated their patriarchal underpinnings. Rarely did the media coverage interpret this efflorescence of cultural expression as a serious effort to dismantle the cult of masculinity; rarer still was the argument made that undermining patriarchy was intrinsic to deepening democracy in a gender-unequal country like India.

It was unsurprising, therefore, that of the two competing tropes that marked public discourse on the Delhi gang rape—the projection of a climate of fear along with the regressive call for capital punishment that was pitted against a demand for enhancing women's freedom and sense of safety in public places—it was the former that gained salience in the public sphere. The ugly undertow implicit in the loud demand for capital punishment suggested that it was the forces of patriarchal regression that had gained pole position during this period, with help from mainstream and social media. It fed into a familiar, time-worn narrative that protection of a community's 'daughters', 'daughters-in-law', and 'wives' were linked directly to the protection of the community's religion, honour, and ways of life, and provided justification for 'Love Jihad' vigilantism and the institution of anti-Romeo police squads like those set up by Adityanath, once he became the chief minister of Uttar Pradesh in 2017.

Although the Justice Verma Committee report had categorically rejected the death penalty as a legal option, the Criminal Law (Amendment) Act of 2013 for the first time brought capital punishment into the ambit of the law for rape. This was a direct capitulation to the demand for such a measure that had emerged from the streets during these protests. The amendment made to the Juvenile Justice Act in 2014, one of the first legislative interventions of the new BJP-led government, lowered the age at which juvenile delinquents could be tried as adults, from eighteen years to sixteen years. Although the move was fiercely contested by child rights activists and sections of civil society, the government was successful in pushing it through. Legal academic Ved Kumari, a strong opponent of the move, traced the political support for it to the fear psychosis created during the Delhi gang rape protests.[81]

The protests have sometimes come to be regarded as instances where the media were used as a major tool to create awareness on sexual violence at a mass level. Such technological reductionism fails to answer the basic question: Why was it that the media could help to create an unprecedented, leaderless upsurge against sexual violence, but could not address the root causes for the social crises that had caused it in the first place?

There was little attempt by media professionals in the course of their reporting to focus on the discrete issues the gang rape raised. The irony, for instance, in the fact that many young male protesters during this period were shouting sexualised expletives against the rapists—'the usual maa-behen. Police ki maa ..., Sarkaar ki behen ... a bizarre sense of support'[82]—in their ostensible support for Jyoti Singh; how was this to be understood? Or, to take another example, the idea that 'real men don't rape', which became fashionable at that time, was allowed to gain traction without questioning the patriarchal assumptions that underlay the construction of the 'real man'.

Any hope that the protests would lead to a sustained interrogation of the lack of gender justice for survivors of sexual violence in the country was belied. The promised foregrounding of the issue of sexual violence in public discourse never materialised. The misogyny that undergirded the public statements of notables—whether it was the supposed godman, Asaram, who had averred that the gang raped woman was equally responsible for the crime, or Uttar Pradesh politician Mulayam Singh Yadav, who pronounced in another context that *'ladke, ladke hain ... galti ho jati hai* (boys will be boys ... they commit mistakes)'—revealed how untouched they were by the protests.

The inability to problematise rape at that juncture and see it as an act of power, not a crime of passion, gave rise to further failures over time. Despite sexual violence against women emerging as an issue during the General Election of 2014, as we noted earlier, the media largely failed to call out the misogynist, communal, and casteist ways in which it was often articulated. As a feminist activist argued at the time of the 2014 election, 'the discourse on gender in these elections is deeply disturbing. In previous years, perhaps women were ignored or taken for granted. Now, women need to worry about how they are being talked about—and what kind of politics is being done in their name.'[83]

One of the most conspicuously negative aspects of the media coverage was its failure to make the connections between sexual violence and entrenched misogyny; the structured silences and gaps in planning and policymaking in terms of gender equality; the lack of women's representation in legislative bodies; the low value accorded to women's labour; the indifference to infrastructure that impacts women's safety directly, like safe public transportation in cities or sanitation facilities in rural India. The dominant image of Jyoti Singh as victim, as the living dead—the *'zinda lash'*, in Sushma Swaraj's words—persisted and ended up dehumanising her. Such a construction was directly related to the manner in which the media are structured to actively encourage conformism. Social media like Facebook, for all its promise of being different from mainstream media, ended up supporting the status quo. By allowing an opinion to get validated instantly by ten others, pressuring the eleventh person to fall in line and by putting a premium on 'virality', it is inherently designed towards rewarding consensus.

These failures were particularly troubling since the case came to be a central point of reference for reportage on crimes against women in India. In fact, every subsequent case of rape was measured by the metrics of this case, which meant that crimes committed by strangers were privileged, despite the fact that most rapes in India are actually perpetrated by relatives or acquaintances. The media's deliberate attention to the former category at the expense of the latter, one commentator argued, 'reinforces a particular notion about the prevalence of rape as a crime committed by a deviant few and does not push the public to ask uncomfortable questions of themselves and society'.[84]

The media also proved unequal to unravelling the other, multiple social crises behind the incident, including the narrative of vicious urban disparities and discriminations that thread their way through this story. The Justice Verma Committee Report, which came out in January 2013, went much further down that road than the media ever did. In contrast to the holistic reading of violence offered by the Verma Report, media content during those two weeks were marked by major epistemological gaps and discontinuities. A Delhi-based psychoanalyst suggests that perhaps it may have been less distressing for the average Delhiite to view this brutal attack as the 'work of "psychopaths"'.[85] But was the media guilty of going along with this comforting assumption because they wished to spare their readers/viewers the trauma of confronting the fury residing below the 'civilised' selves of ordinary people? This would be a plausible, if not conclusive, surmise. The fact remains that the media narrative did not confront the demons within society or bring into view what Deepak Mehta, quoted earlier, had referred to as the 'honey badger'. If the media had played a genuinely liberatory role, they would have tried to find ways to address the underlying issues which, despite extensive reportage, remained invisible, including possible answers as to why the rapist-murderers did what they did.[86]

In the end, while there was some possibility in this moment of public outrage for the media to have helped transform public discourse and usher in substantive, systemic social change, it would appear that they chose not to use it. They preferred instead to deploy their physical and intellectual resources to exploit a singularly fraught case of sexual violence to cater to their own requirements of market consolidation.

NOTES AND REFERENCES

1. Ravi Sundaram, a professor at the Centre for the Study of Developing Societies, remarked at a conference on the media how surprised he was to see women holding placards condemning rape in Hampi, Karnataka, while the protests were going on in Delhi.

2. Maitrayee Chaudhuri, 2017, *Refashioning India: Gender, Media, and a Transformed Public Discourse* (New Delhi: Orient BlackSwan), 236.

3. Poulami Roychowdhury, 2013, 'The Delhi Gang Rape: The Making of International Causes', *Feminist Studies* 39 (1), 282–92.

4. Indira Jaising and Ritu Menon, 2015, 'Ethics and Theatrics On "India's Daughter"', *Economic and Political Weekly* 50 (2), 28 March.

5. Jakob De Roover, 2015, 'India's Daughter and BBC—Belgian Professor Speaks Out', Niti Central, 11 March. Available at http://www.niticentral.com/2015/03/11/indias-daughter-and-bbc-belgian-professor-speaks-out-306333.html (accessed April 2015).

6. 'Activists write to NDTV on India's Daughter', SIFY, 5 March. Available at http://www.sify.com/news/activists-write-to-ndtv-on-india-s-daughter-news-national-pdfqBcadbjcia.html (accessed August 2015).

7. Leila Seth, 2014, *Talking of Justice: People's Rights in Modern India* (New Delhi: Aleph Book Company), 6–7.

8. Verma Committee Report, 2013. Available at http://nlrd.org/womens-rights-initiative/justice-verma-committee-report-download-full-report.

9. Pamela Philipose, 2014, 'The clamour, the silence', *The Indian Express*, 16 December.

10. 'Respondent Opinions on Issues They Want Addressed by Their Elected Representatives' (October 2013–April 2014), Institute for Development and Communication, Chandigarh.

11. Rainuka Dagar, 2015, 'Gender Narratives and Elections', in Paul Wallace (ed.), *India's 2014 Elections: A Modi-led BJP Sweep* (New Delhi: Sage Publications), 86.

12. 'Fashion shoot on Nirbhaya gang rape triggers outrage', *The Times of India*, 5 August 2014.

13. Gitanjali Joshua, et al., 2015, 'Locating Hyderbad for Feminism in the Present Struggle against Violence', *Economic and Political Weekly*, 50 (44), 31 October.

14. Vasundhara Sirnate and Nithya Nagarathinam, 2015, 'What enables rape reporting?', *The Hindu*, 25 April.

15. Seth, *Talking of Justice*, 16.

16. Raymond Williams, 1989, *Politics of Modernism against the New Conformists* (London: Verso), 134–35.

17. Robin Jeffrey and Assa Doran, 2013, *Cellphone Nation* (New Delhi: Hachette India), 2.

18. '27 Million Smartphone Users in Urban India', 11 July 2012. Available at http://www.nielsen.com/in/en/press-room/2012/smartphone-incidence.html (accessed January 2015).

19. Vikas S. N., 2013, 'Facebook India Active Users Up 59% To 71M In Q4-2012', 6 February. Available at http://www.medianama.com/2013/02/223-facebook-71-million-india-users-2012/ (accessed 18 January 2015).

20. 'In India, 1 in 4 Online Minutes are Spent on Social Networking Sites', 20 August 2012. Available at https://www.comscore.com/Insights/Press-Releases/2012/8/In-India-1-in-4-Online-Minutes-are-Spent-on-Social-Networking-Sites (accessed 18 January 2015).

21. 55th Annual Report of the Registrar of Newspapers for India.

22. TRAI Consultation Paper, 2013, 'Issues Relating to Media Ownership'.

23. 'Online news readership in India grows to 9.4 million daily', 7 October 2013. Available at http://www.afaqs.com/news/story/38877 Online-new-readership-in-India-grows-to9.4-million-daily-visitors:-comScore (acccessed 24 January 2015).

24. Shakuntala Rao, 2014, *Covering Rape in Shame: Culture, Journal of Mass Media Ethics* (SUNY-Plttsburgh: Department of Communication).

25. Interview with activist Prabhleen, August 2014.

26. Interview with television anchor Ravish Kumar, January 2013.

27. Supriya Chotani, 2013, 'Television News Media and Facebook as Mediating Spaces of Protest in India', digitmed.wordpress.com, 13.

28. Interview with women's activist Nilanjan, August 2014.

29. Saifuddin Ahmed and Kokil Jaidka, 2013, 'Protests against #delhigangrape on Twitter', *JeDem*. Available at http://www.jeedem.org,54.

30. CMS Media Lab Analysis, 2013, Centre for Media Studies, New Delhi.

31. Pamela Philipose, 2013, 'Anxieties in the Republic Media: Metamorphosis and Popular Protest', *Economic and Political Weekly* XLVIII (6).

32. Interview with college student Gurpreet, August 2014.

33. 'Blog: Why I began Facebook campaign after Delhi gang-rape'. Available at http://www.ndtv.com/delhi-news/blog-why-i-began-facebook-campaign-after-delhi-gang-rape-508123 (accessed 13 July 2016).

34. Interview with Kavita Krishnan, July 2014.

35. Hamid Dabashi, 2012, *The Arab Spring; The End of Postcolonialism* (London: Zed Books), 18.

36. Interview with social activist Manak Matiyani, August 2014.

37. Pierre Bourdieu, 1998, *On Television* (New York: The New Press), 23.

38. Ahmed and Jaidka, 'Protests against #delhigangrape on Twitter'.

39. Ibid.

40. Interview with Siddharth Varadarajan, then editor-in-chief of *The Hindu*, August 2014.

41. Flavia Agnes, 2015, 'Why India loves Nirbhaya, hates Suzette', *The Asian Age*, 20 March.

42. Rao, *Covering Rape in Shame*.

43. 'Upper castes dominate national media, says survey in Delhi', *The Hindu*, 5 June 2006. Available at http://www.thehindu.com/todays-paper/tp-national/upper-castes-dominate-national-media-says-survey-in-delhi/ (accessed July 2015).

44. Press Trust of India, 12 September 2012. Available at http://articles.economictimes.indiatimes.com/2012-09-05/news/33616265_1_internet subscriber-base-cent-users-internet-access (accessed September 2015).

45. Anand Teltumbde, 2013, 'Delhi Gang Rape Case: Some Uncomfortable Questions', *Economic and Political Weekly* XLVIII (6).

46. Tithi Bhattacharya, 2015, 'India's Daughter: Neoliberalism's dreams and the nightmares of violence', *International Socialist Review* 97, 1–4 July.

47. 'First time since fateful night, girl meets friend', *Hindustan Times*, 22 December 2012.

48. Douglas Kellner, 2003, *Media Spectacle* (London: Routledge), 92.

49. Interview with university student Shraddha, August 2014.

50. Interview with youth activist Prabhleen, August 2014.

51. Annual Report of the Reserve Bank of India, 2011–12.

52. 'Need rules to handle flash mobs: Chidambaram', *Hindustan Times*, 26 December 2012.

53. 'Congress plans Rs 100 crore social media war chest', *Governance Now*, 19 January 2013.

54. Debal K. SinghaRoy, 2014, *Towards a Knowledge Society: New Identities in Emerging India* (New Delhi: Cambridge University Press), 218.

55. Manuel Castells, 1994, 'European Cities, the Information Society, and the Global Economy', *New Left Review* 204.

56. Dhunu Roy, 2010, 'City Makers and City Breakers', in Maya Dayal and Ravi Dayal (eds), *Celebrating Delhi* (New Delhi: Penguin/Viking, 2010), 154.

57. Interview with Deepak Mehta, August 2014.

58. Jean Dreze and Amartya Sen, 2013, *An Uncertain Glory—India and its Contradictions* (New York: Allen Lane), 228.

59. Ibid., 227.

60. Henry Jenkins, 2006, *Convergence Culture: Where Old and New Media Collide* (New York: New York University Press), 2.

61. Ahmed and Jaidka, 'Protests against #delhigangrape on Twitter'.

62. Mohan J. Dutta-Bergman, 2004, 'Complementarity in Consumption of News Types Across Traditional and New Media', *Journal of Broadcasting & Electronic Media* 48 (1).

63. Sashi Kumar, 2014, *Unmediated: Essays on Media, Culture, Cinema* (New Delhi: Tulika Books), 9.

64. Ursula Rao, 2011, *News As Culture: Journalistic Practices and the Remaking of Indian Leadership Traditions* (New Delhi: Cambridge University Press), 54.

65. Interview with youth activist Dhruv Arora, August 2014.

66. Ibid.

67. Interview with Siddharth Varadarajan, then editor-in-chief of *The Hindu*, August 2014.

68. Paul Mason, 2013, *Why It's Still Kicking Off Everywhere: The New Global Revolutions* (London: Verso), 66.

69. John Bellamy Foster and Robert W. McChesney, 2011, 'The Internet's Unholy Marriage to Capitalism', *Monthly Review* 62 (10).

70. Miriyam Aouragh, 2012, 'Social Media, Mediation and the Arab Revolutions', *tripleC(2)*. Available at http://www.triple-c.at/index.php/tripleC/article/view/416 (accessed February 2015).

71. Seth, *Talking of Justice*, 16.

72. Joanna Jolly, 2016, 'Rape in India: Is the English-language press falling back on stereotypes?', *Columbia Journalism Review* 20 July.

73. Roychowdhury, 'The Delhi Gang Rape'.

74. Jatin Anand, 2013, 'Ranga-Billa redux: How rapists were sent to the gallows', *The Hindustan Times* 9 January.

75. Pratiksha Baxi, 2012, 'We must resist the cunning of judicial reform', *Kafila*, 29 December.

76. Interview with feminist activist Madhu Bala, August 2014.

77. Interview with Kavita Krishnan.

78. Pratiksha Baxi, 2011, 'In Defence of the Besharmi Morcha', *Women's Feature Service*.

79. A. Shakil, 2013, 'Protests, the Justice Verma Committee and the Government Ordinance', *Economic and Political Weekly* XLVIII (6), 9 February.

80. Justice Verma Committee Report, 2013. Available at Fuhttp://nlrd.org/womens-rights-initiative/justice-verma-committee-report-download-full-report.

81. From a lecture delivered by Ved Kumari, titled 'In the Aftermath of Nirbhaya', September 2014, Centre for the Study of Law and Governance, JNU, New Delhi.

82. 'Arrogance vs angst: a blog by a protester at Raisina Hill', blog by Nishtha Gautam. Available at http://www.ndtv.com/india-news/arrogance-vs-angst-a-blog-by-a-protester-at-raisina-hill-508378 (accessed 5 April 2015).

83. Kavita Krishnan, 2014, 'Political Discourse on Gender Hits an All-time Low', The Hindu Centre for Politics and Public Policy. Available at http://www.thehinducentre.com/verdict/commentary/article5968909.ece (accessed April 2015).

84. Divya Arya, 2015, 'Reporting Sexual Violence in India: What Has Changed Since the Delhi Gang Rape', *Economic and Political Weekly* l (34), 31 October.

85. Rakesh Shukla, 2014, 'The Rage of Angels: Anger, Fury, Brutal Rape, Protests, Police Action', *International Journal of Applied Psychoanalytical Studies* 11 (2).

86. Interview with Deepak Mehta, August 2014.

four

SCRIPTS, TWEETS, POSTS, AND VERDICTS

Electoral Discourse in a Mediatised Age—I

NARENDRA MODI

Elections are symbolic affirmations of a country's functioning democracy. Yet, in a very real sense, they also reflect assertions of asymmetrical power that contribute to legitimising the decision-making authority of those who stand for office and win.

Three principal forces interact and seek to influence each other in these assertions of power: partisan elites and their supporters; the electorate; and the media. The inter-linkages between the three entities have often been studied in order to gauge political prospects and electoral outcomes, but they also offer a useful framework through which to assess the level of mediatisation of politics within a particular society. The media, which once functioned as merely channels of communication within the election process, have now emerged as independent power centres operating 'autonomously, according to its own economic and symbolic logics'.[1]

The capacity of the media to set political agendas, which has been defined as the 'assignment of special relevance to one particular issue or set of information by the source of the message ... with the expectation that the audience will respond with heightened attention to the content and format of the message',[2] has also been noted. Early theorists of the media's agenda-setting potential, Maxwell E. McComb and Donald L. Shaw, based their research on an election scenario. During the 1968 presidential election in the US, voters in North Carolina were asked to name the most important issues of the day, and their responses were found to closely reflect the pattern of news coverage in the newspapers, television and radio stations they had accessed. The conclusion McCombs and Shaw drew was that 'media are the major primary sources of national political information' because they force attention to certain issues and build up the public images of political figures.[3] Subsequent theorising by them and others on the subject brought about a more nuanced understanding of the phenomenon by unpacking the manner in which the media sought to set the agenda through the framing of their content. Here, the existing ideologies of voters were always taken into account, since the media's capacity for agenda-setting was invariably heightened when it conformed to what the audience was already inclined to believe.

The media's agenda-setting potential has been the subject of much debate in recent times. Castells argued that 'because the media constitute the main source of socialized communication—that is communication with the potential to reach society at large—the framing of the public mind is largely performed through processes that take place in the media'.[4] Other theorists saw this as too technologically deterministic, pointing out that the media and communication technologies were located within the dominant structures of power, and that this factor greatly influenced their agenda-setting.

The advent of the internet and social media, creating extensive socio-technical networks for electoral purposes, has complicated the argument further, since the very patterns of communication have now changed. It was possible for political entities and actors to achieve an even wider dispersal of their messaging through self-communication in a financially affordable way. Michael J. Jensen noted that 'The monological flow of communications between parties and publics is now a dialogical flow with low cost means of communicating.'[5]

These are useful theoretical perspectives to understand how the changes in communication technologies and the political universe have influenced and been influenced by each other. It should also not be forgotten that the communications landscape in India has been shaped by political interests. Robert W. McChesney points out that the communications revolution in the US was the 'the result of structures and markets created and shaped by policies and extraordinary public subsidies'.[6] He termed the result a 'bad system', built as it was on policies all driven by opaque government decision-making.

A similar critique could be extended to India, since media growth here has followed the same trajectory, particularly in the years following economic liberalisation. The opening up of the economy to global capital from the early 1990s was coterminous with the market-driven communications revolution in the country. This led to piquant and sometimes ironic realities like that nugget from Census 2011, already noted, that while the country had approximately 60 per cent of total households that had access to television, less than 47 per cent of Indians had an indoor toilet.

Policymaking, a good deal of it taking place behind closed doors, increasingly aimed at privileging economic growth and allowing politically well-connected interests to prosper. Significant changes in the ownership structures of media houses, their business models, as well as the programmes they generated, complemented this flourishing.

Take the example of the opening up to private capital of a hitherto strictly State-controlled sector like television, a prime contributor to the politics of culture in the country. The exponential rise in private television channels within India from the early1990s left the State broadcaster, Doordarshan, in a state of paralysis, and brought in its wake new content, the success of which was measured by new metrics such as television rating points (TRPs) and levels of advertising revenue. 'In this new competitive environment, content in general and the old-fashioned portrayal of "national" culture in particular has undergone redefinition'.[7]

While this story is often told in terms of an 'invasion from the skies' by foreign satellite companies, it was an invasion that was made possible through State endorsement. Before foreign entities could get a foothold in the country, there had to be policy changes to expedite the circumvention of 'the tight national controls on the terrestrial broadcast spectrum'[8] and allow them access to vast markets without having to make the heavy investment required for building terrestrial transmitters.

If a supportive political environment had major consequences for the way media grew and developed, the reverse was equally true. The post-liberalisation media scenario in India altered the format and discourse of politics and introduced many new elements into its practice, including some that were clearly indefensible. Nalin Mehta quotes the experience of an unnamed TV executive who had joined a new TV channel launched by a real estate company and learnt that his employer, given the imminent election to the Uttar Pradesh assembly, was busy striking deals with politicians for coverage.[9] The propensity of politicians and political parties to run television channels to buttress their own constituencies, either openly or through surrogate companies, had major impacts on Indian democracy, since these channels often served as ventriloquist dummies for their respective interests.

Meanwhile, communication technologies in India were growing with rapidity, driven by powerful political backers. Within a short span of time, profitable linkages between politicians, big business, and the telecom sector became the reality even as the beeping intruder—the mobile phone—transformed personal communications and sociality, captured in the 1998 Bollywood hit song, 'What is mobile number?/What is your smile number?' from the film *Haseena Maan Jaayegi*. The scandals involving Sukh Ram in the mid-1990s and A. Raja a dozen years later, both unsurprisingly ministers of telecommunications at the federal level, were symptomatic of these murky goings-on—the first involved corruption in the issuing of licenses for services like emailing and paging; the second reflected the malfeasance marking the distribution of the electromagnetic spectrum.

All governments, whether they were led by the Congress or the BJP, were goaded by a combination of self-interest and corporate coercion to frame policies that benefited private telecommunications interests. While the social benefits of the unprecedented expansion of the country's telecom infrastructure unleashed by such political interventions were undeniable—it was no mean achievement to enable mobile phone usage to rise from 23 million in 1999 to 900 million by 2012—it was also true that 'officials, corporations and politicians could benefit each other through collusion in the distribution of public property—in this case Radio Frequency'.[10]

If television changed the contours and content of political discourse in the 1990s, so too did new communication technologies two decades later. In *Cell Phone Nation*, Robin Jeffrey and Assa Doron recall the role of the cell phone in gathering 'flash mobs' of protesters that ensured the end of President Estrada's rule in the Philippines as early as 2001, and point out how mobile phones 'augmented bicycles, conviction and organisation to bring the Bahujan Samaj Party to power in Uttar Pradesh (UP) in 2007'.[11]

In this way mass self-communication, expedited by vastly expanded and improved networks of mobile telephony and the internet, came to be coterminous with mass communication, often supplementing it in emphatic ways. But the darker consequences of the new scenario need to be underlined as well. Mobile phones and internet connectivity in India have been used to deepen cultural, religious, and caste identities and widen cleavages between communities to create situations of political turbulence for electoral considerations. In the lead-up to the General Election of 2014, riots were systematically engineered in Muzaffarnagar, in western Uttar Pradesh, India's most electorally significant state, and a region that had never witnessed communal tensions earlier, through the calculated use of social media in August–September 2013. Rumours and falsehoods were fanned in real time as fake images and unverified media content designed to stoke communal hatred were circulated through the use of social media platforms, which helped to create an alternate news simulacrum.[12] The politicians behind such exercises were hardly held to account for the resulting deaths and mass displacement of families. On the contrary, they went on to gain even greater political profile as members of the state legislature and Parliament.

NEW MEDIA ON POLL PODIUM

In this chapter and the next, we will look at the elections to the Delhi Assembly in 2013 and 2015 and the Sixteenth General Election of 2014. It could be argued that these three elections, taken together, marked the apogee in the deployment of mediatised political mobilisation in India and tested the efficacy of social media as tools of political communication for the first time in the country.

This phenomenon, which could be seen as part of an international trend, came into view most conspicuously during the Barak Obama presidential election of 2008. Although web pages and other internet-based communications tools had become part of electoral strategising in various parts of the world, including in the United States much before Obama's first election campaign, what made this particular presidential bid so striking was the strategic manner in which he and his team used the entire range of new communication technologies and social media to create what has been termed the 'first 21st century campaign'[13] in the US.

Since the Obama presidential campaigns emerged as something of a template for the election campaign conducted by the BJP in the 2014 general election, it may be useful to consider it more closely. An account of the 2008 Obama campaign from within it by an election volunteer highlighted how it had benefited from deploying no less than sixteen social media networks, which included Facebook, YouTube, and Twitter. Each of these was integrated seamlessly and efficiently into campaign planning and organisation. 'The campaign's use of blogging, social networks, text messaging, email, and video heralds a new era of integrated digital communication that is simultaneously widespread and intimate.'[14]

Among the first efforts the team made was to revamp the old website that Obama had used, and fashion it as a mothership on which it located a blogging site, a campaign schedule, a video channel called BarackTV, and a social network called my.barakobama.com. These efforts had one central emphasis: to build voter empathy and enhance interactivity.

The manner in which Facebook was used is a case in point:

> In a tech first, in March 2007, the Obama new media team developed an innovative FB application that harnessed the power of interactive media. This linked the users of MyBO account with the FB account, seamlessly importing their FB contacts in MyBO and publishing the myBO activities onto FB's newsfeed. The Obama FB application allowed the campaign to transfer each community's members' list of family and friends into an audience for campaign activities .... A small widget was added to a user's FB profile page which continued a stream of the O camp's most recent videos and news items.[15]

It was through detailed online surveys that the Obama campaign could bring the interests and inclinations of the constituency within its sweep and ensure that campaign information tailored to its profile could reach it. In the process, the campaign got these varied individuals and constituencies to actually work on the presidential candidate's behalf. Within a day of the announcement that Obama would be standing for the elections, 1,000 grassroots organisations had already been created using the site's online tools. Individuals in all fifty states created more than 35,000 local organising groups, hosted over 200,000 events, and made millions upon millions of calls to their contacts, thus exponentially expanding the campaign's reach. This deployment of user-generated content was a key innovation of the campaign's media strategy, as those persuaded by the messages put out responded in multifarious ways to them, by blogging, posting, tweeting, and sharing images and videos.

Two other aspects of this campaign were highlighted in subsequent research. The first was the manner in which US media had evolved into a

> hybrid arrangement where traditional and news sources coexist, complement, compete, and conflict with one another .... Even as most citizens continued to receive much of their campaign information from television news and established newspapers, candidates were able to bypass media gatekeepers and get their message out to voters directly via an assortment of digital platforms.[16]

The Obama campaign understood the importance of media convergence and user-generated content, and used both to great advantage.

Noteworthy in this context was the emergence of a category in the US that the Pew Internet & American Life Project termed the 'online political users'—people who went online for news of the campaign and of politics more generally; who communicated on the internet with others about politics; and who received and shared content using internet platforms. Significantly, more than half of them were younger than thirty-five years.[17]

Equally impressive, it seemed, was the fund mobilisation that the campaign achieved. According to the rhetoric of Obama campaigners, it was grassroots activism that egged individuals and local communities to contribute, but in actual fact the lion's share came from corporate backers who understood that an Obama presidency would be in their interest. Big money had always played a dominant role in all US presidential bids, but the Obama campaigns of 2008 and 2012 marked new highs in such funding. In an important analysis of the 2012 victory, John Nichols and Robert McChesney dismiss the tall claims of grassroots activism having beaten big money. Looking back at the 2012 election, which they pegged at around $10 billion—the most expensive in US history—they point to 'powerful interests—freed to, in effect, buy elections, unhindered by downsized and diffused media that must rely on revenue from campaign ads'[18] setting the rules of engagement. Those interests, they argue, have so dominated the field that democracy in the US was turning out to be a 'dollarocracy'.

As for the argument that the internet could prove to be some sort of leveller in this scenario, Nichols and McChesney dismiss that possibility outright, pointing to the fact that the internet itself has become a site of domination and control. They refer to the scandal over the surveillance attempts of the National Security Agency, which became public knowledge in 2013, as confirmation of this trend. They perceive the emergence of Big Data in the hands of corporations and politicians as the other big threat to democracy. 'We are entering a new political age in which candidates and parties will maintain extraordinary dossiers on prospective voters. They will tailor messages to demographic groups, to donors and ultimately to individual voters.'[19] The prophecy was to prove extraordinarily accurate in November 2017, when Donald J. Trump became the forty-fifth president of the United States. In India, too, the General Election of May 2014 proved to be the most expensive in the country's history. It saw both 'powerful' interests funding a party and a prime ministerial candidate that best suited their interests, and the use of 'extraordinary dossiers on prospective voters' to achieve victory.

LOK SABHA POLLS: 2004, 2009

All these aspects of the Obama elections—online activism, user-generated content, an active youth cohort that was willing to engage with the election campaign through social media, databases of disaggregated data on voters according to their social profile and voting predilections—was to become part of the political scenario in India.

It was not always like this, of course. Myron Weiner, writing about the 1977 general election, had noted that because of high levels of illiteracy, low newspaper circulations, and governmental control of radio and television, popular participation in elections took place largely through public meetings.[20] This was to change dramatically over the next quarter century, both in form and content.

> The BJP showed an early propensity to use computers for election data crunching. In 2003, James Manor had made special note of the BJP's data gathering drive in the context of the Madhya Pradesh state election of that year: 'This writer gained access to a pre-election strategic survey of the state, developed for the BJP by professional analysts at a think tank.' In thirty-one years of studying state elections, he has seen nothing to rival it. It ran into 452 pages, excluding an extensive introduction and annexures. It contained extremely detailed information—constituency by constituency—on caste composition, local conditions and problems, other parties, voters' perceptions, and the party's chances of winning.[21]

The BJP also discerned early the possibilities of new communication technologies to buttress its own presence. One of the first steps that it took in 1998, when it came to power as part of the National Democratic Alliance (NDA), was to set up the National Task Force on Information Technology & Software Development. While successive Congress Party governments had also liberalised the telecommunications and media sectors from the mid-1980s onwards, it was the BJP again that proved more adept at harnessing their potential, as reflected in its use of audiovisual technologies to ignite the popular imagination during the Ram Janambhoomi agitation of the late 1980s.[22] Predictably, it was also the first political party in India to host its own website as early as 1998.

The BJP's enthusiastic embrace of mediatised political communication became very evident in its campaign for the 2004 General Election, which political scientist Niraja Gopal Jayal characterised as 'the first election in which political communication came to be conducted in the corporate vocabulary of image making, branding and marketing'.[23] That general election campaign was the first that featured political advertising on television, with its theme of 'India Shining', which the party had hoped would win it another term in office by creating a 'feel good' mood among voters. According to media monitoring agency TAM India, between December 2003 and January 2004, advertisements that showcased the message of 'India Shining' were shown 9,472 times[24] across media platforms. So ubiquitous was the campaign that the two words 'India Shining' came to occupy cult status in popular vocabulary thereafter.

Corporatised ad campaigns apart, the BJP also set aside a small part of its substantial campaign budget for an innovation not many had heard of in India: an e-campaign, which saw the use of the World Wide Web for the first time in electioneering. This was a nod not only to the new communication technologies that were now available, but also to an emerging generation of media users in the country.

Internet use had risen exponentially from the beginning of the decade—from 5.5 million, or 0.5 per cent of the population, in 2000, to 39.2 million, or 3.6 per cent of the population, in 2004.[25] While this number may appear modest, it represented a cohort of young, articulate, urban-based men and some women who, given their ability to use newer media, was a potentially valuable electoral asset. Both the BJP and the Congress Party hosted websites, and although the content put out was largely in English and the interactivity that was to come a few years later with Web 2.0 was not available, these sites were useful for information dissemination and the projection of party ideologies and personalities through vision statements, candidate profiles, and the like. Personal engagement with the voters at that point was largely through the uploading of contact details and registration forms. Sometimes websites were also set up with the specific intent of exposing rivals, as for instance when the Congress Party sought to expose the BJP through a website named www.nationbetrayed.com.[26]

The BJP, followed by others, also began to successfully experiment with mobile telephony to enhance its voter outreach by capitalising on a constituency that had not existed earlier—that of the mobile phone user, who were more likely than not to be prosperous, urban, young, and male. By the year 2004, mobile telephony in India had struck roots in the country, having risen from

4 million users in 2000 to 48 million by 2004, with penetration levels rising from 0.3 per cent of the population to 4.5 per cent during this period.[27]

In fact, there was an additional dividend in taking recourse to these new media platforms. The Election Commission of India (ECI) was regulating very strictly any possible misuse of mainstream media for electoral gain, and the unregulated sectors of mobile telephony and internet media offered alternative media platforms that allowed political parties to escape such rigorous monitoring in a cost-effective manner.

The second generation of mobile telephony allowed the use of SMS. The BJP was the first party to make political use of this facility. A contemporary newspaper report on the party's poll preparations noted this: 'Pick up your telephone ... and you may hear ... Atal Bihari Vajpayee, delivering his one-minute election campaign message .... your e-mail account ... may be flooded with messages from the ... BJP. And ... you may find an SMS message from the party.'[28] There were also mobile caller tunes that could be downloaded and people could listen to then Prime Minister, Atal Bihari Vajpayee, by dialling a dedicated phone number.

Careful micromanagement of these various media platforms showcased the party message. A team set up under the direct supervision of then Union Minister of Information and Broadcasting, Pramod Mahajan, comprised young computer geeks, many of them trained in the best universities of the country and the world, who compiled databases, monitored media coverage, and devised appropriate messaging. The BJP did not win the 2004 election despite these efforts, but there can be no denying that its 2004 campaign emerged as something of a harbinger to the party's subsequent electoral forays. In fact, every major political party felt pressured to follow in its lead.

By the time of the 2009 general election, internet users in the country had doubled in number with a user base of 81,000,000[29] since the general election of 2004. Half of these users were online four to six times a week, spending on an average 15.7 hours, twice the time spent in 2004.[30] The country's mobile telephony base now covered 44.7 per cent of the population,[31] and the communication tools experimented with in 2004 now proved far more effective because of the rapid expansion in telecommunications infrastructure in the country during the intervening years.

By 2009, seven national parties and forty-eight state parties had their own websites[32] and with Web 2.0 now affording greater interactivity, they could build up their own online communities of supporters. Similarly, short mail messages, which in 2004 had been sent out in bulk, could now be dispatched from personal phones. The 2009 election was to see mobile phone election campaigning reaching its zenith in India, emerging as the chosen media platform to reach voters in rural areas. It was estimated that anything from three to four billion SMSes were sent out at this point.[33]

The BJP continued to outflank its rivals in media strategising by consciously evolving into the most high-tech political party in the country. As media analyst Mahima Kaul put it in an interview to me,

> I remember Prodyut Bora, the national convenor of BJP's information technology cell, presiding over the BJP's digital war room before the 2009 general election. Although the party did not win that election, it was taking the baby steps that would allow it to transition to its successful 2014 campaign. A fully trained cadre that was used to blogging and using social media was now available for the party.[34]

Months before the actual campaign began for the 2009 general election, Bora was working on an ambitious plan to provide all state party headquarters with WiFi connectivity, linking them through IP video telephones and unified messaging networks.[35] The calculation was that with a large proportion of internet users living in India's eight biggest cities, accounting for at least fifty Lok Sabha seats, it made eminent sense to pursue a cyber trajectory with seriousness. It was a similar calculation that prompted the party to buy up 200,000 key words for internet ads in 50,000 websites.[36]

Not only did Bora revamp the existing BJP website, but a separate website for the party's prime ministerial candidate,

L. K. Advani, was also set up—the first time the leader of a major political party in India had a personalised website. Advani—now in his early eighties—had the most active presence on the internet among his peers. His efficient campaign team ensured that chats, blogs, and videos were being constantly uploaded on YouTube and various websites. The opinions and creative expression of political sympathisers through their personal Orkut and Facebook accounts were also used optimally by the party as an auxiliary flank—a strategy that was to come to fruition under Narendra Modi five years later.

By 2009, there were an estimated two to three million bloggers in India, and several bloggers sympathetic to the BJP's ideology of Hindutva began to act as the party's foot soldiers. Rajesh Jain, a Mumbai-based techie and entrepreneur, was a good example of this community. A hundred days before the election, he had blogged that he wished to be publicly identified with the BJP, and that he was working with a group of like-minded professionals to create a 'Friends of BJP' group with the aim of ensuring that L. K. Advani becomes the prime minister and the party notches '200+ seats in the 15th Lok Sabha'. Jain's blog noted that 'Technologies like the Internet and mobile give us the tools to self-organise and make our voices heard. The India of 2009 is very different from that of 2004. The 2009 Elections will be the first where urban India can actually make a difference.' The numerous positive responses this blog received were clear indication of the emergence of an articulate section of young urban voters with rightwing sympathies and expectations, who were impatient with the Congress-headed dispensation ruling the country. On 29 January 2009, shortly after Rajesh Jain's blog appeared, one Prashant Solanki responded enthusiastically:

> Congratulations, I really admire ur thoughts & actions. India needs political stability as well as security & for that a national party has to emerge with 200+ seats. There should be no dominance of regional parties at centre as they halt development of whole nation for their interest in their state. I am with you to support & promote BJP with 200+ seats. Vande Matram.[37]

MODI EMERGES

This quick overview of recent electoral history would indicate that for the BJP, the use of the media has always been an extremely important feature of its electoral campaigning, more so than for its political rivals. This was dictated by the fact that its traditional voter base also happened to have a preponderance of voters who were urban, upper caste, upper class, educated, prosperous, and consequently more literate, thus making a strong media outreach electorally rewarding for the party. Yet, even by its own formidable standards in mediatised electioneering, the sixteenth General Election of 2014, which brought Narendra Modi to power, marked a quantum leap in the use of media platforms, and demands a more detailed examination.

It has sometimes been argued that the breakdown of communication creates conditions for polarised politics. Contemporary India, however, seems to demonstrate a countervailing trend: better communication technologies and the deeper mediatisation of society contributing to both the articulation and practice of polarising politics. The masterful manner in which Narendra Modi deployed both mainstream and social media to assist him in his rise to power as a champion of Hindu nationalism, at both the State and federal levels, is a clear validation of this proposition. The evolution of the man and his media strategies which helped him to emerge from an unknown RSS *pracharak* to become the prime minister of the country has a long back story, which will be revisited in these pages.

THE EARLY MODI

Most studies of Modi's use of the media have tended to focus on the period beginning from 2002, when he won the Gujarat assembly election for the first time, to 2014, when he emerged as prime minister after the General Election. Yet, years earlier, as a little known RSS *pracharak*, Modi had already perceived the importance of gaining the attention of the national press through the staging of out-of-the-box events tailored for media attention. In 1988, twelve months after he was deputed by the RSS to work as the organising secretary of the BJP's Gujarat unit, the 'Nyaya Yatras' he organised had caught the eye of the nationally circulated magazine *India Today*, which, in its report of 15 January, noted that jeeps dressed up as chariots were being drawn by partymen. This succeeded in projecting the party, hitherto 'an ineffective minority in the state Assembly', as a force to reckon with outside the state.

Yatras as public events designed to attract wide media coverage were popular in the late 1980s and early 1990s. In 1989, Modi assisted in the scaling up of a yatra to national proportions when L. K. Advani embarked upon his Somnath to Ayodhya rath yatra on 25 September 1990. It was Modi, as the man in charge of the Gujarat leg of this yatra, who is believed to have suggested that the yatra begin at the Somnath temple, because it would capture public interest by 'evoking the destruction and plunder of Somnath, which is part of the folklore of Gujarat'.[38]

Here again, getting a captive media was an important part of the arrangements made. According to one journalist who was part of the press entourage, over 300 journalists accompanied Advani during this journey—many funded by the BJP directly.[39] Another remembers Modi's 'eye for detail', how almost instantly he became 'Narendrabhai' to all participating journalists, and how, every evening, they would receive a printed sheet with the exact programme for the next day. 'Modi would personally ensure that the media was provided every facility to cover the yatra. Fax machines were made available at every place along the yatra route, with the BJP local office bearing all expenses. Modi even occasionally suggested the storyline and what could be highlighted!'[40]

> A year later, he once again put his stamp on the media coverage of Murli Manohar Joshi's Ekta Yatra, which set out from Kanya Kumari in December 1991 with the objective of unfurling the national flag at Lal Chowk in Srinagar on Republic Day 1992. Once again it was Modi's attention to detail in terms of media coverage that was

> conspicuous. He was very aware that he needed the media to be on his side to make the Ekta Yatra a success, and consequently he was several steps ahead of his peers and rivals within the party when it involved media management. 'Back in 1991, Modi instructed the small band of loyalists, who were deputed to him to carry several fax machines and coordinate with the party units in the towns and cities designated as "media halts" to ensure that small media centres were set up for the purpose.'[41]

However, apart from managing the press in those days, his role as party spokesperson had also grown in importance. A correspondent with *The Times of India* at that point recalled how he was advised by senior BJP leaders to treat Modi 'as a single-point source of information'.[42] It was not until he was appointed National Secretary (Organisation) in 1998 and moved to Delhi that Modi was able to build close ties with national newspapers and television channels of the day on a more regular basis. Since ensuring good media coverage for BJP leaders was among his responsibilities, he had to organise regular press conferences, a task he recalled during a meeting with mediapersons after he became prime minister. 'I used to arrange chairs here waiting for you. I had a beautiful relationship with you and it helped me in Gujarat.'[43]

The transition Modi made from being the backroom manager of media information to being a part of media content itself was now beginning to take place, assisted by his own regular appearances on television. A television anchor recalls one instance when, after a scheduled BJP representative had dropped out at the last minute, he called Modi as a fill-in. Although he was fully aware that he was only a last-minute replacement, Modi made sure to show up because he was unwilling to give up a chance to appear on national television.

Another television anchor of that time, Rajeev Shukla, also recalled Modi's eagerness to be interviewed and how he had come to his studios to be interviewed at short notice. The interview Shukla conducted for his 'Ru-Ba-Ru' series showed the BJP national secretary as a modest man, taking his own laundry in from the clothesline outside his nondescript living quarters at 11, Ashoka Road, the BJP's headquarters in Delhi. Interestingly, the fact that he was computer savvy and loved to browse on the internet was also highlighted in that programme, with Modi claiming that he understood the 'potential of information technology' because of his God-given curiosity about the world. This was confirmed later in an interview he gave to Lance Price in 2014, in which he revealed that his internet habit started as long ago as the late 1990s.[44]

The media access was exploited not only for party publicity, but was also used to take on his political rivals and help his own ascendance to power, as Modi himself has publicly acknowledged. Among his rivals was former mentor Keshubhai Patel, who was then the chief minister of Gujarat. A well-known editor of a national magazine, the late Vinod Mehta, recalled Modi having visited him in his office with 'a file containing damaging material about the sitting Gujarat chief minister Keshubhai Patel .... The next thing I heard was that he had become the chief minister in place of Keshubhai,' Mehta wrote.[45]

Media access also offered Modi an opportunity to project his own ideological convictions. The party press conferences held by the BJP in Delhi during the Kargil war of 1999 were exercises in jingoism and nationalism. During television appearances, he conveyed his opinions unambiguously. Asked during one TV debate about how to respond to provocations from Pakistan, his answer was: 'Chicken *biryani nahi*, bullet *ka jawab* bomb *se diya jayega*—we won't give them chicken biryani, we will respond to a bullet with a bomb.'[46] Another instance of such direct speaking was when he was a guest on a prominent news show after the Twin Towers in New York were attacked. He is quoted as having said, 'It has taken an attack like 9/11 for India's pseudo-secular media to finally use a word like Islamic terrorism ....'[47]

'Pseudo-secular', a term that Advani had borrowed from Anthony Elenjimittam's 1951 book, *Philosophy and Action of the R.S.S. for the Hind Swaraj*, and which he used widely during the Rath Yatra days, was understood as shorthand for 'minority appeasement'.

Modi's adoption of the term to define the mainstream media would indicate, therefore, that he already had a strong antipathy to national newspapers and television channels for what he perceived as their elitist, secular bias and their anti-Hindu agenda. It was a relationship that would deteriorate markedly during and immediately after the Gujarat riots, even while support for him from the Gujarati media grew exponentially. More important to note is the manner in which Modi was able to pit the two contending narratives generated by the English-language media and the Gujarati-language media against each other in order to win the empathy of the Gujarati voter.

Modi defined himself as a politician in a hurry in his first interaction with the press as Chief Minister of Gujarat, when he is reported to have announced, 'I have come here to play a one-day match ... I need fast and performing batsmen to score runs in the limited overs game.'[48] He later clarified that his words were misreported, and what he had really meant was that 'just as in a one-day cricket, achieving a given run-rate is critical, he had appealed for a better "work-rate" to fulfil the Government's promises to the people',[49] given that there were only 12,000 hours to go before the next Assembly elections.

What was not to be disputed was the spectacular manner in which party workers celebrated his swearing-in as Chief Minister of Gujarat on 7 October 2001. Held in an enormous *shamiana* set up at the Gandhinagar helipad ground, it was a major media event, with national newspapers devoting serious coverage to it,[50] and proved to be a template for several such spectacles that would mark his career in the years to follow.

The media in 2002, it should be emphasised, had a greater capacity than earlier to circulate information and images of events, with local cable television, the incipient presence of websites, digital cameras, and mobile phone texting now available. Modi, as chief minister, wanted to use every tool available to communicate his message, going by the recollections of Manish Bardai, a publicity agent who worked for Modi after his chief ministerial appointment. 'At the beginning, back in 2001, no political people were using advertising agencies apart from in election campaigns. It was unusual. He said he wanted a fresh approach to communication.'[51]

GUJARAT POGROM

The curiosity in the media that Modi initially attracted could be attributed partly to the fact that it was for the first time that an RSS *pracharak* had made it to the high office of chief minister. But the events that took place four months later—the burning of coach S6 of the Sabarmati Express at Godhra, resulting in the deaths of fifty-nine Hindu pilgrims on 27 February 2002, and the communal pogrom that engulfed the state from the following day—were to change irrevocably the manner in which the media framed him. He emerged from that interregnum as a deeply polarising figure: painted as a champion of Hindus, defender of Gujarati pride, by one section of the media; and as a betrayer of the constitutional responsibility to protect minorities and complicit in the genocidal violence that ravaged Gujarat, by another section. In defending himself against the criticism of the latter group, Modi invariably used arguments that resonated with the former. What was on test was his capacity, both in his personal interactions with the media and through the Gujarat state information department, to publicly defend and justify some of the extremely controversial decisions he took in the immediate aftermath of the attack on the Sabarmati Express, whether it was the handling of the funerals of the victims of the Sabarmati Express attack; the tardy summoning in of the army; or his widely reported observation that *'har kriya ki pratikriya hoti hi hai'* (every action has an equal and opposite reaction), which was often cited in media reports and inquiry proceedings.

Modi denied having made this comment, maintaining that he had 'merely only narrated the facts and justified nothing'.[52] In his first televised address over Doordarshan on 28 February, he dwelt only on Godhra and made no reference to the riots that were already raging in the capital of the state: 'Gujarat shall not tolerate any such incident. The culprits will get full punishment for their sins.

Not only this, we will set an example that nobody, not even in his dreams thinks of committing a heinous crime like this.'[53] This was a pattern that was to emerge in all briefings by the state information authorities thereafter. While the Godhra incident was invariably referred to as an 'inhuman genocide'/'inhuman carnage'/'massacre', the communal riots were termed as 'disturbances' and, sometimes, 'violent disturbances/incidents'.

The only regret he expressed, in an interview with *The New York Times* in June, was that he had not handled the news media more effectively. '"We have 18,600 villages," he said in his office, where a photograph of Gandhi hung on the wall. "Ninety-eight percent of Gujarat was peaceful. Is it not a credit for the administration, the government?"'[54]

Three themes dominated Modi's media management after the Godhra carnage/Gujarat pogrom, which helped him achieve an image makeover over the next few years. The first was the claim he kept reiterating, that he had restored law and order in '72 hours', with emphasis placed on urgently reviving the disrupted economic activity. The 'Resurgent Gujarat' project, which found much support within the state and was assiduously promoted through many public events over the following decade, was conducted under his direct supervision.

The second theme was to cast the various incidents of riot violence—according to a Gujarat state press note—as 'pre-planned, inhuman, collective violent terrorism against Gujarat'[55] and a part of Pakistan's proxy war against India. Expressions like 'Islamic terror', widely used in the aftermath of the September 2001 attacks on the Twin Towers in New York, were freely deployed in order to frame the Muslims in Gujarat, who were collectively marked as having been responsible for the Godhra carnage.

This also helped the chief minister to emerge as 'Chhote Sardar', the new iron man of Gujarat, with its referencing to Sardar Vallabhbhai Patel, Gujarati freedom fighter and the country's first home minister. One of the posts from a supporter on Narendra Modi's own website, www.narendramodi.org, hailed the chief minister as a god and 'asli mard' (real man) for protecting Hindus.[56] Being cast as 'Chhote Sardar' or an 'asli mard' was reflective of Modi's growing popularity among large sections of Gujarati society as a strong man leading the way out of chaos.

The third effort was to target that section of the national media which had covered the riots extensively and had mounted an unrelenting critique of the chief minister's handling of them. Very early on, the Modi government attempted to turn the tables on its critics by suggesting that it was precisely such widespread media coverage that had fanned the violence. It had argued before the National Human Rights Commission, for instance, that while major acts of violence were contained within seventy-two hours, 'on account of widespread reporting both in the visual as well as the electronic media, incidents of violence on a large scale started occurring in Ahmedabad (and) Baroda cities and some towns of Panchmahals, Sabarkantha, Mehsana, etc.'[57]

There was also a concerted attempt made to promote the narrative of the local media. Newspapers like *Sandesh* and *Gujarat Samachar*, which had 'vitiated the atmosphere by spreading false and dangerous news',[58] were hailed, with the chief minister personally expressing his high appreciation for their restrained coverage in the best traditions of journalism. One senior journalist who was at the receiving end of state hostility—his channel was even banned for a day—had observed, 'by attempting to pigeonhole a section of the media as the so-called "secular Taliban", the aim appears to be to create a divide between the Hindutva patriots versus the anti-national pseudo-secularists'.[59]

Images that emerged from the theatre of violence—the one of a Muslim tailor, Qutubuddin, pleading for his life was a prime example—came to be interpreted by the citizens of Gujarat along two different registers reflected their respective frames of ideology and location. This conforms to the argument that 'publicity works through linguistically stratified media and does not operate in a single linguistic register', and that while the information generated may be extensive, the 'absorption of their import was contingent on prevailing frames of understanding'.[60]

Narendra Modi and his state government were conspicuously successful in portraying the national media's denunciation of the handling of the riots as a direct attack on Gujarat and Gujaratis—and, by extension, Hindus and Hinduism. This fed off a widespread perception, sustained, if not created by the Gujarati-language media, that the majority community was correct in responding to attacks on it through violence, and that the national media, seen as 'outsiders', had no right to besmirch the state through their 'unprincipled' coverage.

A good example of such positioning was a state press release of 9 March, cited in the Editors Guild report, that was headlined, 'We will not surrender to the elements out to malign Gujarat says the Chief Minister'. The maligning of Gujarat was to become the central focus of the pre-election Gaurav Yatra that Modi was to embark upon in September 2002, and the speeches he made conformed to the earlier messaging: othering the Muslim community, focusing almost exclusively on bringing those behind the Godhra attack to justice, and countering the 'pseudo-secular' media narrative: 'I am determined to take out the yatra and tell the world the Gaurav Gatha (Story of Pride) of ... the state .... Gujarat was not a state of murderers, rapists as the pseudo-secularists ... and power hungry Congress leaders are attempting to project.'[61] Communication through every means possible, from CDs to wall posters, in strict synergy with ground mobilisation was the key to the success of the Gaurav Yatra that saw him reach out to all 182 political constituencies of Gujarat. 'Modi wanted to contact at least 1 lakh people every day .... It took the shape of a full-fledged political yatra when election dates were announced. The yatra covered 4,200 km during which Modi addressed 400 rallies in 146 constituencies.'[62] It helped him to both protect and popularise his ideological franchise and build a pan-Gujarat political constituency for himself, which was so fiercely loyal that he was to emphatically win every single state election in the decade that followed—not just in the one that took place in the riot year of 2002, but in 2007 and 2012 as well.

It could be argued that the attack on the Sabarmati Express and the genocidal violence that followed was the crucible in which Modi's long-term media blueprint was conceived and tested, one that helped him to ascend the long stairway to the most powerful office in the country, that of prime minister. The blueprint conceived of three major pillars, each buttressing the other. The first of these was the conscious and consistent projection of a larger-than-life mass leader committed to neoliberal development ('Vikas Purush'), with the capacity to transform the state and the lives of those who trust in his vision. In order to achieve this, the other two pillars were crucial—the direct and indirect control of the media through a strategy of patronage and management; and the creation of a parallel media system that allowed for self-projection through self-communication.

A compact disc, 'Two minutes to the truth', that the Modi government released in September 2002 and distributed not only among his supporters and within his state, but also as a giveaway with the English-language magazine *India Today*, in order to reach a national audience, provided a hint of how the Gujarat script was to be changed. Focusing on Godhra, after all, may be politically useful, but potentially disastrous for the economy of the state, and Modi realised this. The effort, therefore, was to shift to the script of modernity and 'governance', with a lot of the narrative focused on Gujarat's 15 lakh smart cards and e-governance. The chief minister was also presented in it as a savvy user of information, who reads newspapers on the web and video-conferences with rural Gujarat every evening.[63] This messaging was based on a reading that the people of a trade-centric state were hankering for stability and peace so that they could carry on with their lives, a mood that was captured in opinion polls conducted during the 2002 state elections.

There were several elements to this project of enhancing Modi's image that went beyond projecting him merely as a Hindutva icon. He was the proverbial 'strong man' who protects the state from terrorists through a 'strong policy against terrorism'[64] and a commitment to the RSS vision of nationalism, as well as a 'vikash purush', or development man. Both images resonated in the media and helped define Gujarat as a state ranking high in terms of a secure social environment and ease-of-doing-business parameters, and where there was a commitment to Hindu nationalism along with a market-friendly economy. Over the years, both were successful tropes and contributed immensely in achieving Modi's famous 2014 victory.

CHANGING THE MEDIA SCRIPT

Of the two image-building exercises, the first was more easily achieved because Hindutva has become almost naturalised in post-riots Gujarat and was being reinforced through everyday politics and media coverage. Every once in a while, Modi burnished his Hindutva credentials through hard-hitting speeches and even the occasional book. *Jyotipunj*, for example, a 200-page volume which came out in 2008, venerated RSS workers and had a lengthy chapter on M. S. Golwalkar.

Emerging as the 'development man', however, needed more attention, but paid handsome dividends both within mainstream media and corporate India. The effort here was to segue the agenda of Hindu nationalism into a neoliberal model of development through politics that 'de-politicized local-level issues, problems and protests'.[65] What was most marked in this discourse was the new familiarity that characterised the relationship between Modi and business tycoons/CEOs.

It could be argued that had the post-Godhra violence not occurred, there would have been no great requirement to undertake such a complex exercise. But opprobrium from a range of institutions and actors, from the Supreme Court of India and the Confederation of Indian Industry (CII) to international governments that refused him visas, from the chairperson of the National Human Rights Commission to then Prime Minister, A. B. Vajpayee, demanded such a concerted effort. As it turned out, it proved extremely advantageous for Modi personally.

Within days of winning the December 2002 election, Modi set himself to the task of furthering this goal. At the first ever Pravasi Bharatiya Divas organised by the Government of India to network with the Indian diaspora, which took place twenty days after the victory, Modi struck a chord with a community that had always bemoaned the bureaucratic hurdles that had come in their way of doing business in India, with his vision of e-governance that would usher in a regime that was transparent and unfettered by red tape.[66]

He had, just before the pogrom had broken out, organised the Resurgent Gujarat to attract investment to the state. Now, in the face of criticism of the communal situation in the state from some strong voices of corporate India during a CII meet in February 2003—widely reported in the mainstream media[67]—he felt driven to create a corporate body that would be personally aligned to him. Borrowing from the nomenclature of the earlier meet, it called itself the Resurgent Group of Gujarat, and comprised corporate entities which incidentally included Gautam Adani, a businessman who later came to be identified very closely with Modi. The group not only supported his model of doing business, but also defended him politically and anchored the biennial Vibrant Gujarat Business Summits, which over the years attracted a great deal of traction, both nationally and internationally.

The Vibrant Gujarat Business Summits, interestingly enough, helped to change the media script as well by drawing unqualified support from mainstream media. Their news reports on these events were swamped by unverified and unverifiable data about the stream of dollar investments coming into Gujarat, altering the very tonality of media coverage on Gujarat. By 2003, the green shoots of this new approach were evident. A news report of October that year read: 'For a state that got international attention in the past couple of years for just bad news ... there is finally some good news .... Vibrant Gujarat...may well give the state the much needed push towards the path of development.' It went on say,

> For Modi, a lot depends on the real success of Vibrant Gujarat .... Since assuming office, his Government has mostly had its back to the wall, defending itself from attacks by the intelligentsia as well as the judiciary for the unstable communal situation prevailing in the state and the Government's pathetic record on human rights.[68]

The language adopted in this report is still somewhat ambivalent: the mild criticism of the chief ministerial human rights record is leavened by an incipient approval of the assiduous pursuit of foreign capital. But what is interesting and should be underlined is the manner in which Modi had now become Vibrant Gujarat, and Vibrant Gujarat had become Modi.

Over the next decade, this tone of approval became increasingly accentuated, driven by Gujarat state's corporate-friendly policy-making, public relations, and the growing persona of Modi himself. References to the post-Godhra violence, almost mandatory in any news reporting on Gujarat earlier, were slowly dropped. This outcome was the result partly of Modi's own media strategy, as we shall see, but also because of a tacit understanding within the corporate media to hold back on the issue while focusing on the development narrative, because 'Modi was Mr Development. He gave development political weight and theological force. His speeches were sermons on development. Development became the new collective morality.'[69]

An often cited example of policy translating into popularity in corporate circles was the manner in which Gujarat, by offering attractive tax breaks and land, became the preferred destination for the Tatas once it decided to close down the Nano plant at Singur, West Bengal. It was seen as 'Modi's final makeover', a moment when he transited from 'being Hindu Hriday Samarat to Vikas Purush'.[70] But even three years earlier, Gujarat had been judged as the 'Number 1 state in economic freedom index' by no less than the Rajiv Gandhi Institute for Contemporary Studies, a think-tank seen as close to the Congress Party.[71] The way in which this recognition from an unlikely source was promptly highlighted through large newspaper advertisements under catchy captions like 'Always

Enterprising Gujarat', testified to the fact that Gujarat also had one of the most efficient publicity machineries, comprising nationally and internationally renowned public relations giants.

The PR machinery became even more sophisticated as the decade progressed. APCO Worldwide, to cite one example, was hired in 2009, and its forty-five member team spread out over twenty countries made sure that Modi became a global figure, appearing on the cover of international publications. The *Time* (Asia) cover on him in March 2012, under the title 'Modi Means Business', projecting the possibility of the prime ministerial post coming his way, was evidence of this. Interestingly, the very fact that *Time* magazine had put him on centre-stage in this way triggered effusive coverage in the Indian print and visual media. They read it as Modi having arrived internationally.

By now, the media were conducting opinion polls projecting him as the country's best chief minister and, as the decade progressed, as the person most suited to be the prime minister of the country. A January 2013 'Mood of the Nation' poll conducted by *India Today* is a case in point. It showcased Modi as the most preferred choice for prime minister, hailing his transition from being 'an ubiquitous office bearer in Delhi to the anti-hero of 2002 riots to the highest priest and practitioner of development politics with a national fan following' as 'one of the most captivating transformation sagas in Indian politics'.[72] As proof of this, it cited Gujarat as unarguably the best governed state in the country, with a growth rate that was higher than the national average.

The term 'Gujarat Model' now began to gain increasing currency. It was a concept based on the understanding that both the state and the citizens of Gujarat had flourished because of a government that delivered social and economic goods to them effectively. A post-election analysis in 2007 by a journalist supporter argued that the 'Gujarat Model is not in conflict with the Bharat model. What has clicked in Gujarat is a leadership style built on innovation, dedication and a resolute defiance of a compromised Establishment. A Modi folklore has been created .... It has corresponded with subliminal perceptions of good leadership.'[73] More rigorous analyses of the phenomenon argued that although the 'Gujarat Model' was based on social polarisation, those who stood to lose—largely Muslims, Dalits, and Adivasis—did not constitute more than 30 per cent of the population. In contrast, the beneficiaries were not just the Hindu middle class, but those at the lower rung who aspired to move into the middle class, a large enough cohort that could bring Modi to power over three consecutive state elections.[74]

The media allowed the concept of the 'Gujarat Model' to grow in the public imagination until it became a national-level commonsense, ultimately helping Modi and his party to emerge victorious in the 2014 general election. The striking aspect about it was that it was never rigorously interrogated. In fact, it had become shorthand for the 'developmental' possibilities under a Modi regime and enthused even rural folk in 2014. The general election saw BJP's rural vote share rise by 5 per cent. The reason the term carried conviction, according to one commentator, was that Modi did 'deliver some tangible benefits to the upper middle class that is vocal, controls the media and hence is influential in shaping public opinion'.[75]

The fact was that the obverse side of this story never came into view because of the fixity with which the media focused on the state's growth figures, which, the state government claimed, had risen at the rate of 10.24 per cent between 2002 and 2012.[76] There was little questioning of the communally polarised geography or the resource extractive nature of this growth. The high subsidisation of private investment with public money, the urban beautification projects that displaced large communities of the poor, the low wages of agricultural labour, the extreme deprivation marking Adivasi pockets, none of this received much media attention. National Sample Survey Organisation (NSSO) figures, cited by Jayati Ghosh, revealed that while Gujarat's per capita income was around 20 per cent higher than the per capita income for the country as a whole, rural wages and urban wages were about 20 per cent and 15 per cent lower, respectively.[77] But such data was lost in the bedazzling patina of the 'Gujarat Model', with its futuristic visions of highways and optical fibre networks, bustling ports, and rapid industrialisation. If, on the rare occasion, an issue like undernutrition and malnutrition of women and children in Gujarat came under the media scanner, it was largely by happenstance, as was the case when *The Wall Street Journal* asked Modi in August 2012 why around half of Gujarati children under five were stunted, or too short for their age. His reply—that this was the result of beauty-consciousness among young girls who were worried about putting on weight—did attract prominent coverage in the Indian media as well, and provoked some media scrutiny into the reasons for these high malnutrition levels in a state as prosperous as Modi's Gujarat.[78]

The paradigm shift that occurred in the media narrative on Gujarat during the decade from 2002 to 2012, which invisibilised the post-Godhra violence and visibilised the Gujarat growth story, allowed rising economic growth, and corporate investment to meld with the majoritarian Hindutva ideology, took place at a time when the national media were also being re-defined by the same corporate forces. The rapid growth of private entertainment-based television content, new advertising-driven business models, the arrival of the large, vertically integrated media models, and growth of information technologies contributed to making the mass media, in Adrian Athique's words, 'an exemplar and cheerleader for the liberalization economy'.[79] It would follow from this that the emergence of Modi as the icon of the liberalising leader would also find favour with media managements and editors, and they in turn, through their agenda setting and news priming and framing strategies, helped to create the turbo charge that brought Modi to power at the Centre. By 2014, Narendra Modi had become a 'simulacrum, a media artifact regarded as more true than any amount of information and, in fact, capable of correcting that information'.[80]

This could not have happened without the active agency of the protagonist of this story. In all his interactions with the media, Modi's first effort was to try and control the way in which the media interpreted his involvement in the 2002 communal violence.

Initially, all the accusatory questions put to him on his handling of the riots were met, as we saw, with a mixture of insouciance, accusation of bias, and an outright rejection of charges. An exchange with Prabhu Chawla on his television show, Seedhi Baat, is a case in point.[81] When told that he was responsible for the killing of 1,100 innocents, he disputed the figure. When asked what, according to his estimation, was the correct toll, he diverted the conversation, saying that if there had been no Godhra, the riots would not have taken place.

By April 2004, however, after having won a successful election, he was fielding the inevitable 'riot question' with far more confidence. A 'Walk the Talk' interview with Shekhar Gupta, conducted on the Sardar Sarovar dam walkway, had Modi already keeping the conversation focused on subjects like the river grid that the state had achieved and how it was successfully focusing on the education of the girl child. But when asked a direct question about the riots, he maintained that it is sad when anyone is killed—'insaan, insaan hi hote hain' (a human life is a human life)—but immediately went on to deny the charge that the Gujarat police had killed more Muslims than Hindus during the violence, accusing his interlocutor of having an agenda. The expression he used in that interview, 'If I am guilty, hang me!', was to become a familiar refrain of his in the future.

This was the tone and argument he would henceforth adopt with regard to any public reference to the riots: a general expression of sadness that such violence had occurred, but a strong denial of any responsibility. Even a decade later, in an interview with Reuters, he denied any wrongdoing in handling the riots, adding,

> [S]omeone else is driving a car and we're sitting behind, even then if a puppy comes under the wheel, will it be painful or not? Of course it is. If I'm a chief minister or not, I'm a human being. If something bad happens anywhere, it is natural to be sad.[82]

Right through the decade, the shadow of the riots dogged Modi, often enlarged by circumstances over which he had no control, as for instance when the US rejected his application for a diplomatic visa in 2005 or when the president of the Indian National Congress, Sonia Gandhi, famously implied in an election speech delivered in December 2007 before the Gujarat state election that the leaders of Gujarat were merchants of death ('maut ka saudagar'). In each of these instances, Modi was successful in turning the subsequent coverage to his advantage, by implying that it was his anti-conversion stand that had led to the visa denial in the first instance, and that the Congress Party was soft on terror in the second.

By the time his first term as an elected chief minister came to an end in 2007, Modi was drawing a firm line between media houses he considered sympathetic to him and those that he had long dismissed as pseudo-secular. Towards the latter, he was now adopting a far more combative tone. Just before the Gujarat assembly election that year, he had reluctantly agreed to an interview with Karan Thapar, who was then anchoring an interview-based show, 'The Devil's Advocate', on the English-language channel CNN-IBN. Not known to pull his punches, Thapar, after a few lines of niceties, came straight to the riots, asking Modi why, despite him being an efficient administrator, he is often referred to as a 'mass murderer'. A contemporary news report captures what happened next: 'Modi first asked for water, then removed the microphone from his shirt and told Thapar that he cannot continue the interview, observing calmly, "These are your ideas, you go on expressing these. I can't do this interview."'[83] Two months later, in his reply to a showcause notice issued by the Election Commission on the eve of the elections for his use of intemperate language vis-à-vis the Sohrabuddin encounter case, he denied the accusation and attributed it to 'unverified and false media reports'. In fact, Modi himself marked 2007 as the year when he stopped engaging with the mainstream media in India over the riots. Seven years later, on the verge of becoming the prime minister of India, he remarked, 'I answered every top journalist in the country from 2002 to 2007 (on the riots) but noticed there was no exercise to understand the truth.'[84]

Modi's counter-strategy was to encourage captive TV channels and newspapers, such as the NaMo Gujarat television channel instituted in October 2012, just before the 2012 state election, to broadcast all his speeches and rallies live across the state. More important was the way social media was increasingly used to put across important information, forcing older media to regularly reference his Twitter feeds and YouTube posts in the news discourse as part of their political coverage.[85]

Towards mainstream media houses and individual journalists, he adopted a conscious policy of patronage and punishment. Only those who were prepared to uncritically relay content emanating from the corridors of power or were happy to tailor their perspective to his, would pass muster. In fact, the contract that image management company APCO Worldwide signed with the Government of Gujarat went beyond generating stories favourable to Gujarat; it was also required to review content in order to 'gauge the tonality of coverage and identify journalists who can further be Media Ambassadors for Gujarat'.[86]

Evidence of how closely Modi's team was monitoring and managing mainstream media coverage surfaced, for instance, in August 2012, when the Gujarat chief minister demanded action from the Election Commission against the state Congress party for boycotting the news channel TV9, arguing that this amounted to suppression of the media. The Congress party had boycotted the channel because it claimed it was conducting itself as a 'Modi channel', with biased coverage in terms of content and time, giving the Congress only '20% time while Gujarat government and BJP's news coverage 80% time'.[87]

When the contracts signed with APCO Worldwide and Mutual PR, for international and national coverage, respectively, came to an end in 2013, the Gujarat government put out a 'Request for Proposal' from public relations companies interested in gaining its account. This time is required them not just to monitor the media, but 'manage any crisis' created by negative coverage—presumably by ensuring rebuttals and counter-narratives. The document reflected an amazingly wide spectrum of tasks, apart from putting out content featuring 'positive growth and developments happening in the state at regular intervals, or as and when asked to do so by the Commissionerate of Information'.[88] The detailed list of expectations ranged from 'publication of at least 6 major stories from the State in a quarter based on the input provided by the State Government in national news papers', to 'coverage/telecast of at least one major story every month in a major TV news channel'.[89] With General Election 2014, the priority was to project 'Shining' Gujarat, given how central that discourse was in Modi's pitch for prime ministership. But there was an anxiety, too, that was reflected in this document: the public relations company that made the cut would also have to monitor 'impending stories about Gujarat State/ leadership' and closely manage any crisis arising as a consequence.[90]

Modi's growing resistance to subjecting himself to the intrusive questioning of mainstream media interlocutors, with their inevitable references to unanswered questions linked to a violent past, led to him adopting various methods of non-discursive communication. While discursive communication through mainstream media is necessarily open to engagement and rational argumentation, non-discursive communication draws on a range of social interactions and communication tools and is much more open to control. One communication theorist explains what is implied here: 'The prevalence of digital tools, as well as the importance of emotions to inventing and composing, both make it necessary to reiterate how language is much more than words. Language included non-discursive forms of meaning-making, forms that take advantage of image, emotion and nonsequentiality.'[91]

Since affect—which takes advantage of 'image, emotion and nonsequentiality'—rather than deliberation was being sought by Modi, a range of communication technologies, strategies, and activities were marshalled to achieve this. He understood almost intuitively that the body itself can also become a site of non-discursive communication and was extremely conscious of the importance of body image. As he revealed in a 1999 television interview, he was always careful to dress well, doing so neatly, if austerely.[92] By the mid-2000s, there was a re-imagining of that body image, with the austerity of the early phase as an RSS worker consciously discarded to project a more market-friendly, contemporary mien.

Modi now emerged as a style icon in his own right, sporting tailored kurtas, designer waistcoats, Western suits, jeans, and fashion accessories like ten gallon hats, Bvlgari glasses, Movado watches, and Mont Blanc pens. 'For him they symbolize his commitment to modernization, ambition and good-quality products.'[93] The mainstream media ensured that these details were transmitted to the public through a great deal of soft focus coverage and often fulsome prose, all of which helped in the iconisation of the chief minister. Take this newsmagazine report on the pre-Navratri festival mood in Gujarat in 2013: 'Known for having created a brand around him, now Brand Modi has spilled onto the Navratri Festival. Modi Tattoos, Modi Kurta and also Modi Suits, Fabrics and Sarees have found their way into the market ... we look at some emerging trends surrounding Modi theme this season.'[94]

Roadshows, Modi masks, kites bearing legends like 'I Love Modi', 3-D projections of speeches that allowed audiences to witness them in multiple locations, and later—as the 2014 general election grew closer—the setting up of Chai pe Charcha stations and the use of 'Selfies with Modi' were all instances of non-discursive communication that also translated into mainstream and digital media content.

USE OF DIGITAL MEDIA

It was the use of digital media for controlled communication, however, that came to define Modi's communications strategy. Digital media served a dual, if contradictory, purpose. On the one hand it made him appear approachable and ready to engage with people; on the other, it precluded the necessity of having to really engage with the mainstream media. Communication scholars have defined Modi's use of Twitter as 'part of a larger theatrical of political narrative that reinvents the political actor and what he represents through a relatively manageable media outlet that at once allows for one-way pronouncements alongside the spectre of interactive conversation'.[95]

There were many aspects of the digital media that exercised a powerful appeal for the politician in Modi. It symbolised modernity and tied in with his political argument, albeit one marked by rather uncertain logic, that intractable problems like mass poverty and low human development indicators could be addressed effortlessly with information technology. The fact that it was the chosen media of the most articulate demographic cohort in the country—the young adult—was an additional attraction. Not only was this cohort important in electoral calculations, but association with it also imbued Modi himself with the same characteristics of contemporaneity and freshness of appeal. There was also the realisation that multiple digital platforms used together aggregated the messaging in a virtuous cycle. Above all, social media allowed for cost-effective, mass self-communication at a time and manner of one's choosing—crucial for a politician looking to intervene in public conversations.

Older politicians have found it difficult to make such a transition in their media messaging. Modi, in contrast, has been a nimble adapter to changing media technologies. By the early 1990s, as we saw, he had adapted to the computer, and a mobile phone was his constant accessory by the second half of that decade. He once recalled that he was the first to use a digital camera in the 1999 elections, by which time he was also a regular browser of the internet. As he revealed to his biographer,

> Another example of my forward thinking relevant to the technology world is my prediction around WhatsApp. When WhatsApp had just started, and long before it had become popular I was telling people to start using this as a means for communication as it would be a major messaging platform in the days to come.[96]

After Modi's swearing in as Gujarat chief minister in 2001, a personal website, www.narendramodi.org (in English), was set up. The Gujarati version of it followed as soon as the technology to accommodate regional language fonts was available. The police of his state were one of the earliest to deploy videography for surveillance, and the Gujarat government to use the SMS for its outreach purposes, such as conveying information about government jobs and public examinations. By early 2009, Modi was on both Twitter and Facebook. During the 2012 Gujarat state election, there was a well-calibrated consolidation of his presence on digital platforms, which now also included a personal channel on YouTube.

Apart from marshalling a wide range of digital platforms for his media game plan, care was taken to ensure the timeliness of the messages. The synchronisation of the message with actual developments taking place on the ground has been regarded by communication strategists as key to its success. This was a lesson learnt by the Gujarat chief minister from the days of the post-Godhra violence, when the powerful counter-narrative to mainstream media content generated by his state information department could win him wide public support. Once digital media options were available, Modi was quick to use blogs, posts, and tweets for essentially the same purpose.

Take the Modi's blog, 'Letter to my countrymen', for instance. It appeared on his website in 2010 at the point when he was appearing before the Special Investigative Team (SIT) set up by the Supreme Court. Written in order to exonerate himself before the public, he accused vested interests of coming together to spread lies, adding that the machination will come unstuck, 'for people have seen through this charade'.[97] His tweet of 26 December 2013, 'Satyamev Jayate! Truth alone triumphs', made a similar claim of exoneration after a metropolitan court in Ahmedabad thought it fit to reject riot survivor Zakia Jafri's petition against him in connection with a case in which her husband and sixty-seven others were killed by a mob at the Gulbarg Society during the 2002 violence. He followed it up with a blog the next day, in which he reiterated that his government had controlled the violence more efficiently than any other government had done when faced with a similar situation. According to one observer, those words, coming a few months before the 2014 general election, signalled that Modi was now seized of the need to 'change his image to be more acceptable to a larger audience'.[98]

Digital media helped immeasurably in enabling Modi to emerge as the BJP's prime ministerial designate by trimming the rough edges of his political persona and burnishing his pan-national credentials, although the exercise sometimes came a cropper. When the Uttarakhand floods of June 2013 occurred, Modi was the first national-level leader to react by tweeting, 'Seeing extremely disturbing visuals of floods in Uttarakhand. We stand by the people during this hour & pray things get back to normal soon.' This was followed up by a personal visit to Dehra Dun. It proved to be a rare instance of a Modi public relations exercise failing spectacularly, because his publicity team overplayed its hand by framing him as a courageous leader-rescuer shepherding 15,000 Gujarati pilgrims out of the flood-ridden state. The backlash was swift[99]—the claim was deemed fraudulent by both mainstream and social media.

Such slips were rare. Modi's moves to appear prime ministerial were by and large successful. By October 2012, he had a support base of a million-plus on both Facebook and Twitter, and he was also registering an emphatic presence on Google Plus. While all of this was typically done by a team of young professionals, supervised by trusted officials, he remained the chief architect of his electoral media plans.

Arvind Gupta, who headed the information technology and media cell, later revealed that Modi's prime ministerial campaign actually dated back to 2010, when there was a leadership crisis within the BJP.

> I then offered my services full time. That was how a small team we set up began its baby steps. A big part of it was evangelisation. We set up systems independent of the party and got ready to play for the quarter finals. We tested our platform from 2010 to 2012. What you saw in 2014 was a platform tested before.[100]

Both in tone and tactics, the 2012 campaign for the Gujarat assembly election in December was conceived by his handlers as a sort of dry run for the general election that was to follow two years later. The search for a more pan-national appeal began with his Sadbhavna Yatra of 2012—essentially an amalgam of mainstream media, social media, and personal interaction—embarked upon in September 2011 with the primary intent to establish connect with Muslims, even as the consolidation of Hindu sentiment carried on apace. In June 2012, as the 150th anniversary of Vivekananda was being celebrated, Modi appropriated the spiritual icon by putting out daily tweets of him, which in turn became talking points within the larger media universe.

The jibes against the Congress Party leadership, including the calculated infantilisation of Rahul Gandhi as 'Rahul Baba'; the concerted attempts to speak the language of the young adult and the use of media platforms they frequent; or even a detail like the image of him bonding with his mother after the 2014 verdict were all first employed in 2012, before being refined and repeated in 2014.

The hyper-mediatisation of both campaigns ensured that they were also hyper-personalised. Both were shot through with the singular image of the ever tireless, ever waving, ever articulate Modi in missionary mode—celebrated through slogans like 'Nayana sinhasan mate, Gujaratna sinha sanamn mate' (for the throne of justice, for felicitation of a lion of Gujarat), or in 2014 with the ubiquitous 'Ab ki baar, Modi sarkar' (this time, a Modi government)—endlessly circulated through word and image.

Social scientist Ghanshyam Shah points to the way Modi presented himself as the primary candidate on behalf of all the party candidates, to the point of rendering the party and other contestants almost irrelevant. In Gujarat in 2012, he kept reiterating that he was the candidate in all 182 seats and that every vote cast for the BJP was a vote for him.

> The same strategy was followed in the 2014 Lok Sabha campaign in the country replacing 'Gujarat' with India. He told voters of the country, 'Aaj khud apne liye vote maang raha hoon ... meri appeal hai har gaali aur kuche se, aap ka vote seedhe, seedhe, mujhe milega

> (Today I am seeking a vote for myself. I want to tell all voters that your vote will reach me directly).[101]

The other conspicuous commonality between the 2012 and 2014 campaigns was the active wooing of the youth segment. The Google Plus Hangout as a potential magnet for the youth was tried in August 2012. A post on Modi's website claimed it to be a mega success, viewed by people from 116 nations and generating 1,66,000 clicks and 70,000 tweets. The experiment was deemed successful enough to be tried again before the 2014 election, with popular film star Ajay Devgn anchoring both sessions.

Once the 2012 Gujarat election was won, Modi lost no time in effortlessly switching to a pan-national projection. Nowhere was this more evident than in two highly mediatised speeches that had millions participating as part of television and online audiences. They took place between the victorious Gujarat verdict in 2012 and the General Election triumph of 2014. The first was delivered as a victory speech on 20 December 2012, and the chosen language of address was Hindi, rather than Gujarati, which had been the preferred language for the victory speeches of 2002 and 2007. Additionally, the valedictory tone that interlaced his words, the employment of phrases like, 'forgive me if I have committed any error', also seemed to signal an imminent shift from Gandhinagar to New Delhi. The seriousness with which he took mainstream media coverage of that particular event was made patent when he interrupted his speech to instruct BJP workers not to crowd out the cameras, saying, 'let the media do their job'. In that statement was the recognition that the old hostility towards mainstream media had long ebbed, and what was now at play was a new partnership of sorts in order to bring the Modi project of becoming prime minister to fruition.

If the first speech was nuanced, the other, delivered on Independence Day 2013, was unambiguously direct. Delivered from Bhuj, against a backdrop that recalled Delhi's Red Fort from where Prime Minister Manmohan Singh had just delivered his formal Independence Day address, Modi broke all political conventions by mocking the former's speech and its 'gissi pitti sochch' (worn-out shibboleths), attacking the Congress' 'dynasty politics', and openly demanding a debate on development. National television channels, which normally ignore Independence Day speeches in state capitals while focusing on the Red Fort address, gave live coverage to Modi's address, billing it as a 'Battle of the Speeches', with streamers that went 'Narendra Modi's Independence Day Challenge to the PM' and 'Who Will India Listen To?'

There was a fair degree of criticism from political commentators on this projection of an alternative prime minister on a day that called for national unity. Modi's supporters, however, argued that it all amounted to how India received the message. 'I would say it was net positive. The backdrop of the Red Fort, what he said, how he said it, made all the difference.'[102] Yet to be named as the BJP's prime ministerial candidate, Modi, through this audacious, highly mediatised move, had commandeered for himself at a notional level the premier position on the national centre-stage.

The year 2013 was a period of uncertainty. Since controlling the mainstream media discourse had become crucial, the approach was to generate as many photo-ops and media interactions as possible, while efficiently neutralising negative stories.

The well-publicised interaction with the students of Shri Ram College of Commerce in Delhi in February of that year, or the Rewari rally in Haryana with ex-servicemen in September, relayed on every media platform, proved to be important building blocks for a victorious verdict in 2014. Excerpts from the Rewari speech were tweeted and carried live on Modi's own channel, and its transcript was made available on his website. It was also podcasted on the internet and accessed through telephonic dial-ins. 'It was part of a conscious effort to use social media to force the newspapers, TV and radio to take notice of every speech and to cover them in a way that reflected the priorities of the campaign.'[103]

Modi finished 2013 with another mega event, Run for Unity, designed to create an alternative nationalist movement discourse that would bypass the Nehru–Gandhi family and claim Vallabhbhai

Patel for the party, by staging what Modi's website claimed was the 'largest mass run/walk of its kind in the world'. This effort to iconise Patel through this event in support of a statue of his made of material—pieces of iron—brought in by several social groups, from farmers to young people, recalled the mass mobilisations on the Ram Mandir issue in the 1990s, when bricks for the temple were requisitioned from supporters all over the country.

It was in the effective handling of potential informational landmines, however, that the real communications skill and quickness of response was tested. The Cobrapost.com expose on the surveillance that the Gujarat government had allegedly conducted on a young woman broke in late November and had a brief run on almost all media platforms under the eponymous term, 'Snoopgate'. It demanded quick damage control, which really meant media control. Editor-in-chief of the IBN 18 Network, Rajdeep Sardesai, remembered a telephone call from Modi's right-hand man, Amit Shah, requesting him to remove the report.[104]

Ultimately, that story was managed skilfully, not so much through direct censorship as by the media's own reluctance to address the core issues that it raised, including the alleged overreach of a sitting chief minister/prospective prime minister and the damaging implications that state surveillance had on individual liberties. While news sense required that the story be covered, the anxiety to move on and let the prime ministerial designate escape the force of its velocity was patent. Within a few weeks, the sensational 'Snoopgate' story was as good as dead, despite several subsequent attempts to revive it by interested persons and rival parties. Once the dates of the general election were announced in March 2014, the steamroller impact of the Modi media machine ensured that almost all coverage remained positive.

It helped that the RSS, the world's largest non-government organisation with an estimated 1.5 to 2 million regular participants, put its full weight behind the Modi bid to become prime minister. On only two occasions had the RSS been fully engaged in parliamentary elections—'once in 1977 for the Janata Party and in 2014 for the BJP'.[105]

INDIA'S MOST MEDIATISED GENERAL ELECTION

The Sixteenth General Election of April–May 2014 has been recognised as the most mediatised in India's history. The mainstream media were continuing to grow, with three of the five top-selling newspapers being Hindi-language ones. The multi-edition *Dainik Jagran* headed the list, with a daily readership of 16.63 million readers. At this point there were 788 television channels in the country and India had become the third largest television market in the world, with close to 154 million TV households, after China and the United States.[106] Of these, around 392 were said to be news channels and the elections brought a fresh spurt of growth in this segment.

Parallel to the growth of mainstream media was the explosion in the communication technologies sector. Mobile telephones were ubiquitous with 2G-GSM networks covering 87 per cent of the population.[107] Even radio had not commanded such mass presence. Simultaneously, with telecom operators bringing down tariffs on 3G services sharply, the sales of smartphones had also registered a marked rise by late 2013, with a considerable number of Indians now accessing the internet through their mobile phones. The Internet and Mobile Association of India (IAMAI) estimated that by June 2014, smartphone users accounted for 76 per cent of the country's internet user base of 243 million.[108] In synchrony with this growing internet presence was social media usage. Of the various platforms, Facebook's user base had touched 100 million, while that of Twitter was around 33 million, with LinkedIn, Pinternet, and Instagram also very much in circulation,[109] along with WhatsApp, which had been acquired by Facebook in February 2014.

These were the resources that the Modi campaign exploited to the hilt, achieving a synchrony of media presence across platforms in a way that recalled the careful preparations that he had once put into winning the war of public perception a quarter of a century earlier, during the Advani rath yatra. Journalists covering the event organised for the release of the BJP manifesto in April 2014 were handed over a pen drive carrying the manifesto and a small video on the party. The event itself was featured in newspapers, television, and social media sites like Facebook, and publicised on WhatsApp and through mobile dial-ins.

The publicity was based on the proactive strategy of 'replicate and pervade',[110] so that its information got stamped on popular consciousness. One scholarly journal editorialised:

> If Modi holograms and masks served as evocative substitutes to his physical presence in mass rallies, his virtual presence loomed large across the media. Even in the regional language media, both television and print, while local issues naturally occupied centre stage and even where the BJP may have had little or a marginal scope or role, the Modi factor, like a subliminal awareness, informed the proceedings.[111]

Such nuanced critique was rare. Most publications adopted a stance of consistent, sometimes fulsome, support for Modi. The *Dainik Jagran* editorial that greeted the Modi victory could be seen as representative of the sentiments prevailing in the Hindi print media as a whole. Titled 'Janata ka Jawab' (The people's answer), it noted that Modi had been 'ridiculed on many occasions, even at times being insulted and cast as a tyrant by many so-called intellectuals in India and abroad. To them Modi has given an apt answer by winning with a handsome margin.' The implication here was that the 'handsome' victory was sufficient in itself to validate the new prime minister, no matter what his historical record may have been.

The cover stories over the years of the popular news weekly, *India Today*, tell their own story. In 2002, the magazine carried four cover stories on Modi the first three of which were unqualifiedly negative, as their headlines would indicate: 'Agony of Gujarat: Blundering Modi' (18 March), 'Modi the Untouchable' (8 March), and 'Hero of Hatred' (29 April). The fourth, even as Modi's campaign for the 2002 election was gathering steam, reflected a guarded change in tone; it acknowledged that the majority of Gujaratis were backing him: 'Exclusive Gujarat Opinion Poll: Riding the Hate Wave' (15 November). By early 2003, the tone had become more accommodative: 'Narendra Modi: Master Divider' (6 January). Over the next few years, cover stories on Modi were less frequent, but increasingly celebratory: 'Gujarat Elections—Modi On Trial' (7 December 2007), 'Hat in the Ring' (3 October 2011), 'King Modi Seeks Delhi Throne' (5 November 2012). By 2014, in the run-up to the 2014 elections in April–May, the magazine abandoned any pretence of balance and carried as many as six Modi cover stories in the five months of the campaign, most of which bordered on the reverential. The post-victory cover story of the 26 May issue showed Modi in a Napoleanesque pose under the bannerline, 'The Conqueror'.

Television channels, some of which had mounted a no-holds-barred scrutiny of Modi's handling of the 2002 massacres twelve years earlier, had by 2014 turned into unabashed votaries of his prime ministerial candidature. A combination of powerful corporate support for the Modi candidature—the stock markets greeted his victory with a 5 per cent jump—and a perception that his popularity was good for TRPs and reader interest made for the hard-nosed calculus behind such coverage. Sardesai writes how 'TV channels aired Modi's speech without any advertising breaks (it would become a familiar practice over the next 12 months, causing loss in revenues to news channels) .... In the TRP (Television Rating Point) war, Modi was already the winner.'[112]

All this was testimony to the chief protagonist's skilful management of the television media. Those media houses that were seen as recalcitrant and critical were punished through the simple expedient of being boycotted. In the run-up to the 2014 elections, when Modi allowed himself to be open to television interviews, his resentments were made clear. NDTV, for instance, was the only major news network that was not given an interview, possibly because of its stance on the Gujarat pogrom. In contrast, he extended full cooperation to those who had afforded him soft interviews. An appearance before the victory verdict of 2014 on Rajat Sharma's Aap ki Adalat on India TV was a case in point. As the channel's editorial director, who resigned subsequently, was to reveal, the show was designed to showcase the Modi persona to the extent that even the studio audience was packed with Modi supporters, who kept cheering his every word.

Such coverage was prompted by the business model of television companies. Television news gathering is prohibitively expensive and hardly revenue generating—80 per cent of the Rs 2,000 crore that came in as television advertising revenue for the year 2013–14 went only to the top ten players.[113] Most news channels existed for reasons other than profitability, including influence peddling, a trend that had figured in the consultation paper of the Telecom Regulatory Authority of India (TRAI):

> Media outlets owned/controlled by political/business entities may try to sensationalise a news item to undermine the interests of their opponents with scant regard for the overall national interest. Instances of such irresponsible reporting and sensationalisation are not uncommon during, say, political elections, when controversial news items/videos/visuals are bandied in the public domain through media outlets.[114]

Ashutosh, who later joined AAP and went on to play a leadership role in that party, reveals how, during that election campaign, many news organisations came under intense pressure to present a point of view that was favourable to Modi, with all opposing viewpoints edited out. He claims that several newspersons expressed their helplessness over not being allowed to file stories that were critical of Modi. 'I don't know if it was done at the behest of the Modi camp or if there was some kind of monetary temptation (as massive sums were paid to every news channel in the form of ads) or if the owners had decided not to antagonize Modi.'[115]

The combination of external pressure from corporate interests and internal pressure from owners and managers of media houses had visible impacts: BJP received nearly 40 per cent of primetime television coverage, with coverage of Modi accounting for a 37 per cent share. Both figures, incidentally, were higher than the percentage of votes that went to the party.[116] The clear dereliction of professional norms, inherent in the way the media favoured Modi through self-censorship and self-selection, hardly registered with the voting public. The general presumption was that media reports accurately reflected the truth.

Mainstream media election narrative, even if disproportionately favourable to the BJP, is difficult to control completely, which was why Modi's self-communication strategies through digital media proved so useful. Bypassing the gatekeepers of mainstream media, social media succeeded in large measure to set the news agenda for all media platforms, including that of mainstream media, through timely tweets, posts, and videos.

> By 2014, we did three key things: we built a great tech platform that was sustainable; created believers through social media; created volunteers, again through social media while unifying them on the 'Slogan 272 Plus'. It was a 360-degree campaign, from online professionals and brand ambassadors to some 22 lakh on-the-ground volunteers speaking different languages and spread over 400 constituencies working out of their own aspiration, using their own tools and creating free media content for us.[117]

A major innovation of the Modi campaign, according to commentator Christophe Jaffrelot, was the recruitment of 'vote mobilisers' and 'building—parallel to the BJP apparatus—structures of activists paying allegiance to him personally'.[118] Arvind Gupta, as Modi's digital pointsperson, called them by various appellations, including 'evangelists' and even 'yodhas' (warriors), who, while acting separately, were confined to watertight groups, but could freely interact, influence, and draw from each other thanks to communication technologies. 'No party leader in India had ever had such an array of organisations and structures in place ready to support their bid for power.'[119] Some, like the NaMo volunteer programme, were strictly self-driven, others like NitiDigital operated in tandem with the Modi campaign, and still others like the Citizens for Accountable Governance worked within the ecosystem of the party's election outreach. Finally, there was a category of free-ranging volunteers whose fealty to the Modi cause was expressed largely through the virtual takedown of anyone who held a contrary view through targeted, if anonymous, abuse, otherwise known as trolling. This was the first evidence of the BJP's notorious army of trolls, who were to acquire even greater profile as the years went by. Once he became prime minister, Modi even invited 150 of these 'yodhas', people whose handles he follows, to tea at his official residence in Delhi on 1 July 2015.[120]

The cumulative impact of this mobilisation was to amplify the anti-incumbency sentiment against the UPA while projecting a wave in Modi's favour. A political analyst termed the strategy as one of creating a 'political "discourse" that was remarkably homogeneous', by moving 'from "manufacturing consent" to "manufacturing dissent" against the existing government'.[121]

The general elections had already expanded the use of social media in India greatly. According to Facebook data, from 7 April, the day the polls were announced, to 12 May—the final day of the nine-phased process—29 million people in India had put out 227 million posts, comments, shares, and likes on its site in the specific context of the elections, with an additional 13 million making 75 million interactions involving Modi. While platforms like Facebook, YouTube, Linkedin, Pinternet, and Instagram were used by the Modi team in relatively straightforward ways as bearers of information, images, videos, appeals for support, and the occasional observation, it was Twitter—there were 15.8 million Twitter users in India in 2014—which was the chosen weapon for the thrust and parry of political one-upmanship. It helped to make a man who had refused to engage with an untutored mainstream media now emerge in public perception as India's most approachable and communicative political leader.

A closer reading of how Twitter was harnessed for this messaging is instructive and 'exemplifies the power of social media in shaping the citizenry's imagination of its political leader'.[122] The shaping of popular imagination, however, was not a spontaneous phenomenon and could not have been achieved on this scale without close professional guidance and the wide-ranging involvement of a group that Gupta had evocatively described as 'evangelists'. A study conducted by Pal, et al. on Modi's tweeting patterns from 2009 onwards reveals three striking aspects. First was the remarkable functionality of their messaging. If the tweets sent out between August 2012 to January 2013, which had the Gujarat 2012 elections as its principal focus, and where voters were largely Gujarati, had Hindutva as their main theme. By the time of the general election campaign—when the broadest support base for the prime ministerial aspirant was being sought—it was the issue of development that was predominant.

The second trend they flagged was evidence of a committed base growing substantially in the period of the campaign between March and May 2014. Until February 2014, retweeting was the primary form of engagement of Modi followers, but once elections were announced and until the verdict came in, favoriting had become the preferred mode—a sign, according to the authors, of the crystallisation of the mass fan base.

The third aspect was the conscious policy of 'follow backs' that allowed Modi and his team a two-way engagement with those who were following him, a large proportion of whom were ordinary people. This was a departure from celebrity tweeting patterns, which are usually one-way. It recalled the first Obama presidential campaign that had, as early as 2008, understood the importance of online reciprocity with followers/friends and the value of user-generated content.

During the 2014 campaign, Modi consistently adopted a tone of warm friendship to his significant Twitter followers, while successfully projecting to the general public that he was a technology-savvy leader aligned with the aspirations of a new India. Mainstream media's coverage of his tweets extended their impact further. His tweet of 22 April 2014, for instance, distancing himself from the communal statements made by political leaders aligned to the BJP, was widely picked up by several mainstream newspapers.[123]

Twitter was put to three main uses: to set the political agenda on his terms; to attack opponents and shore up the enthusiasm of his support base; and to enhance his own personal appeal.

Coming to the first—setting the political agenda—the attempt was always to frame the election as a pathway from economic slump to economic progress for all. In March, two weeks after the ECI had declared polling dates, Modi tweeted: 'Give us 60 months to serve you. We don't want to enjoy power but want to be Chowkidars who will guard people's money.' A similar missive was tweeted on 21 April: 'Give us 80 Lotuses from UP so that India gets a strong Govt. Cong, SP & BSP should not open their accounts in UP.' Agenda setting was also achieved through critiques of the ruling Congress-led government: 'Why is Cong hesitant to bring back black money? Because they know who it belongs to ... NDA will bring back every Paisa that is stashed abroad' (30 March). This particular tweet was retweeted and favorited 1,833 times and 822 times, respectively. Some of these tweets had a strong nationalist pitch: 'Today, we should think on how India can become self-sufficient in defence manufacturing. How can we strengthen R&D in defence sector' (11 May).

For a more synoptic view of the Modi agenda, links to his interviews, speeches, and manifesto pledges were tweeted regularly, through both his personal Twitter account and those of the party and followers. As Pal, et al. emphasise, political appeal in a general election has necessarily to be broad-based, unlike in a Gujarat election where overt Hindutva messaging had always guaranteed electoral dividends. In the Modi campaign of 2014, religious polarisation was certainly resorted to, but the exigencies of a prime ministerial campaign required such references to be almost always tangential. There were, for instance, disparaging references to the 'pink revolution', code for cow slaughter and the meat trade which, for BJP constituents, are strongly associated with Muslims. Modi made it a point, moreover, to regularly tweet about his visits to temples. On 26 March, he tweeted: 'Jai Mata Di! On way to Vaishno Devi from Sanjichhat'; a few weeks later, he sent out an image of himself within the Sri Venkateswara Swamy temple in Tirupathi with the words: 'Offered prayers at the Tirumala Temple. I prayed to Lord Venkateswara for the peace & prosperity of our nation' (1 May). Yet care was taken not to allow Hindutva radicals within the party to run away with the agenda: 'Petty statements by those claiming to be BJP's well wishers are deviating the campaign from the issues of development & good governance' (22 April).

Twitter was useful for such quick course correction, partly because its then 140-character limit precluded the need for an elaborate argument. The impression that the BJP was too urban-centric, for instance, was countered by tweeting greetings for Akshaya Tritiya: 'May this day bring prosperity in our lives. I also pray for the success & wellbeing of our hardworking farmers' (2 May). Campaigning in rural UP, he again tweeted: 'If the nation has to move ahead then the farmers and the villages have to prosper' (8 May).

A succinct format and real-time immediacy also make tweets useful for both polemical and empathetic exchanges—the second major use that the Modi campaign made of Twitter. A tweet, sent out on 26 April, attempted to do both: 'I want to thank friends on social media for relentlessly puncturing one lie after another spread by Congress & questioning their leaders.' It was a direct encouragement from him to his followers to attack the rival party. Often the responses from his followers on the Gandhis, in particular, were ugly. When Modi recalled a speech of his in a tweet, 'Give me blood, I will give you freedom. I told people, "Give us support, we will give Surajya"' (27 April), a follower, Sanjay Patel, responded immediately with this tweet: '@narendramodi but country still need blood of gandhi family .... sorry sir but they hv to be completely removed for country sake.'

Modi's attack on the Congress Party was a constant theme: 'Political untouchability is in nature of Congress. Ministers meeting other CMs are questioned & Pakistan leaders are served chicken biryani!' (2 May), or again, 'Campaign for 2014 Elections is reaching its final stages but no Congress leader has talked about development issues. Very sad' (6 May). But his sharpest comments were reserved for Rahul Gandhi. The terms he used in his campaign speeches in reference to Rahul Gandhi, like 'shehzada', also showed up in his tweets: 'Shehzada should tell us about R(ahul), S(onia), V(adra), P(riyanka) model. This RSVP model has looted India' (19 April). Throughout the campaign, he kept returning to 'Rahul baba': 'The way Rahul Baba is making statements with a dash of comedy in them, I think the TV show of Kapil Sharma may soon have to shut shop' (27 April).

The Congress' counter-offensive was also strategically deflected. Priyanka Gandhi's statement in Amethi that Modi was indulging in 'neech rajniti' (low-level politics) was quickly turned into a caste slur, both in the course of a public speech and as a personal tweet: 'As I belong to a socially backward section, they consider my politics to be neech rajniti .... Some people cannot see that it is due to the renunciation, sacrifice and hard work of people of backward castes that the country has reached its current heights' (6 May). Interestingly, it was the same tactic that was used to counter Mani Shankar Aiyar's statement that Modi was a 'neech aadmi' in the run-up to the Gujarat assembly election in December 2017.

In the 2014 campaign, displays of wounded feelings were often resorted to. When Modi was barred by the ECI from holding a rally in Varanasi for security reasons, party functionaries were quick to take up the issue. While his supporters waged the battle for him in this crucial phase of the campaign, the tweets from Modi himself claimed the moral high ground: 'My profound apologies to Ganga Maa for not being able to perform Aarti today. Wish these people know that a Mother's love is above politics' (8 May).

Self-projection was a major aspect of the tweeting and Modi constantly tweeted details about his campaign and himself, revelling in the popular adulation coming his way. He tweeted about the tirelessness with which he went about his campaign: 'Campaigned in Himachal Pradesh & Uttarakhand. People in these states feel betrayed due to misgovernance both in Centre & in their states' (29 April), or 'In traditional headgear at the rally in Arunachal

Pradesh' (31 March). Occasionally tweets were constructed to whet the anticipation and curiosity of supporters: 'Will address Bharat Vijay Rallies via 3D technology. This is the 3rd round of these 3D rallies. Looking forward' (17 April). The sheer scale of the campaign was repeatedly invoked: 'By the end of the campaign I would have addressed 1350 3D rallies & joined Chai Pe Charcha, that was held across 4000 locations,' or '8 months, 5800+ rallies, Charchas, programmes, 3 lakh+ KMs ... an extensive, innovative & satisfying journey' (10 May).

To expand his social media following, several stratagems were adopted. One was to personally call out to the main users of Twitter—the youth. He did this in various ways, but most specifically in urging them to vote, with the underlying assumption that they would vote for him. The attitude adopted was companionate: 'I particularly call upon my young friends to go & vote in large numbers. The youth of India must show the way!' (21 April). A few weeks later, the tone grew importunate: 'My special request to the youth—go out & vote and take your family and friends along to the polling booth!' (12 May). The response was enthusiastic, as this return tweet from ArunK8mec would indicate: 'Spent money on travel, took off from work and now my duty is done. Voted with lot of expectations @narendramodi sir. We need good government' (24 April). Each tweet of this kind helped to enthuse others. In the US, incidentally, Facebook had come up with a button that said, 'I Voted'. Research found that it 'had driven a small but measurable increase in turnout, primarily among young people.'[124]

An attempt was also made to court social celebrities who themselves enjoy great fandom, and thereby access their sizeable following. This would conform to what has been theorised as a 'two-step flow', when opinion leaders follow other opinion leaders to create a 'community of influencers'.[125] Modi's call on the celebrated southern superstar, Rajinikanth, was a good example of this. On 13 April, he tweeted a photograph of himself with 'Rajinikanth ji' and posted it on Facebook. That one visit drew the attention of more than 2.2 million social media users. A few days later he greeted novelist Chetan Bhagat on his birthday with the following tweet: 'Dear @chetan bhagat, many many happy returns of the day! Sharing the selfie you took last evening' (22 April). It received 2,508 likes and was retweeted 2,172 times—evidence once again of not only Modi's, but also Bhagat's fan following.

The tweeting of selfies was yet another strategy. A selfie tweet that went viral showed an image of Modi in the polling booth with his inked finger holding up a lotus icon: 'Voted! Here is my selfie', the text read. The move contravened election rules that make it illegal for a party symbol to be displayed within the precincts of a polling booth, but it buttressed a key BJP gameplan to involve young people by inviting them to post their selfies in, and eventually these individual selfies were used to create an online mosaic of Modi. The selfie was a cheap, intimate, and self-perpetuating platform for building political presence and allowed for a 'do-it-yourself form of virality, ensuring that the "NaMo" (short for Narendra Modi) syndrome never went out of circulation'.[126] As Modi later explained to Lance Price, 'The selfie was a natural reaction and just for social media. It was part of what I was always doing and the youth of the nation were in my mind when I did it.' Adding, 'Our message got the attention it deserved to keep the election momentum going.'[127]

As soon as the verdict was clear, a personal stamp was immediately placed on it, with a tweet bearing a photograph of himself with his mother and the words, 'Sought blessings from my Mother', going on to assume instant virality (16 May). The image and tweet immediately recalled the Obama victory tweet of 7 November 2012, when an image of the President with wife Michelle and the words 'Four more years' proved to be one of the most retweeted tweets ever.

The big difference between the BJP's general election media campaigns of 2009 and 2014 was that in the latter instance, proliferation of social media platforms and greater media convergence greatly facilitated the presidentialisation of the campaign in a manner that synchronised with the Modi brand of stand-above-the-rest assertion, which cast his party in his own image. The media strategy also aimed at taking the older media to the newer media space. The 'old-fashioned' mass rallies conducted by him, for example, were made to circulate endlessly on virtual platforms through videos, tweets, and posts.

> Traditionally, the most visible and high impact campaign events were big public rallies that were mostly, and are still, held in 'maidan' or the public grounds in most cities that are meant for holding large public events. But Mr. Modi did not hold fewer rallies than the other party leaders, indeed, he held far more. He simply added another highly visible communication layer to his campaign over which he and his followers had direct control—social media updates via Twitter, Facebook, and Google+, among others.[128]

Old systems of mass contact were similarly refined and modernised through the use of media. Prashant Jha notes in the context of the Uttar Pradesh election of 2017 how the party created support structures for their candidates in the fray, which included teams to supervise their daily schedule and even handle their Facebook pages and WhatsApp campaigns.[129] This was an approach that had marked the 2014 campaign as well.

Such electioneering, however, was highly capital-intensive and needed deep pockets. It helped Modi's cause greatly that some of India's most prominent corporates supported him, having perceived him as the candidate best placed to support a neoliberal economic agenda aligned to their own. As one analyst put it, 'never in the country's history has the fraternity of leading corporate CEOs united so strongly and volubly to promote a single politician to prime ministership as they did for Modi',[130] a support that resulted in his campaign expenditure touching stratospheric heights. According to Price, 'it is quite possible that this was the most expensive election anywhere in the world, surpassing even the seven billion dollars spent during the American presidential election of 2012.'[131]

The 'transition in political culture in contemporary India signifies the ways in which the Indian nation has been reimagined in the context of liberalization.'[132] The new mediatised electioneering that emerged during the 2009 general election reflected just such a transition, but it was only with the 2014 Modi campaign that the process came to acquire stability.

NOTES AND REFERENCES

1. David L. Swanson and Paolo Mancini, 1996, *Politics, Media, and Modern Democracy: An International Study of Innovations in Electoral Campaigning and Their Consequences* (Westport, CT: Praeger), 11.

2. Manuel Castells, 2013, *Communication Power* (Oxford: Oxford University Press), 157.

3. Maxwell McCombs and Donald Shaw, 1972, 'The Agenda-setting Function of Mass Media', *Public Opinion Quarterly* 36, 176–87. Available at https://www.unc.edu/~fbaum/teaching/PLSC541_Fall06/McCombs%20and%20Shaw%20POQ%201972.pdf (accessed November 2015).

4. Castells, *Communication Power*, 157.

5. Michael J. Jensen, 2016, 'Social Media and New Information Dynamics in Political Campaigning'. Available at https://ecpr.eu/Filestore/PaperProposal/c95aab93-e083-4474-8821-e37eb9f98efe.pdf (accessed 2 December 2017).

6. Robert W. McChesney, 2007, *Communication Revolution* (New York: The New Press), xii.

7. Sunetra Sen Narayan, 2014, *Globalization and Television: A Study of the Indian Experience, 1990–2010* (New Delhi: Oxford University Press), 89.

8. Adrian Athique, 2012, *Indian Media* (Cambridge: Polity Press), 54.

9. Nalin Mehta, 2015, *Behind a Billion Screens: What Television Tells Us about Modern India* (New Delhi: HarperCollins), 35.

10. R. Jeffrey and Assa Doron, 2013, *Cellphone Nation* (New Delhi: Hachette India), 57.

11. Ibid., 220.

12. Pamela Philipose, 2014b, 'Violence, Just a Click Away: How Communal Violence has a Domain in Cyberspace', *DNA*, 2 September.

13. Ronald Brownstein, 2008, 'The first 21st century campaign', *National Journal* 19 April. Available at http://freerepublic.com/focus/f-news/2003853/posts (accessed November 2015).

14. Rahaf Harfoush, 2009, *Yes We Did: An Inside Look at how Social Media built the Obama Brand* (Berkeley: New Riders Press), xiii.

15. Ibid., 139–40.

16. Diana Owen, 2009, 'The Campaign and the Media', in Janet M. Box-Steffensmeier and Steven E. Schier (eds), *The American Election of 2008* (Lanham, MD: Rowman & Littlefield Publishers Inc.), 9.

17. Aaron Smith, 2009, 'The Internet's Role in Campaign 2009', Pew Internet, Science & Tech, 15 April. Available at http://www.pewinternet.org/2009/04/15/the-internets-role-in-campaign-2008/ (accessed November 2015).

18. John Nichols and Robert W. McChesney, 2013, 'Dollarocracy', *The Nation*, 11 September. Available at https://www.thenation.com/article/dollarocracy/ (accessed November 2015).

19. Ibid.

20. M. Weiner, 1978, *India Votes: 1977* (Washington: American Enterprise Institute for Public Policy Research).

21. James Manor, 2004, 'The Congress Defeat in Madhya Pradesh', *Seminar* June, 68. Available at http://www.india-seminar.com/2004/534/534%20james%20manor.htm (accessed December 2015).

22. Nalin Mehta, 2008, 'India Talking—Politics, Democracy and News Television', in Nalin Mehta (ed.), *Television in India: Satellites, Politics and Cultural Change* (London: Routledge), 48.

23. Niraja Gopal Jayal, 2004, 'A Malevolent Embrace? The BJP and Muslims in the Parliamentary Election of 2004', *India Review* 3 (3).

24. 'India Shining amongst biggest ad campaigns', Rediff.com, 24 February 2004.

25. 'India Internet Usage Stats and Telecommunications Market Report'. Available at http://www.internetworldstats.com/asia/in.htm (accessed December 2015).

26. Shyam Tekwani and Kavitha Shetty, 2007, 'Two Indias: The Role of the Internet in the 2004 Election', in Randolph Kluver, Nicholas Jankowski, Kirsten Foot, and Steven M. Schneider (eds), *The Internet and National Campaigns: A Comparative Study of Web Campaigning* (New York: Routledge), 153.

27. 'Indian Mobile Service Sector—Struggling to maintain sustainable growth, 2011', Cellular Association of India, PWC, 8. Available at https://www.pwc.in/assets/pdfs/publications-2011/pwc-coai-white-paper-indian-mobile-services-sector.pdf (accessed December 2015).

28. Neena Vyas, 2004, 'Pick up the phone, it may be the PM', *The Hindu*, 25 February.

29. 'India Internet Usage Stats and Telecommunications Market Report', Available at http://www.internetworldstats.com/asia/in.htm (accessed December 2015).

30. Priya Shah, 2010, 'Indian Political Communication and Digital Technology', *Scribd.* Available at http://www.scribd.com/doc/46046810/Indian-Political-Communication-and-Digital-Technology#scribd (accessed December 2015).

31. 'Indian Mobile Service Sector'.

32. Bhaskar Mukherjee, 2009, 'Link analysis of Indian political parties' web sites: A temporal comparison', *Annals of Library and Information Studies* 56, September.

33. Kavita Karan, 2012, 'E-Engaging India: E-democracy Strategies for Empowerment and Civic Participation', in *Digital Democracy: Concepts, Methodologies, Tools and Applications* (USA: Information Resources Management Association).

34. Interview with social media professional Mahima Kaul, conducted on 6 October 2015.

35. Marco Fioretti, 2008, 'Indian political party turns to FOSS', *linux.com,* October 20. Available at http://archive09.linux.com/feature/150549 (accessed December 2015).

36. Shah, 'Indian Political Communication and Digital Technology'.

37. Rajesh Jain, 2009, 'Emergic Rajesh Jain's Blog I Support the BJP'. Available at http://emergic.org/2009/01/29/elections-2009-i-support-the-bjp/ (accessed December 2015).

38. Quote by senior journalist Rajiv Shah in Kingshuk Nag, 2013, *The NaMo Story: A Political Life* (New Delhi: Roli Books), 55.

39. K. K. Singh, 2011, 'Down the Memory Lane: Advani's Rathyatra of 1990 to Construct Ram Mandir!', Blog, 10 October. Available at http://kksingh1.blogspot.in/2011/10/down-memory-lane-advanis-rathyatra-o-f.html (accessed April 2016).

40. Rajdeep Sardesai, 2014, *2014: The Election That Changed India* (New Delhi: Penguin Viking), 5.

41. Nilanjan Mukhopadhyay, 2013, *Narendra Modi: The Man, The Times* (New Delhi: Tranquebar Press), 180–81.

42. Nag, *The NaMo Story*, 57.

43. 'PM's Diwali Mangal Milan with the Media', 25 October 2014. Available at http://www.narendramodi.in/pms-diwali-mangal-milan-with-the-media-6790 (accessed April 2016).

44. Lance Price, 2015, *The Modi Effect: Inside Narendra Modi's Campaign to Transform India* (London: Hodder & Stoughton), 137.

45. Vinod Mehta, 2014, *Editor Unplugged: Media, Magnates, Netas and Me* (New Delhi: Penguin India), 243.

46. Vinod K. Jose, 2013, 'The Emperor Uncrowned: The Rise of Narendra Modi', *The Caravan*, 1 March.

47. Sardesai, *2014*, 10.

48. Jose, 'The Emperor Uncrowned'.

49. 'Rights and Wrongs: Ordeal by Fire in the Killing Fields of Gujarat', Editors Guild of India Fact-finding Mission Report, 2002.

50. 'Modi sworn in Gujarat CM amidst fanfare', *The Hindu*, 7 October 2001. Available at http://www.thehindu.com/2001/10/08/stories/02080001.htm (accessed April 2016).

51. Price, *The Modi Effect*, 54.

52. 'Rights and Wrongs', Editors Guild Report.

53. Ibid.

54. Celia W. Dugger, 2002, 'Religious Riots Over Indian Politics', *The New York Times*, 27 July. Available at http://www.nytimes.com/2002/07/27/world/religious-riots-loom-over-indian-politics.html?pagewanted=all (accessed April 2016).

55. B. G. Verghese, 2010, *First Draft* (New Delhi: Tranquebar Press), 447.

56. 'Rights and Wrongs', Editors Guild Report.

57. Ibid.

58. Siddharth Varadarajan (ed.), 2002, *Gujarat: The Making of a Tragedy* (New Delhi: Penguin India), 271.

59. Rajdeep Sardesai, 2002, 'Did the media ransack shops, take lives, Mr Modi?', *The Indian Express*, 7 March.

60. Arvind Rajagopal, 2010, 'Violence, Publicity and Secularism: Hindu-Muslim Riots in Gujarat', in Chris Berry, So-young Kim and Lynn Spigel (eds), *Electronic Elsewheres: Media, Technology, and the Experience of Social Space* (Minneapolis: University of Minnesota Press), 159, 165.

61. 'Modi determined to take out Gaurav Yatra', rediff.com, 12 August 2002. Available at http://www.rediff.com/news/2002/aug/26guj1.htm (accessed April 2016).

62. Sudesh Verma, 2014, *Narendra Modi: The Game Changer* (New Delhi: Vitasta), 153.

63. Pamela Philipose, 2002, 'The Portable, Moveable Modi', *The Indian Express*, 25 October.

64. Narendra Modi's reply to a show cause notice issued by the Election Commission', 8 December 2007.

65. Shiv Visvanathan, 2012, 'Janus Shut the Door', *Outlook*, 25–31 December.

66. Mukhopadhyay, *Narendra Modi*, 342.

67. 'Modi rebuffed at CII meet', *The Hindu*, 7 February 2003. Available at http://www.thehindu.com/thehindu/2003/02/07/stories/2003020705420100.htm (accessed April 2015).

68. Uday Mahurkar, 2003, 'Modi Makeover', *India Today*, 13 October. Available at http://www.thehindu.com/2003/02/07/stories/2003020705420100.htm (accessed April 2016).

69. Shiv Visvanathan, 2014, 'Narendra Modi's Symbolic War', *Economic and Political Weekly* XLIX (22), 31 May.

70. Mukhopadhyay, *Narendra Modi*, 365.

71. 'Rajiv Gandhi Foundation Finds Gujarat Number 1 State', *The Economic Times*, 21 May 2005. Available at http://articles.economictimes.indiatimes.com/2005-05-21/news/27510532_1_economic-freedom-gsdp-total-cases (accessed April 2016).

72. Sardesai, *2014*, 110.

73. Swapan Dasgupta, 2007, 'The Modi Charisma', *The Times of India*, 30 December. Available at http://timesofindia.indiatimes.com/swapan-dasgupta/right-wrong/The-Modi-charisma/articleshow/2661475.cms (accessed April 2016).

74. Christophe Jaffrelot, 2015, 'What "Gujarat Model"? Growth without Development—and with socio-Political Polarisation', *Journal of South Asian Studies* 38 (4).

75. Ghanshyam Shah, 2015, 'Mega Marketing and Management: Gujarat's 2024 Elections', in Paul Wallace, *India's 2014 Elections: A Modi-led BJP Sweep* (New Delhi: Sage Publications), 280.

76. From a speech delivered by Narendra Modi at the Annual Plan Discussion in the Planning Commission, New Delhi, 18 June 2013. Available at http://planningcommission.nic.in/plans/stateplan/Presentations13_14/gujrat2013_14.pdf (accessed April 2016).

77. Jayati Ghosh, 2014, 'Gujarat model: The real story', *Frontline*, 22 August. Available at https://www.frontline.in/columns/Jayati_Ghosh/gujarat-model-the-real-story/article6279847.ece (accessed January 2016).

78. 'No, Mr. Modi. Beautiful People Are Not Malnourished', *FirstPost*, 30 August 2012. Available at http://www.firstpost.com/india/no-mr-modi-beautiful-people-are-not-malnourished-434694.html on April 25 (accessed April 2016).

79. Adrian Athique, 2012, *Indian Media* (Cambridge: Polity Press), 54.

80. Arvind Rajagopal, 2014b, 'Two Tyrants in the Age of Television', *Economic and Political Weekly* XLIX (8), 22 February.

81. http://prabhuchawla.com/video-search.php?q=narendra+modi&submit=.

82. 'Modi's "puppy" remark triggers new controversy over 2002 riots', Reuters, 12 July 2013. Available at http://in.reuters.com/article/narendra-modi-puppy-reuters-interview-idINDEE96B08S20130712 (accessed May 2016).

83. 'Modi walks out of TV interview after being quizzed on riots', Rediff.com, 20 October. Available at http://www.rediff.com/news/2007/oct/20modi.htm (accessed May 2008).

84. 'I spoke to media on 2002 riots, none tried to understand the truth: Modi', *The Business Standard*, 17 April 2014. Available at http://www.business-standard.com/article/elections-2014/i-spoke-to-media-on-2002-riots-none-tried-to-understand-the-truth-modi-114041600587_1.html (accessed May 2016).

85. Sahana Udupa, 2015, *News, Publics and Politics in Globalizing India: Media, Publics, Politics* (New Delhi: Cambridge University Press), 210.

86. Appu Esthose Suresh, 2013, 'Makeover Gurus', *The Indian Express*, 20 October.

87. 'Gujarat Congress boycotts TV9, Modi wants Election Commission to intervene', *Desh Gujarat*, 26 August 2012. Available at http://deshgujarat.com/2012/08/26/gujarat-congress-boycotts-tv9-modi-wants-election-commission-to-intervene/ (accessed February 2016).

88. Jatin Gandhi, 2013, 'The Modi Mythology', *Open Magazine*, 18 July.

89. Ibid.

90. Ibid.

91. Joddy Murray, 2009, *Non-discursive Rhetoric: Image and Affect in Multimodal Composition* (New York: State University of New York Press), 2.

92. Ru Ba Ru, 1999: Narendra Modi interview with Rajeev Shukla. Availablle at https://www.youtube.com/watch?v=shyXSvQW4_w (accessed May 2016).

93. Price, *The Modi Effect*, 180.

94. 'Modi tattoos, Modi kurtas ... it's Modi, Modi everywhere this Navratri', *India Today*, 5 October 2013.

95. Joyojeet Pal, Priyanka Chandra, and V. G. Vydiswaran, 2016, 'Twitter and the Rebranding of Narendra Modi', *Economic and Political Weekly* LI (8), 20 February.

96. Price, *The Modi Effect*, 138.

97. Nag, 2013, *The NaMo Story*, 163.

98. Ashutosh, 2015, *The Crown Prince: The Gladiator and the Hope* (New Delhi: HarperCollins), 99.

99. 'In the cross-hairs of Rambo's para-truths', *The Telegraph*, 25 June 2013. Available at http://www.telegraphindia.com/1130625/jsp/frontpage/story_17045317.jsp#.VzwKR-R8uev (accessed May 2016).

100. Arvind Gupta, at a discussion on the 2014 General Election at the Observer Research Foundation, New Delhi, July 2014.

101. Shah, 'Mega Marketing and Management', 266.

102. Arvind Gupta discussion; see n49.

103. Price, *The Modi Effect*, 102.

104. Sardesai, *2014*, 181.

105. Walter K. Andersen and Shridhar D. Damle, 2018, *The RSS: A View to the Inside* (New Delhi: Penguin/Viking), 3.

106. 'Govt says TV industry to be Rs 50,140 crore in 2014', IndianTelevision.com, 19 February 2014. Available at http://www.indiantelevision.com/regulators/i-and-b-ministry/tv-industry-valued-to-be-at-rs-50140-crore-in-2014-mib-140219 (accessed May 2016).

107. Joss Gillet, 2014, 'Measuring mobile penetration: Untangling "subscribers". "mobile phone owners" and "users"', GSMA Intelligence. Available at https://www.gsmaintelligence.com/research/2014/05/measuring-mobile-penetration/430/ (accessed May 2016).

108. 'India to have 243 million internet users by June 2014', Press Trust of India, 29 January 2014. Available at http://www.thehindubusinessline.com/economy/india-to-have-243-million-internet-users-by-june-2014-iamai/art (accessed May 2016).

109. '10 Important Statistics about Digital and Social Media in India', blog by Harsh Ajmera, Digital Insights. Available at http://blog.digitalinsights.in/important-statistics-digital-and-social-media-users-in-india/05224987.html (accessed May 2016).

110. 'Fourth Estate That Vanished', Editorial, *Economic and Political Weekly* XILX (21), 24 May 2014.

111. Ibid.

112. Sardesai, *2014*, 118.

113. '3 dozen in 5 months: News channels crowd news space', *The Indian Express*, 5 May 2014. Available at http://indianexpress.com/article/india/india-others/3-dozen-in-5-months-new-channels-crowd-news-space/ (accessed May 2016).

114. 'Consultation Paper on Issues Relating to Media Ownership', Draft, Telecom Regulatory Authority of India (TRAI), 2013.

115. Ashutosh, *The Crown Prince*, 223.

116. S. Rukmini, 2014, 'Modi got most prime-time coverage: Study', *The Hindu*, 8 May. Available at http://www.thehindu.com/elections/loksabha2014/modi-got-most-primetime-coverage-study/article5986740.ece (accessed May 2016).

117. Arvind Gupta discussion; see n49.

118. Christophe Jaffrelot, 2015b, 'The Modi-centric BJP 2014 election campaign: New techniques and old tactics', *Contemporary South Asia* 23 (2), 156.

119. Price, *The Modi Effect*, 98.

120. Swati Chaturvedi, 2016, *I Am A Troll: Inside the Secret World of the BJP's Digital Army* (New Delhi: Juggernaut), 17.

121. Zoya Hasan, 2014, 'Manufacturing Dissent: The Media and the 2014 Indian Election', The Hindu Centre for Politics and Public Policy, 2 April. Available at http://www.thehinducentre.com/verdict/commentary/article5843621.ece (accessed June 2016).

122. Pal, et al., 'Twitter and the Rebranding of Narendra Modi'.

123. 'Modi tweets disapproval after Sena leader calls Muslims "deshdrohis" at his rally', *The Indian Express*, 23 April 2014.

124. Alexis C. Madrigal, 2017, 'What Facebook Did to American Democracy', *The Atlantic*, 13 October.

125. Harsh Gangadharbhatla and Masoud Valafar, 2017, 'Propagation of user generated content online', *International Journal of Internet Marketing and Advertising* 11 (3).

126. Anirban K. Baishya, 2015, '#NaMo: The Political Work of the Selfie in the 2014 Indian General Elections', *International Journal of Communication* 9, Feature 1686–1700. Available at http://ijoc.org/index.php/ijoc/article/viewFile/3133/1393 (accessed November 2015).

127. Price, *The Modi Effect*, 171–78.

128. Taberez Ahmed Neyazi, Anup Kumar, and Holli A. Semetko, 2016, 'Campaigns, Digital Media, and Mobilisation in India', *The International Journal of Press/Politics* 21 (3).

129. Prashant Jha, 2017, *How the BJP Wins Inside India's Greatest Election Machine* (New Delhi: Juggernaut), 85.

130. Achin Vanaik, 2016, 'India: Liberal democracy and the extreme right', in Leo Panitch and Greg Albo (eds), *The Politics of the Rights* (Monthly Review Press), 176.

131. Price, *The Modi Effect*, 229.

132. Leela Fernandes, 2007, *India's New Middle Class: Democratic Politics in an Era of Economic Reform* (New Delhi: Oxford University Press), 41.

five

Scripts, Tweets, Posts, and Election Outcomes

Political Discourse in a Mediatised Age—II

ARVIND KEJRIWAL

The manner in which an unknown political entity, the Aam Aadmi Party (AAP), which had debuted just a year earlier, catapulted itself to power in December 2013 was assisted considerably by the innovative use of the media. The emergence of this phenomenon for the first time in India drew considerable public attention, and even came to be regarded as a 'game-changer not just for the newcomer party but also a test for the use of social media in politics'[1].

The IAC protests had provided Arvind Kejriwal, and those who gravitated towards him from within the IAC fold, with valuable insights into how the perception management of people on a mass scale could actually be made to translate into political connect. The euphoria of that early phase of party formation was captured by an AAP volunteer who had joined in the IAC activities in early 2011.

> Anna Hazare's fasts had served as a catalyst. They struck a chord with people that no political party had so far achieved in recent times, not even the Left parties, and forming a political party was the logical next step. In a way those protests helped us sow the seeds of a new kind of politics. It made us realise how to use media to articulate issues that other parties saw as insignificant, as for example a toilet in a basti (shanty town), which is a huge issue for those affected. It

> also taught us how important it was to reach out to young people and forced us to use media content and technologies that could do this. During the Anna fasts, I remember listening to some of the conversations that were going around. It somehow made people feel alive. Even school kids in Punjab were talking about Anna.[2]

In 2011, the IAC mobilisations at their height were able to harvest the public support that came with media convergence. The Anna team, as we saw, projected its messages through social media even while gaining considerable mainstream media traction. This goodwill had begun to dissipate after the third Anna fast at the MMRDA grounds in Mumbai, and had all but evaporated by 2012. Speculative stories soon began appearing about the growing differences between Hazare and Kejriwal, with journalists eliciting information on this from both men with the sole intention of pitting one against the other. 'Anna publicly contradicted everything Arvind said,' recalls Mayank Gandhi, a senior leader from Maharashtra, who left the party later.[3]

The break-up between the two leaders on the question of forming a political party was widely anticipated and details of the acrimony that marked the eventual parting made for colourful media coverage. A *Times of India* report of 19 September 2012, for instance, was an amalgam of speculative information from anonymous sources: 'The discussions saw a section alleging that Hazare was "exploited" by the Kejriwal group. It was countered by others saying "people in Delhi have made Anna what he is now".'[4]

In the immediate aftermath of the IAC break-up, it was Kejriwal rather than Hazare who demonstrated a greater dexterity in making political use of the media. A senior anchor with CNN-IBN recalls the manner in which Kejriwal called upon Delhiites to take part in a dharna in October 2012:

> ... he wasn't going to make this a routine news event. He asked the gathered crowds to burn their electricity bills and then climbed up on the electricity pole himself. Pandemonium broke out, the police rushed in, water cannons had to be used. Kejriwal had got his breaking news TV moment.[5]

By proposing a new political party, Kejriwal had neatly turned the tables on Hazare. That, however, was not his primary intention. Many who know Kejriwal offer a less complicated reason for why he pursued the idea of a political party: personal ambition. If ambition was indeed the driving cause, Kejriwal took care to frame it in self-righteous terms, averring that setting up a party was not about grabbing political power, but about bringing political power back to the people. The AAP website later explained the decision to join politics thus.

> For almost two years we tried every single way available to plead our cause to the government .... But despite the huge wave of public support in favour of a strong anti-corruption law, all political parties cheated the people of India and deliberately sabotaged the Janlokpal Bill. The time for peaceful fasts and protests is gone. This is the time for action .... Our aim in entering politics is not to come to power; we have entered politics to change the current corrupt and self-serving system of politics forever.

During the IAC protests, Kejriwal had displayed the ability to turn even inimical questions posed to him to his advantage, and this ability became even more apparent in his new political avatar. When the media reported how Hazare had forbidden Kejriwal to use his photograph and the IAC symbol for his politics, Kejriwal responded by declaring that he, on his part, would always carry Hazare's photograph in his heart—a statement designed to make the older man appear churlish and signal that he, Kejriwal, at least was unwilling to play up to the media game of pitting one against the other.

This intuitive way of countering media hostility was in full view during Kejriwal's first appearance on Aap ki Adalat, one of Hindi television's most watched shows. Telecast on 25 November 2012, around the time AAP was being officially launched, he appeared wearing a Gandhi cap which now bore the legend, 'Main Hoon Aam Aadmi', instead of the older 'Main Anna Hoon'. The language he employed during the programme was hard-hitting and colloquial, each sentence crafted as a soundbite. The entire effort was to convey the impression of an honest, 'ordinary' man in a hurry to clean up the system before the country was completely destroyed. There were issues that he articulated, like the alleged money laundering of the Ambanis, that were designed to unsettle the anchor of the show, given the dependence of mainstream media houses on corporate support. Kejriwal, though, was not fazed, and went as far as to call for an alternate media after accusing newspapers and television channels of trivialising serious issues and putting out false news.

That first Aap ki Adalat encounter in its mock courtroom setting provided an early foretaste of the cat-and-mouse game that was to be played between the party and the mainstream media in the days ahead. The questions that came at Kejriwal from the Aap ki Adalat anchor were critical, yet the manner in which he responded to them, his diatribes against the powerful, and his repeated declamations that he was prepared to go to jail if his accusations against them were proved wrong, went down extremely well with the studio audience, whom he addressed as the 'janata' (citizens), investing it with the symbolic power of larger society. Inherent in the exchange was a contradiction that the new party was to soon face: its efforts to gain mainstream media support in order to build a credible public image would often run counter to its bid to take on issues that resonated with the public.

The party's rhetoric against large Indian corporates was a case in point. When Kejriwal addressed press conferences, during which tapes of the conversation between Nira Radia and Atal Bihari Vajpayee's son-in-law were played, and allegations aired against the UPA government for allowing Mukesh Ambani's Reliance Industries to gain enormous profits through its gas pricing policy, it struck a chord with the average citizen, but caused immediate disquiet within mainstream media. Analysts point out that it was only when AAP became a political party and began to take on the forces of big capital that the 'mutual love affair' between the media and Kejriwal, that was much in evidence during the IAC protests, ended.[6]

Signals were soon sent out from media bosses to their employees to go slow on AAP coverage, often prompted by direct pressure from corporate backers. In his book *Rogue Elephant: Harnessing the Power of India's Unruly Democracy*, Simon Denyer refers to a letter from Reliance Industries that took media houses to task for broadcasting Kejriwal's accusations against the company. While Denyer could get neither the representatives of these media houses nor those of Reliance Industries to comment on this, a reporter in a major television network confirmed to him that there were in-house instructions that Kejriwal's accusations were not to be telecast unless the channel had carried out its own investigation.[7]

Disapproval within the media for the AAP brand of politics manifested itself in different ways, and ranged from sharply critical reports of the party to the manner in which any disparaging comment made against Kejriwal and the AAP by political critics was played up. Every time a Ram Jethmalani pronounced that Arvind Kejriwal's political party was a foolish project, or a Digvijay Singh termed him a megalomaniac, their statements would figure prominently in the news. There was also a great deal of television content devoted exclusively to tarnishing AAP and Kejriwal, based on sting operations, interested leaks, and hostile questioning at press conferences.

The run-ins between the anchor of a re-launched Hindi news channel, India News, and AAP developed into major public confrontations during this period. In a Facebook post of 17 February 2013, Kejriwal accused the channel of 'spewing venom against us' because of political vested interests, ending with the observation that 'if such people start running TV channels and owning media houses, then the challenge before the people of this country is very big'. Another major face-off between the two took place in November, just ten days before the Delhi election of 2013 was to take place. When News Sarkar, an affiliate of India News, conducted a major sting operation showing AAP candidates accepting money from random sources, the party filed defamation cases against both entities on the ground that only edited versions of what really transpired were broadcast, and were therefore fraudulent. In all party media briefings, it was consistently suggested by AAP spokespersons that a lot of money was flowing into mainstream media coffers from powerful entities intent on destroying the party.

PREPARING FOR ELECTION 2013

The occasional friendly story apart, throughout 2013—an important election year for the party because the Delhi assembly election was to take place in December that year—media hostility towards AAP was unrelenting. As Denyer put it,

> The problem for Kejriwal, though, is that he expected the media to join him in the battle against the entire establishment, an elite that many senior editors were part of socially, and perhaps also financially. Once again Kejriwal had ridden the media tiger beautifully for a while, but was in the end at risk of being thrown off and devoured. Big businesses had invested in Indian media companies partly to buy insurance from such charges, and Kejriwal could not break those kinds of bonds single-handedly.[8]

The media's virtual blackout of AAP after it took on Reliance was, according to one commentator, a major factor in its embrace of a politics that was 'post-ideological in a profound sense', and which saw the media as part of the power bloc that it was opposing.[9]

What was perhaps mainstream media's most potent weapon against AAP, and one that was particularly damaging for a fledgling party looking to shore up its profile, was the blanking out of its activities. The impact of this was keenly felt in the early months of 2013. Two programmes were now embarked upon—the filing of Right To Information (RTI) requests and interactions with Resident Welfare Associations (RWAs). AAP also turned to activism on issues of water and electricity, conducting *jan sunwai*s (public hearings) to make visible public grievances, especially in the densely populated resettlement pockets of the city. In other words, AAP chose a model of intense face-to-face campaigning on issues that touched a chord with people through grassroots mobilisation, which pitted the broom wielding, Gandhi topi wearing 'aam aadmi' against a corrupt and unaccountable power elite—represented in AAP's patois as 'lal bhatti wallahs' (those who rode on VIP cars installed with red beacons as a sign of their status).

Very little of this early phase of activism undertaken by the new party figured prominently in mainstream media coverage. AAP chose to bridge this lack of visibility in the mainstream media space by reporting upon and documenting its own work through social media platforms. The indifference of the mainstream media continued even after Kejriwal embarked on a physically debilitating fast in March 2013 against high power tariffs. A *Times of India* report on it, which appeared under a facetious headline, '13 days on, Arvind Kejriwal still on fast track', noted that the media coverage for the fast had been poor.[10]

An interesting point to note about the mainstream media hostility was that it did not seriously damage AAP's electoral prospects. On the contrary, it seemed to have added to the party's credibility in the eyes of a growing *'mohalla'* (local neighbourhood) public. This would also suggest that there was already a great disconnect between mainstream media discourse and public conversations at the urban grassroots, with issues of concern for the latter rarely figuring in the news priorities of the former. The fact that Kejriwal and his political colleagues chose to speak directly to the local communities through their programmes, rather than through PR agencies and media institutions that were perceived as being the megaphones of vested interests, helped to shore up AAP's reputation of being people-centric. It also promoted among a growing section of the electorate a sense of personal connect with the party.

The AAP capitalised on this politically by calling out mainstream media silences through social media posts. A statement put out by the party on 19 June 2013 highlighted this aspect specifically:

> Many of us might have realized that media is not covering any of AAP activity, they have been instructed to make sure AAP does not get any attention due to the upcoming election. What is more upsetting is that some crafted stories are being produced to tarnish the image and create negativity about AAP.

Social media was used in a strategically complementary fashion to create a parallel public conversation that was framed as one shorn of the falsehoods that marked mainstream media content.

What was striking was that the tweets and posts that went out on behalf of the party were largely functional, seeking to introduce candidates, raise funds for the party, convey manifesto highlights, and the like, but the tweets of leaders, in contrast, were intimate and often passionate.

Even as the party built its digital intimacy with audiences, its leaders did not forget a lesson learnt during the IAC campaign. They were conscious that social media communication could never be an end in itself and that communicating directly with people through jan sabhas, rallies, and meetings was crucial in building the perception that the party was responsive to their quotidian needs and aspirations. A case in point was Arvind Kejriwal's famous exhortation to the citizens of Delhi to stop paying their electricity and water bills during his two-week fast in March 2013. He followed it up with a personal tweet, stating that he had stopped paying his electricity bills 'in solidarity with whole of Delhi, as part of civil disobedience movmnt'.

There was a deliberate calculation behind this focus on the high costs of power and lack of water, as Kejriwal revealed to Ashutosh. 'He said that elections were not fought with the minds but with hearts. People had to fall in love with you .... He told me that in order to win elections it was important for him to create waves, many waves, one after another.'[11]

Waves of course need issues that touch the lives of regular people, but the injunction to stop paying electricity bills provoked a lot of adverse comment in the mainstream media. It was perceived as an attempt to undermine the rule of law and the fear was that economic reform could be derailed. One prominent commentator accused Kejriwal of 'seeking to go beyond reforms' under the guise of participative democracy: 'He wants to unsettle India and keep it in a state of permanent turbulence.'[12] The response in the shanty towns and middle-class colonies of Delhi, however, presented a sharp contrast to these status quoist rumblings. This move was, in fact, received with a rare exuberance and AAP could successfully mobilise nearly a million people through its constant tweeting and hosting of special 'signature' camps to support a petition stating that they would stop paying their dues to power companies. The campaign, cast as a non-cooperation movement/civil disobedience movement, sought to conflate in the popular mind the non-payment of utility bills with the national struggle for independence.

To build on this popular connect, other communication tools, from street theatre to pamphlets and posters, were also deployed. An essay written by Kejriwal on direct democracy, published in 2012 in the form of a book under the title *Swaraj*, proved popular with the reading public. One of the ideas he had expounded upon in this slim volume was that of mohalla sabhas, or local neighbourhood bodies taking decisions for their respective neighbourhoods through a process of community discussion. It was an untried idea, but the attempt was to project it as a blueprint for change. Many discussions were organised around it, including in prestigious institutions like the Indian Institution of Technology, Delhi.

The party's most potent strategy to counter mainstream media's hostility and indifference was, without doubt, the systematic use of social media, an approach that had brought in demonstrable results during the IAC protests in 2011. An AAP volunteer was quoted as saying, 'I think technology has been our savior.'[13] But technology without groundwork could not have delivered results. AAP's strategising ensured that the use of communication technologies was twinned to activity on the ground. For instance, Thunderclap, an app designed to amplify conversations within the cyber community, which helped AAP reach an estimated 3.5 million just before polling began, would have proved ineffectual without the careful coordination of user response. It was the synchrony between online and offline activities that multiplied the impact of both.

Through steps similar to those undertaken during the heady IAC protest days, AAP built its public identity through internet and social media tools. Its multilingual and accessible website—the nerve centre of all its digital activity—profiled the party by spelling out its ideology, showcasing its constitution and election manifesto, and explaining how its internal complaints committee functioned. The website had a video link and a section for blogging, and allowed its supporters to send donations and access transcripts of speeches made on AAP platforms and information on party events.

While the website remained the unifying platform, other resources like YouTube, Facebook, Twitter, and Google Plus were used to build a distinct identity for the party and the leader from the moment the party was formed. The speech Kejriwal made on the day the party was launched was uploaded on all its social media platforms and received thousands of supportive responses. One even anticipated the future: 'I am requesting delhi people to vote aam aadmi party, because the future of india is on you, aam aadmi party must win, to spread the party all over india ....'

The party as well as its leaders had separate Facebook pages, but interesting to note was how the AAP Facebook community worked to amplify, even glorify, the party message. By early 2013, there were at least twenty-five Facebook pages projecting Kejriwal as the country's future prime minister, with one of them, 'We Want Arvind Kejriwal as Indian PM', having attracted 24,661 likes.[14] This particular page had come up in late 2012 and had helped to iconise Kejriwal within the IAC community. A post of 6 October 2012 on this page defended Kejriwal's right to protest by going on hunger strike, berating many 'paid news channels' for questioning his methods. It compared him to Gandhi, a comparison that had, up to this point, only been made with regard to Hazare. The post ended with the line: 'If AK is a criminal, then our beloved Bapu was the biggest criminal by the logic of such people.'

Ever since its inception and up to the 2013 election, AAP used its website, Facebook, and Twitter accounts in distinctly differing ways to carve out a political space, but the website emerged as a platform for the party to talk to itself. The first challenge was to build a disciplined cadre within a party composed largely of disparate individuals who were often strangers to each other, and who now needed to bond together as a political formation. Regulatory tweets to volunteers often went out from the leadership, like this one from Kejriwal on 19 May 2013: 'I strongly condemn the foul language by some on Twitter. They cannot be AAP volunteers and could be impersonating.'

More complex than building a cadre within was the task of building a cadre without—the imagined community of AAP supporters. The party website, which facilitated donations to the party or allowed browsers to access videos of speeches and network with volunteers, helped immeasurably in achieving this. The effort constantly was to invest any involvement with the party as synonymous with nation-building. This lofty aim proved subsequently to be a source of embarrassment for the party, as we shall see. In the early days, however, donating money was about furthering the fight against corruption, and signing up for an internship meant the promise of being a part of the Kejriwal team to 'help bring clean governance in the country'.

Invocations of AAP as the 'hope for the future' were also projected systematically. The first public meeting in Roha, Maharashtra, in December 2012, for instance, was presented as evidence that 'AAP is the only hope' in a situation where people despaired over the credibility of all political parties. The party's special anthem, 'Main Hoon Aam Aadmi', worked on the same sentiment. The first message put out by the party on 1 January 2013 captured a sense of optimism by cleverly playing on the word 'aap' in the line: '"Delhi Hogi AAP Ki"—Delhi will be yours, come let us give our country a better future.'

This imagined community of party supporters was not circumscribed by bureaucratic norms of affiliation. The invitation to attend the party's founding meeting in November 2012, put out as a Facebook post, promised that every person attending it could register himself/herself as a founder member of the party. Similarly, the party attempted to transcend limitations of location, as implied in a post put out in May 2013 stating that Non-resident Indian in twenty US cities had extended support to AAP.

If this strategy recalled that of the IAC campaign, so too did the consistent foregrounding of the theme of corruption in the social media messaging. In the early days of the party, there were many frontal attacks on a corrupt corporate India. A press release, put out by the party in early December 2012, was uploaded as a Facebook post of 9 December: '"A few days ago, I exposed that Anil and Mukesh Ambani have Swiss bank accounts. They have not admitted their fraud. I have the Swiss bank account numbers of Anil and Mukesh Ambani here with me. Shall I read them?" Arvind Kejriwal asked a packed hall at the Times of India Literary Carnival on Sunday.'

This commitment to deliver graft-free politics was made over and over again, especially as AAP got into election mode. By June 2013, six months before the elections, Kejriwal was reiterating this foundational principle in a tweet: 'We will walk the talk. There wud be absolutely no compromise against corruption.' And then again: 'Laloo made crores in fodder scam. But no order for recovery of that money. Just 25 lakh fine and few years in jail. A sweet deal.' Anti-corruption and the promise of a Lokpal law remained arguably AAP's single most important ideological thrust in this period, inherent in the much retweeted line: 'Hum chunav ladenge, jeetenge, aur khud apna Lokpal Bill laayenge' (we will fight, win and ourselves bring in our own Lokpal Bill). Some image-building was also called for, as Gandhi notes: 'We had to build his image as an angry young man, willing to do whatever it took to defeat "evil".'[15]

AAP's preparations for the first election battle it had ever faced had a significant social media component, given the tepid treatment meted out by mainstream media, but its real success lay in having successfully got its 'online team to "act" offline'.[16] The first significant politically invested stance it took was in late 2012, when it seized the Delhi gang rape moment to both network with the civil society groups and individuals involved in those mobilisations as well as to expose the Congress government in power in Delhi. On 29 December 2012, a photograph of Arvind Kejriwal sitting on dharna to protest the gang rape on its Facebook page had the following caption: 'Aam Aadmi Party members sitting silently at Jantar Mantar for peaceful protest'. But AAP was also careful not to be seen to be co-opting the protests for its own purposes.

Shazia Ilmi was one of those IAC activists who chose to go with Kejriwal. She was important, not only for her powers of articulation as a former television anchor, but also as an AAP spokesperson who could emphasise the 'feminist angle', as an AAP member later recalled.[17] Ever since the Delhi gang rape protests, it was clear that women's security was going to be a big issue in Indian politics. Kejriwal, through his personal tweets, almost insinuated himself into them. On 15 March 2013, he tweeted, 'During Damini's gang rape protests, people demanded fast track courts, swift n certain punishment for crime against women.' By June, his political rivals had been brought into the picture: 'Delhi women want to know in these elections "which party can provide me safety?"' He followed this up immediately with another salvo: 'Sheila Dikshit's response after each rape—"what can I do? Delhi police not in my control." Do we want such a helpless CM?' Marking its first anniversary, Kejriwal in a post made it a point to remind the people of Delhi that 'No rape case in Delhi in last one year has seen face of the court apart from the Damini incident. No concrete security measures have been taken and still most of the police personnel in Delhi are engaged in VIP security.'

The other important objective of AAP's self-communication was to expose its political rivals, whether it was Kejriwal's attack on the Congress when he tweeted in November 2012 that there was 'no place for dynastic politics in AAP', or when a Facebook post of 4 December 2012 had him demanding to know whether the Modi government in Gujarat was 'Adani's dukaan (shop)?' The tone grew more strident a few months later as the 2013 election drew closer. Actions on the ground were amplified on social media. The campaign mounted on autorickshaws, the public transport of choice for the city's lower- and middle-class resident, pitted a youthful Kejriwal labelled as 'honest' against an elderly Dikshit, labelled as 'corrupt', and its warning line—If you vote for the corrupt yet again, women will continue to be raped in Delhi—and had a long afterlife on social media chatter.

Defending the party and its volunteers when they were in trouble was yet another use to which social media was put. The beating up and detention of AAP volunteers in June 2012 provoked a series of sharply worded tweets that attacked the Sheila Dixit government and police and included photographs of the injured men. Now that the party was in poll mode, the incident was showcased for electoral advantage, with both Facebook and Twitter being used in real time. Late on the night of 19 June, Kejriwal dramatically tweeted: 'All arrested volunteers being presented before Duty Magistrate. I am reaching duty magistrate's house.'

Controlled aggression had now become the hallmark of his social media messaging. Early the following morning came another tweet: 'Jab tak iss system ko dal nahi dete aur sarkar mein baithe in gaddaron ko jail nahi pahuncha dete, hum chain ki saans nahi lenge' (so long as the system is not changed and traitors sitting in the government are not sent to jail, we will not heave a sigh of relief). It touched an immediate chord, with followers like P. ParthSarathi tweeting back: 'abstly correct sir, we hv to wipe out such rotted system through participeting more & more ppls. Salute to our volunteers.'

An unexpected challenge for the AAP came up a few days before election day when the sensational News Sarkar sting operation of 21 November 2013, showing prominent AAP representatives accepting money, was featured prominently in mainstream media and framed as an expose that 'dented AAP's fairytale in Delhi'. The first response by way of a tweet from Kejriwal on the very day this news broke reiterated AAP's commitment to fight corruption, even if its own were involved: 'Some sting operations done on our candidates .... We will not spare the guilty. We will walk the talk.' Having iterated that basic principle, a strong counter-offensive was soon in the making, with two press conferences held over two consecutive days, videos of which were put out on YouTube by an entity called 'AAP News'. The big message sent out was that the AAP representatives exposed in the sting were clean and that powerful forces were attempting to derail a party of high ideals. Kejriwal's tweet of 24 November, stating that a sum of Rs 1,400 crore had been distributed to some sections of the media in order to 'defame' the party, was then followed by a defamation suit against the portal that had conducted the sting.

A potential reversal was thus converted into a possible gain, with supporters swearing by the party. One of them mailed back:

> When I saw this sting clip I was sock and was really surprise on what is going on. But the way AAP Team handle this sting operation criticism and come up with all proof with fax and figure. I salute you guys and shows full faith in you on behalf of me and my family. The more they pull you, the more you will rise.........For Media as an Indian I don't expect this from you. Please establish your faith again in India before its too late.

SOCIAL MEDIA FOR ELECTORAL DIVIDENDS

Arguably the most consequential move was putting social media to electoral use, since it tested the extent to which they could be used by the party to build political participation in the country. AAP's approach in this regard had two broad components that were equally important: one, to communicate with its volunteers, keep them engaged, and expand their presence; and two, to reach out to, and enthuse, potential voters.

An example of the first intent was a Facebook post of 12 November:

> Delhi election are just 21 days 11 hours and 19 minutes away from us. More than 10,000 volunteers, among them more than 500 NRIs are going door to door right now. More than 21 lakh rupees have been donated today morning by 1642 people...Are you part of the change or just another spectator.

Those interested in joining up as AAP volunteers found it extremely easy to gain entrance since the entry threshold was deliberately set low. A Facebook post of 1 December 2013—three days before polling day—was rife with encouragement: 'Today let us proudly wear our topis and spread the message of AAP....'. Volunteers were to come to any one of the ten metro hubs indicated that was closest to them, meet up with an AAP representative, collect their campaign material, and get assigned to one of the selected forty-seven 'buzz locations' in the area to spread the message of AAP. Common slogans like 'Is baar chelegi jhadu (the broom will work this time)' or 'Is baar ek mauka bhrastachar mukt Dilli ke liye', 'Aap ka ek vote badlega Dilli' could also be downloaded. Getting new volunteers to perform functions that only tried and tested party members would have conducted in more established parties helped AAP to build a visible presence that would have taken many years to achieve in an earlier era. It was also true that volunteers signing up in such a virtual way could hardly be characterised as a stable category, with many coming and going. A core, however, remained and was eventually absorbed within the party.

Coming to the second, equally important, component of the social media election strategy—building a direct bridge with potential voters—many, touched by the Kejriwal message of clean, responsive politics, would eventually self-define themselves as AAP supporters and go on to vote for the party, but this required the seeding of minds with the idea that AAP was a credible political force. Fund-raising campaigns helped to infuse an amorphous political entity with some substance, and catchy slogans like 'Hit a Century for India: Donate Rs 101' were aimed at people who could come in at a low cost to themselves. Information that the party was rapidly gaining support across the country was also put out through tweets like, 'AK in Bangalore on 27th for launch of Aam Aadmi Party—Karnataka'. The results of a poll commissioned by the party, which indicated that 47 per cent of Delhiites wished to give AAP a chance, was widely circulated in the social media and even made their way into newspapers.

By October, the party was election ready with Kejriwal, in what was by now the trademark AAP topi, appealing for votes all over social media. Helping in the effort to convince voters of the rightness of his political cause was an array of cultural personalities who appeal to the youth in particular, like the popular Roadies host Rajiv Laxman, who personally campaigned for the party, wearing AAP topis and waving brooms.

The party took many measures to appear transparent and open, qualities that became less evident after AAP tasted power. New entrants to the party and candidates standing for the election were formally introduced, both on Facebook pages and on YouTube. Ideas for the party manifesto were sought from the public, with a tweet being sent out: 'Have you contributed to #AAP ki Manifesto?' A month before election day, the party's main manifesto was placed in the public domain. It was based, it was averred, not on empty pledges and false promises, but on 'sach ki rajneeti, swaraj ka sankalp' (true politics, the promise of swaraj). What was particularly innovative was the idea of coming up with separate manifestos for each of the seventy constituencies of Delhi, as also separate Facebook pages.

By the time elections were announced, the AAP's twittersphere was alive with calls to close ranks. Supporters were encouraged to keep in touch with the party through cyber platforms and Kejriwal underlined this with his personal message. In Hindi, his tweet read, '*Aap apni party se har samay sampark mein rahe sakte hain. Aam Admi Party ka sandesh logo tak pahunchne mein sahyita karein* (you can stay in touch with your party at all times. Help in taking the AAP's message to the people)'. All his tweets at this point were aimed at making people take ownership of the party and feel positive about themselves as good citizens. On 3 December, he tweeted, 'Delhi Assembly election has already turned into a people's movement. This time, people themselves are fighting elections ....' On the next day, which was voting day, he beseeched them on Twitter early in the morning to 'Vote for any party but do go out and vote'. This injunction to be the good citizen and vote was a strategy that Narendra Modi was to use to good effect during the 2014 general election.

The head of AAP's IT team, Ankit Lal, later claimed that altogether about 60,000 tweets were sent out with pro-AAP hashtags, peaking on voting day—4 December—with 24,000 tweets.[18] However, it was not just the number of tweets sent out that was important ultimately, but their ability to achieve an online-offline dynamic and get people to embrace the party's quest for power. The projection sought to be made was that AAP voters constituted a moral force in and of themselves. On 2 December, Kejriwal tweeted, '*Paise aur daru dekar vote na lenge na hi lene deyenge*' (vote cannot be bought through money and liquor, nor will we allow it to be bought). A day later, on the eve of voting day, his tweet went: 'Delhi Assembly election has already turned into a people's movement. This time, people themselves are fighting elections.'

The turnout of 67 per cent of the Delhi electorate—over 10 per cent higher than the last election in 2008—was attributed to the AAP factor and its promise of a new kind of politics in a state which had hitherto seen bi-polar contests between the Congress and the BJP.

AAP successfully projected itself as a force that would cleanse Indian politics, and not just that of Delhi, and do this by getting people to vote for themselves by voting for the AAP. By winning twenty-eight seats, it conclusively defeated the Congress, a party which had ruled Delhi for fifteen years, but which could only manage eight seats this time. Significantly, Kejriwal could convincingly defeat Chief Minister Sheila Dixit in her own constituency of New Delhi. The AAP also gave chase to the favourites, the BJP, which had won thirty-two seats, but still found power eluding it. Ultimately, with outside support from the Congress, the party ruled Delhi for forty-nine days.

Mainstream media, which had projected just a few seats for AAP, were now forced to take the new party more seriously. One of the first commentators to mark this shift was a prominent newspaper columnist, who observed that 'Aam Aadmi Party's absolutely spectacular political debut is a reminder that India's progressive moment is ripe for being seized through political creativity and imagination.'[19] AAP leader Ashutosh later noted:

> Arvind was hailed as a game changer, a messiah, the one who could stop the Modi juggernaut. The 175-year-old newspaper, The Times of India, had a headline that screamed 'AAP success in Delhi is a political revolution of epic proportions'. This was an unprecedented and historic statement by the press which had never ever commended a political party quite so openly, not even during the JP movement.[20]

Such coverage irked Kejriwal's political critics within mainstream media considerably, prompting one who was sympathetic to the BJP to remark caustically that 'the editorial classes discovered a new messiah in the Aam Aadmi Party leader, Arvind Kejriwal'.[21]

FORTY-NINE DAYS IN POWER

However, it was not long before mainstream media disenchantment over AAP surfaced once again and a great deal of hostile messaging circulated on social media too. This first stint in power was also a period of continuous public scrutiny, all the more because the party and its now iconic leader were anxious to demonstrate, to supporter and detractor alike, a new paradigm for the exercise of power. Even as the party succumbed to the seduction of ruling Delhi by entering into a coalition deal with the Congress—something its leader had once sworn would never happen—it fell back on its own powers of self-communication to try and neutralise the criticism. An online public referendum over whether AAP should take Congress support was an example of this. The verdict apparently was strongly in support of the party going ahead with this arrangement. So AAP did go ahead, inviting 'everybody' to attend Kejriwal's swearing-in ceremony at Ramlila Maidan, with the man himself choosing to take the *aam* Metro to the event. On 29 December 2013, he tweeted: 'Many people asking me for passes for tomo's oath ceremony. No passes needed. All are welcome. Its ur prog. My family will also sit in public.'

This politics of mediatised spectacle was to mark AAP's forty-nine days in power. What became clearer in this early phase of its first government in Delhi was that the party had, to a large extent, become Kejriwal; and Kejriwal, the party. The faultline between him and senior members of the party like Prashant Bhushan was already apparent in the manner in which he publicly disassociated himself from the latter's position on the need to repeal the Armed Forces (Special Powers) Act in Kashmir, stating that it did not have party consensus. The singularity of the Kejriwal appeal was enhanced by his social media messaging, which sought to perceive Delhiites as an extension of his persona. Remarking on a Kejriwal tweet shortly after his swearing-in—'Running 102 fever since yesterday. Severe loose motions. Sad that i won't be able to attend office today'—a commentator noted that 'his Twitter followers found themselves on a whole new level of familiarity with their leader'.[22]

In fact, throughout his forty-nine days of rule, Kejriwal's physical persona constantly coloured his political persona. It included a persistent cough that had by now become his trademark. The projection was that of a frail body combined with an iron will; a tenacity of purpose to go ahead with the agenda, even if it meant braving a cold winter night in the open, despite diabetes and an asthmatic condition. The image sought to be conveyed was of an abstemious, power-shunning, people-friendly chief minister, who always did what was required of him for the greater good. His own blue Wagon R was pitted against the white Qualises and Innovas of the Delhi power circuit, and his preference for modest accommodation juxtaposed with the large colonial-era bungalow that his predecessor in power had once occupied.

But living up to these ideals proved a challenge. Every time he and his party wavered from the norms they had set for themselves, the mainstream media, and social media in synchrony, were quick with critical reports, analyses, and accusations of forgotten ideals. In its report of 3 January 2014, the ABP television network pointedly noted: 'AAP ministers who vowed not to use government vehicles to state assembly before winning the floor test have now been issued Innova cars. So no more travelling in autos. Interesting to watch what CM Arvind Kejriwal has to say on this move.' Kejriwal tried to clarify his position through a tweet the following day, '... and we never ever said that we won't use govt transprt. We said we won't use lal battis. And we stand by that.' A similar script played out over the chief minister's home. Having struck a public stance of refusing a government bungalow, a storm of cynical comments within mainstream and social media followed when he seemed inclined to accept a five-bedroom duplex in Lutyens Delhi. Newspapers, television channels, and influential corporate voices were also disapproving of the culture of 'freebies' that Kejriwal was said to be encouraging with his decision to go ahead and implement his election promise of providing 700 litres of free water to poor households. A newspaper reported that 'many dismissed as impractical and unworkable Kejriwal's decision to provide 700 liters of free water and halve electricity tariffs to Delhi's residents soon after coming to power. The main worry was: Can the state exchequer, already burdened by subsidies, afford a higher dole out?'[23]

There were also the unintended consequences of certain decisions and actions boomeranging on the party and inviting media scorn. The 'Janata Darbar', an event organised by the party that invited people to voice their grievances, and which was designed to once again showcase its charismatic leader, attracted such large numbers that it quickly descended into chaos and the chief minister himself was forced to hastily leave the venue. A similar incident of over-reach was the raid conducted by an AAP MLA, Somnath Bharati, over an alleged 'drug and sex scandal' targeting African nationals in the south Delhi locality, Khirki Extension, which was justifiably labelled as racist, anti-women, and high-handed. It was that particular episode, according to Ashutosh, that turned the tide of media coverage: 'In a complete volte-face the whole ambience changed dramatically when Bharti occupied the headlines. The media which had been singing paeans to the party became critical, then hostile.'[24]

Looking back on those forty-nine days of AAP rule, one can see that the politics of spectacle which had stood Kejriwal in good stead throughout 2013 seemed to fail him once he came to power. One charge—first raised by the BJP and amplified by the media and other opposition parties—which gained salience with the public was that Kejriwal was essentially a time server, who went back on his pledges. Kejriwal's decision to accept Congress support to form the government, even after he had sworn on his children that he would do no such thing, was the initial basis for the 'U-turn Kejriwal' jibe. The party found it difficult to counter this even in the social media space where it had a substantial presence. Typical of such attacks that resonated with the youthful chatterati was a Twitter attack hashtagged #YoKejriwalSoHonest. A 13 January tweet went: '#YoKejriwalSoHonest that in delhi all "U-Turn" boards are being replaced by "Kejriwal-Turn"'.

The more the chief minister tried to demonstrate his commitment to delivering on the poll promises made to the people of Delhi, the greater were the attacks on him. Well-publicised run-ins with the lieutenant governor and protests against the high-handedness of the police force brought little of the popular sympathy he had garnered during his two-week fast in March 2013. On the contrary, his defiance of police orders by threatening a ten-day protest against the alleged police repression of his MLAs during the Khirki Extension raid, even as the Republic Day preparations were in progress in New Delhi, could have lost him some of the middle-class support that had helped him come to power. Even the demand raised by AAP for the granting of full statehood to Delhi proved to be a damp squib.

What must have weighed the most on Kejriwal, sensitive as he was to public opinion, was the apparent dissipation of the anti-corruption crusade—the very *raison d'etre* for AAP's existence—despite exhortations to people to use their mobile phones and conduct sting operations against corrupt officials and the like. This was a dangerous portent for a leader who nursed ambitions to see his party emerge as a national alternative to the BJP after the General Election of May 2014. This factor may well have forced his hand to introduce the much promised Jan Lokpal Bill in the assembly, a few days after his government's anti-corruption wing had registered a case against Reliance Industries' Mukesh Ambani and Veerappa Moily, Union petroleum minister, for colluding to deliver a windfall to the former's company by doubling natural gas prices.

Having staked the continuation of his government on the bill being passed, Kejriwal was left with little option but to resign when it was blocked by the Congress and the BJP acting in unison. Hostile responses to the move reflected the general mood of cynicism towards AAP and Kejriwal at that point. Whether such cynicism was created by political interests or was a spontaneous popular response remains a matter of conjecture, but the tweets against him were unforgiving. One tweet—responding to Kejriwal's earlier tweet claiming the high moral ground by saying that he was prepared to sacrifice the chief minister's chair 100 times to remove corruption from the country—went: 'PM ki kursi ke liye CM ki kursi 100 baar kurbaan (to gain the prime minister's chair, willing to sacrifice the chief minister's chair a hundred times).'

POLITICAL WILDERNESS

The span of a full year between Kejriwal's resignation as the chief minister of Delhi on 14 February 2014 and his return as Delhi's chief minister on 14 February 2015 was a period of great uncertainty. That the AAP could manage only four seats in the General Election of 2014 came as a shock for a party that had begun to believe it had the goodwill of the people, a perception that its supporters on social media had consistently built up. One such message of support, prominently displayed on the AAP website, went: 'Sir, please contest all seat because we want arvind sir our pm, we have no patient for next five year.'

As things worked out, the plan to contest 434 seats came a spectacular cropper. The mainstream media, caught up in reflecting the euphoria of the BJP's massive victory in May 2014, did spare some space for reporting on AAP amidst the ruins of its defeat: 'His party is bleeding volunteers across the country .... The party is losing money—public contributions to the party coffers have shrunk from a peak of Rs 30 lakh a day in April to a few thousand rupees daily in June.'[25]

Criticism of what was termed as the party's abrupt desertion of its responsibilities as the elected government of Delhi was articulated at media fora throughout 2014. The fact that Kejriwal had once proudly declared himself an anarchist came to haunt him now; it was turned into a label of vilification by his political opponents during the 2015 election campaign to the Delhi assembly.

The loss of public support to the party also translated into a loss of personal support to Kejriwal from within the party. As prominent leaders like Shazia Ilmi left the party, inner party dissidence surfaced, with senior leaders Yogendra Yadav and Prashant Bhushan raising questions about party decisions and criticising the centralisation of authority in the figure of Kejriwal, an echo of the sentiments Vinod Kumar Binny had raised earlier that year and which had led to the latter's expulsion. These dissensions also played out in the media and included an angry exchange of letters between Yogendra Yadav and Kejriwal loyalist, Manish Sisodia. As Ashutosh puts it, 'The press revels in such feuds and political letters like those of Yogendra and Manish make good copy .... The two letters became points of animated discussion nationwide.'[26]

These reversals notwithstanding, it was not long before Kejriwal was strategising on his return to power. To counter the negative media campaign against him, he issued a press release on 21 May—four days after the General Election results were announced—saying that his party planned to hold meetings all over Delhi to take its apology to the people and 'begin preparations for seeking a fresh mandate to resume the relief of cheap electricity and free water to the people, apart from providing a corruption-free administration'.[27]

One of his first moves was to build an alternative core team within the party. Neither Yogendra Yadav nor Prashant Bhushan was included; instead, two former journalists, Ashutosh and Ashish Khetan, were inducted. The choice of the new entrants underlined the emphasis that Kejriwal had always placed on mainstream media and the need to counter their hostile coverage by having persons skilled in the currency of their use. By August 2014, three months after AAP's ignominious electoral showing in the general elections, Kejriwal was defending with redoubled passion his record as chief minister in bringing down power and water bills and fighting corruption, even while expressing public regret for having resigned from his chief ministerial post prematurely. His appetite to take on the BJP was on full display. At a public rally, he dared the BJP to get the Delhi lieutenant governor to dissolve the assembly so that elections could be held in the national capital, 'BJP is talking about polls in Haryana and Maharashtra; why is it scared of elections in Delhi?'[28]

The game of brinkmanship over government formation between the BJP and AAP sparked off a great deal of media speculation. In September, after Lieutenant Governor Naseeb Jung invited the BJP to form a government in Delhi, Kejriwal turned up at his door with a CD that charged the BJP of trying to 'buy' an AAP MLA in order to get the numbers to rule the state. The move demonstrated that he had not lost his skill of using social media to keep himself politically relevant. On 11 September, he tweeted: 'We have sent a copy of sting CD to Hon'ble president also.' What was interesting about the responses to it was the trolling that marked them. One tweet went: 'President has a "spam" folder for any docs from Arvind Kejriwal he know he is the king of spamming.' Others included: 'Send one copy to NASA, they will send to Mars' and 'Pata nahin, this guy seems to have a CD factory somewhere'.

Hostile tweets of this kind indicated that the support AAP and Kejriwal had once enjoyed on social media had eroded considerably, for two primary reasons. One was the resurgence of the BJP, which of course had cultivated considerable social media support over time with the iconisation of Narendra Modi after the emphatic general election win in May, followed by BJP victories in the three states of Maharashtra, Haryana, and Jharkhand. The second factor was the negative perception that had now come to be attached to AAP and Kejriwal after their brief brush with power.

PREPARING FOR THE 2015 ELECTIONS

When Lieutenant Governor Najeeb Jung finally dissolved the assembly after a year of President's Rule—the longest span possible under constitutional requirements—the question was: Would AAP be able to win over Delhiites yet again? The mainstream media did not seem to think so. While Kejriwal continued to be burdened with the label of 'anarchist', the Modi mania continued to mark mainstream media coverage. A senior television anchor and newspaper commentator, looking back at the coverage after the AAP win of 2015, concluded that mainstream media had been less than fair in its treatment of the party, with some channels even blanking him and his party out by ensuring that AAP leaders were not called for studio discussions. 'This was "supari" journalism at its worst. By contrast, when Modi entered the Delhi campaign fray with a rally at Ramlila Maidan in January, most channels devoted 24 x7 coverage to the "event". Modi was clearly still box office; Kejriwal was not.'[29]

Given this scenario, we would have to look beyond mainstream media support to discern the resources that helped AAP re-emerge victorious in February 2015. Four factors seemed to have played a decisive role. The first, of course, was AAP's adoption of a clear strategy. Anand Kumar, a member of the AAP executive before he quit the party in mid-2015, recalled how the media had at that point kept reporting that the middle class had deserted the party. This persuaded the leadership to course correct.

> We were all born of the Anna movement. The attitude of disobedience was ingrained in us. The 'sab neta chor hain, sab media chor hain' (all politicians are crooks, everybody in media are crooks) attitude. We saw it as the Lal Batti versus Others. We now felt we had to get out of that approach, rebuild ourselves and re-define the terms of discourse in very conscious, very specific terms. We created the first

> women's forum with links in every ward. Every ward had a committee. Although most of us were 40 plus, we felt we had to reach out to the youth. We had to make young activists feel wanted. We had to start communicating again with people and we began with the bright faced, smiling image of Arvind Kejriwal. Our communication strategies were both vertical and horizontal. We didn't allow it to be anti-rich and pro-poor, we wanted to appear a rainbow coalition.[30]

Kejriwal used mainstream media to convey his intention to win Delhi back again and counter the now popular term used to describe him—'*bhagoda*' (deserter), which even had its own Facebook page. 'We will go among the people, will hold various meetings in Delhi in the coming days. We will apologize to people of Delhi in meetings and gain their trust to ask them to support us with complete majority.'[31] The strategies that had worked for the party in 2013 were now re-tuned and expanded, including the crucial ones of creating a reliable database and choosing candidates early, giving them the space and time to build a personal rapport with constituencies.

Expanding the party's volunteer base was the second big factor. At its peak, AAP was said to have had 1.25 lakh party workers[32] working in many capacities, from publicising rallies and speeches to booth management. As was the case during the 2013 campaign, many of these volunteers were powerful persuaders because they came from the local communities themselves, and appeared to own the party and its campaign. They could also effortlessly seize the opportunity when it presented itself. When Prime Minister Modi's Swachh Bharat scheme took off on 2 October 2014, nearly 11,000 AAP volunteers came out on the streets to clean Delhi, and thus managed to take away some of the credit for the initiative from Modi's party.

Apart from general volunteers, there were those who offered important professional assistance, and this was the third decisive factor. Political analyst Saba Naqvi, in her book *Capital Conquest*, termed this phenomenon 'the power of the 26-year-olds',[33] because many of these individuals were qualified technocrats who made good money in the private sector, but gave freely of their time to the AAP cause. She saw their presence as one of the secrets of AAP's success. As qualified technocrats, they improvised and innovated to expand the party's appeal, even under daunting circumstances. For instance, one of them, having worked with Google Maps, used his expertise to locate areas in Delhi that were the most densely populated for campaign strategising. They also helped to neutralise BJP's election campaign on radio, which had targeted Kejriwal for having deserted Delhi. One BJP radio spot had an elderly female voice complaining bitterly about how her trust was betrayed by Kejriwal because of his premature resignation. Before long an AAP radio ad effectively countered that charge. It featured Kejriwal assuring 'mataji' (the lady in question) that he would ensure that her trust in him was rebuilt.

These 'experts' not only understood the social vocabulary of the aspirational middle class, especially the youth, but also projected a credible alternative model of doing politics by drawing from a broad spectrum of cultural resources, from sophisticated advertising campaigns to street theatre. According to one analyst, this 'effective customisation of strategies used by the left to suit a wider demographic which stretches from the urban middle class to the poor, working class and slum population has helped them (AAP) gain popularity among all these sections.'[34]

The fourth, and very crucial, factor was AAP and Kejriwal's ability to deploy social media for self-communication, much like they had done in 2013, only this time using a wider range of communication technologies. Every social media platform available was exploited in 2015, including WhatsApp and Instagram, which were not in wide use in the earlier campaign. While Facebook and Twitter continued to remain the backbone of their social media campaign, subtle changes were introduced in the way they were used, with a lot more deployment of video content.

A close look at AAP's use of Twitter in 2015 reveals that one of the main aims the party and its leader set for themselves was to *redefine* AAP's identity in order to present it as a responsible political party and dispel the impression that it may prematurely resign and renege on its election pledges if voted to power yet again. At least six weeks before the election date of 7 February 2015 was announced, AAP had decided on its new tagline, 'Paanch saal, Kejriwal' (five years of Kejriwal), which underlined its commitment to serve a full term. The slogan was publicised through hashtags #5SaalKejriwal and #KejriwalFirSe. To further the message, the party tweeted on 24 December: '5 Saal Kejriwal Is Not A Slogan—It's A Pledge For "Good & Corruption Free Governance"'.

This also meant redefining the Kejriwal persona. Every attempt to target him, whether through vituperative advertisements or barbs about being an anarchist and Naxalite, voiced by Narendra Modi in his election speeches, were exploited to fashion the counter-narrative. One Kejriwal tweet targeted the prime minister directly for his attempts to stigmatise him: 'Whl promotng BJP in Delhi, Modi shd knw tht he is PM of India. Didn't expect ds kind of derogatory speech just 4 d sake of votes.' Similarly, the early negative references to the 'common man's muffler' that Arvind Kejriwal sported were now used to create the 'Mufflerman' icon, which implied that an ordinary person can do extraordinary things. 'Arvind was presented as a smiling, positive leader rather than a livid one.'[35]

Videos of Kejriwal's rallies and interviews figured prominently on the AAP website and Facebook page. Now they were also tweeted widely, with continuous effort being made to rid him of the old allegations that his political rivals kept resurrecting. A video posted on its Facebook page of 23 January asked: Kya Arvind Kejriwal satta ke lalchi hain? Kya Arvind Kejriwal ne Dilli ki kursi pradhan mantra banana ke liye chodi thi? (Is it true that Arvind Kejriwal is hungry for power? Is it true that he left his chief ministerial chair because he wanted to be prime minister?). It went on to say: Arvind ne een sab sawalon ke jawab diye, video jaroor dekhiye aur share kare (Arvind answers these questions in this video. Please do watch it and share it).

Adding a certain *joie de vivre* to the campaign was the 'Paanch saal, Kejriwal' ditty, composed by Bollywood music composer

Vishal Dadlani. The words that went, 'Arrey poori bahumat deke toh dekho, aam aadmi ki taakat dekho (oh, give full majority this time, see the power of the common man)', emerged as the unofficial anthem of the campaign, played at rallies and election meetings, used as background music for flash mob dancing by students, and shared innumerable times on social media platforms. It was posted on AAP's Facebook page of 3 January 2015 and on YouTube as a short video, with the caption, 'Jangpura Candidate Praveen Deshmukh at Lajpat Nagar Market singing #5SaalKejriwal'. The post went on to say: 'AAP is blessed to have such amazing volunteers. Do watch and share!'

Another important aim was to project the party as a caring, transparent, responsible, and democratic entity. A Facebook post of 12 January 2015 urged friends to 'Be Our Media' by retweeting and sharing videos put out by the party: 'Aam Aadmi Party has very limited funds to promote our campaigns. Help us spread the word of clean politics.' The video that accompanied this post showed a young Delhi woman seeking an education loan and producing a copy of the AAP pledge to provide good education when asked by the bank manager to produce proof of surety. On Republic Day 2015, a post focused on how the party was committed to ensuring the 'best health-services to the people of Delhi', and again a short video outlined its plans on achieving this outcome.

On the day before Prime Minister Narendra Modi was to make his first poll appearance during the Abhinandan rally of 11 January 2015, held a day before the ECI was to announce the date of the election, AAP was already putting its agenda on the table by using a new hashtag, #DelhiAsksPMModi, designed as a platform for ordinary voters to express their thoughts on current affairs. One tweet under this hashtag went: 'PM addressing Delhi tomorrow for the 1st time. What are your expectations from him tomorrow? Tweet with #DelhiAsksPMModi and we will RT!' RT, incidentally, means re-tweet, and AAP volunteers proved to be indefatigable at re-tweeting all the favourable material that came their way, from supportive tweets to favourable newspaper and television content.

Any information that showed the Centre in a bad light was grist to the AAP social media mill. For instance, when *The Times of India* put out a story on how vegetables prices in Delhi were skyrocketing, it was retweeted immediately with the words, 'Despite Modi Magic, Veggie, fruit prices soar by up to 100%'. Or when the anchor on Times Now channel—not a particular favourite with AAP—rubbished the idea of Kiran Bedi as BJP's chief ministerial candidate, a Facebook post promptly carried a video of the show, with the line 'Do not miss the answers from BJP's representative ...'.

The BJP had not bothered to come out with a manifesto, and this was not lost on AAP. Kejriwal drove this point home in a tweet on 31 January: 'Our manifesto is like Gita to us, like Bible; this is holy for us'. By 5 February, the party's pledges and promises—ranging from 'Revive the Yamuna No encroachments and construction banned' to 'Free ambulance across Delhi for the needy people' and 'Bus Marshals on every bus. Zero tolerance agnst molestation, eve teasing & violence agnst women'—were being tweeted and posted on Facebook. AAP's call for electoral support was always framed in nationalist terms, drawing responses such as one from AAP supporter Uma Singha, steeped in patriotic hues. It went: 'Sabhi deshbhakton se appeal ... bhavishya mein mombati utane se behtar hain aaj jhadu utha liye jaye' (calling all patriots ... it is better to raise the broom now than have to light candles in the future).

Tweets were also aimed to connect with the voter on a range of events and issues. Two days after the Delhi election date was announced, the party was tweeting about a cultural event it had organised, labelled the 'Dance for Democracy'. Its Facebook page invited people 'from all age groups and all areas in Delhi-NCR to be a part of the most sensational Flash Mob campaign ever'. Very thoughtful was the line that followed, 'Don't worry if you are not a dancer, our volunteer teachers will teach you.' Those interested were asked to respond to a WhatsApp number.

The anxiety that the election could be rigged was an issue that exercised many voters and AAP played on this sentiment with panache, expressing its fear that the BJP might try to steal the election. A Kejriwal tweet of 3 February voiced this apprehension clearly: 'Large scale EVM tampering? Yest, during inspection of EVMs in Del cant, in 4 machines, whatever button u pressed, light against BJP lit.' Its Facebook post of the same day took the topic further. Many among AAP's supporters were convinced of this possibility, with one tweeting: 'BE WARNED I have been saying this for the last few months. BJP may have already made arrangements for tampering, rigging the EVMs the booth officers machine connected to the EVMs, and also hacking of EVM from a distance.'

There were many occasions when AAP took to Twitter to respond to attacks, such as accusations of financial impropriety and the like. Four days before the campaigning was to end, on 3 February, a money-laundering charge against the party was brought in by AAP Volunteer Action Manch (AVAM)—a group claiming to be a breakaway faction of the party. Its allegation that AAP had received four donations of Rs 50 lakh each from 'dubious companies' was given back-to-back coverage by TV channels and newspapers. Twitter was used with great care by AAP in a three-pronged response: one, it denied the allegation and attacked the Union finance minister for giving credibility to it; two, it brought in an AAP donor, Jaskirat Mann, to expose the hollowness of the AVAM claim; and three, it highlighted Kejriwal's own 'spotless' image of personal integrity.

By the next day the twittersphere was a noisy space. While Malwinder25 tweeted, 'If this AVAM drama was BJP's ace card ... then guys, u hav totally failed ...', someone going by the name of Chris put out the line, 'FM Jaitley "knows" AAP used fake companies to fund with BlackMoney thru Hawala, but he doesn't order probe. Is the FM endorsing these crimes', while one Sanjeev Goyal came up with the line, 'Dear Arun jatily ji u want to know the details of a company for a political party. Are u really FM of India?' All three tweets were hashtagged JawabDoAVAM. Meanwhile, Vikramadhiman was tweeting, 'BREAKING! Jaskirat Mann traced by @ndtv—says her transaction of 50 lakh rupees to #AAP was white & from Axis Bank & not Canadian dollars.'

With #hawala at midnight and #AAP funding scam becoming the top two Twitter trends, it was time to defend Kejriwal's personal integrity. Supporters chipped in with messages like, 'U can't even Dream of Honesty that @ArvindKejriwal possesses ... Dares to Arrest if Faulty', and 'BJP preaching about political funding is like a carnivore preaching about vegetarianism'. Many of these tweets were retweeted, with AAP leader Mayank Gandhi's statement—'Dirty tricks, masterstrokes, 120 MPs, entire cabinet, big money, Modi rallies—nothing working. The people of Delhi hv made up their minds'—being retweeted hundreds of times.

Responses to political rivals too were invariably couched in tweets, some of them extremely nuanced. In Kejriwal's Twitter face-offs with his direct rival, BJP's Kiran Bedi, he studiously kept away from getting personal, even congratulating Bedi on her appointment as BJP chief minister designate: '@thekiranbedi congrats 4 being nominated as BJP's CM candidate. I invite u 4 a public debate moderated by neutral person n telecast by all.' This was followed with a gentle reprimand: 'Kiranji, i used to follow u on twitter. Now, u have blocked me on twitter. Kindly unblock me.' On 2 February, there was even this tweet: 'Dear @thekiranbedi Ji Welcome to @AamAadmiParty ... please Read this Tweet again after Election.'

While most of AAP's social media messaging was directed at the outside world, a significant proportion of tweets were designed to *enthuse* the party base and keep the spirits of volunteers going. The social media wizardry of Kejriwal and AAP was arguably at its most apparent when it came to celebrating AAP's road shows and rallies or claiming a certain victory. Psephologist and party leader Yogendra Yadav—who was later made to resign a few weeks after AAP returned to power in Delhi—kept the prospects of an AAP victory within everybody's sights by tweeting his projections. His tweet on 3 February went: 'Most of the opinion polls are now reflecting what AAP's internal survey says. Delhi is all set for #AamAadmiKiSarkaar.' A Facebook post the next day echoed this confidence: 'On 7th Delhi will create History and change politics forever, in India and the world.'

When addressing the party faithful through his tweets, Kejriwal invariably adopted the tone of a benevolent elder brother. His tweet sent out on 7.51 am, 7 February, which was voting day, captured this best: 'Sab log naha dhokar aapne aapne Isha ko yaad karke vote dalne jaroor jaana :) aapki aashirwad jeet hogi (Everyone after taking a bath, praying to god, do cast your vote, you will certainly win)'. As voting came to an end, he once again made sure to express his appreciation to the voters of Delhi and the party faithful with the words: 'My sincere thnks n congratulations to all selfless volunteers of AAP, who worked round the clock for their country. AAP is bcoz of u.'

The moment of victory was particularly sweet as mainstream media entered into competitive hyperbole to capture the sheer scale of the victory—sixty-seven seats in a House of seventy—and AAP supporters could bask in a rare moment of unqualified praise from an institution that they had come to regard as hostile. The piquancy of the moment for the party lay not just in the fact that it had managed to conclusively defeat its political opponents, but that it had completely upended a hostile media narrative. Within days of the famous victory, however, evidence of the flaws in AAP's party structure and functioning came forcibly to the fore in a particularly unfortunate manner with the expulsion of AAP founder-members Yogendra Yadav and Prashant Bhushan, along with two supporters, Anand Kumar and Ajit Jha, who were subjected to obstreperous intimidation by party members. While AAP made attempts to justify what was clearly anti-democratic conduct, the episode cast a long shadow on the party and its leader in the days that followed, as reflected in a Mayank Gandhi observation, 'Tragically this unprecedented victory was a curse in disguise. In it lay the seeds of arrogance and the disintegration of the party.'[36]

SIGNIFICANCE OF THESE THREE ELECTIONS

What is argued here is that even if the majority of voters did not access social media directly in 2014, or in the elections of 2013 and 2015, they accessed them tangentially through mainstream media content, which was inevitably influenced by social media content and vice-versa. All three elections provided a template of mainstream media management combined with tech-enabled articulations and self-communication blitzkriegs. This template has been used in every election that followed, and certainly the Seventeenth Lok Sabha Elections will witness a great consolidation and refinement of the template.

There were several similarities between the three elections, including the salience of a central authority figure and the efforts to solicit the support of young voters.

Coming to the first, any highly mediatised election campaign inevitably veers towards a cult being formed around its most prominent candidate, and these polls were no exception. Both Modi and Kejriwal emerged as the central point of reference in their respective campaigns. Both men, through astute information control and perception management at the mass level, could unleash voter anxiety and voter exuberance across temporal and spatial dimensions and emerge as far bigger than their respective parties.

Both promised a dream, embodied by the IAC protests, to make India corruption free. Through its media messaging, the BJP could create the impression that by voting in Modi, India would be on the threshold of discarding the inertia of the past, and embracing a modernity that would bring in good times ('achche din'). Under the leadership of this dynamic, incorruptible change agent and guardian ('chowkidar') of the country's interests, the country's wealth, hitherto mismanaged by an incorrigibly corrupt Congress Party, would be held in trust for everyone to benefit ('Na khaunga, na khane dunga').

For the AAP, similarly, Kejriwal literally embodied the party's name by appearing as the archetypal aam aadmi figure, an extraordinarily 'ordinary person' who will solve the 'ordinary problems' of 'ordinary people' in the city-state of Delhi. Kejriwal grew in the Delhiite's imagination, rising out of an anti-corruption people's mobilisation to create a corruption-free party that 'belonged' to the people, and which could address their everyday problems. Through effective mass communication and self-communication, particularly through Twitter, Kejriwal was able to convince people on a mass scale that by voting for him, they were actually only voting for themselves. He may drive a battered blue WagonR and sport an unfashionable muffler to ward off the winter chill like ordinary Delhiites, but the kiss of power could turn him into a superman.

The image creation in these instances was open-ended and allowed the respective parties to build on the media-fashioned aura of their leaders, creating a certain intimacy between them and the electorate. Both Modi and Kejriwal, even before their formal election to power, took on national institutions in very public assertions of political will. In Varanasi, shortly before polling day on 9 May 2014, when the local administration, in consultation with the Election Commission, cancelled a BJP rally to be held at a particular site in the city because it was considered inadequate to host a mammoth crowd and barred Modi from participating in a public Ganga Pujan, he was quick to tweet his displeasure, claiming that his love for the Ganga was beyond politics. His party meanwhile demanded that the local officers be transferred for this 'biased' treatment. Kejriwal, too, projected forcefully his lack of confidence in the Election Commission's ability to conduct a free and fair election in Delhi in 2015. He repeatedly tweeted his fears of the election being stolen. Both shows of defiance worked to shore up the party bases of the respective leaders, as reflected in the tweets and retweets of supporters.

Crowd responses during public meetings and rallies were also an eloquent measure of the status of the authority figure. The repeated cries of 'Modi, Modi' and the slogan, 'Ab ki baar, Modi sarkar', in one instance, and 'Paanch saal, Kejriwal', in the other—both faithfully reported by the media—reflected the level of idolisation they now commanded. The arbitrary and controlling styles of governance that both men adopted once they were in power could be seen as the logical outcome of such heady adulation.

Commenting on Kejriwal, Srirupa Roy notes the coterie around him and the sense of central command and opacity of decision-making. 'It's all done by a tight clique of men, and personal loyalty to Kejriwal seems to matter greatly in the way the party is structured.'[37] Similar was the case with Modi, with most of the decision-making power within the party coming to be vested in him and his close confidante, party president Amit Shah. The latter's claim to such eminence was his proximity to the leader, but it was a claim reinforced by Shah's own indefatigable drive to centralise party functioning under the Modi leadership and expand the party's presence beyond its traditional bastions through what one political analyst termed as the 'Amit Shah school of election management'.[38] Communication technologies played an important role in achieving this, including the use of a toll-free number read out at rallies that would allow callers to register themselves as BJP members, a stratagem that helped the party expand its membership dramatically.

The second factor common to all three campaigns was the premium both Modi and Kejriwal placed on the young, urban voter. This approach had an unassailable logic to it, given that young people had emerged as an important demographic in mediatised election campaigns the world over. Mason points out that at the centre of the global protests of 2011 was 'a new sociological type: the graduate with no future',[39] and goes on to cite data showing that many of the regions that saw unrest in 2011 were also those with high youth unemployment levels—20 per cent in Africa, 20 per cent in Britain, and 46 per cent in Spain. The global financial crisis of 2008, he argues, had played a role in this by destroying the future prospects for an entire generation in rich and poor countries alike. Free market capitalism, which had offered unending good times to the previous generation, was no longer the genii it once promised to be, and in fact the emerging generation understood well that it was less likely to enjoy the same standards of living as their parents' generation. Other commentators have also pointed to the general consciousness of missed opportunities that marked the Arab uprisings—among a generation that had missed the boom, but was hurt by the bust.

The Indian Census of 2011 revealed that half the country's population was twenty-five years or younger, a figure strikingly similar to the demographic profile of Egypt at the time of the Tahrir Square protests. But even as we note this, it needs to be underlined that the youth in India do not lend themselves to easy comparisons with their counterparts in other countries, precisely because of the numerous variables that define them. These include factors like age, geographical and social location—including urban or rural origins, class and caste backgrounds, educational qualifications, and gender. While some among India's youth may continue in the ways of their parents, or may not have the means to do otherwise, other sections have made life choices strikingly dissimilar to those of their families or communities.[40]

The youth, in any case, do not by themselves constitute a stable social category. Craig Jeffrey, in his work focusing on the lives of Jat male college-going youth of Meerut, reveals the anxiety, ennui, and endless waiting for opportunities of advancement that marked their lives, faced as they were with high levels of unemployment and an unpredictable future. Yet, Jeffrey also emphasises that their shared experience of educational decay and unemployment provided 'political animators with a fund of populist issues—rising costs, corruption, blocked progress and harassment—that can spur students from different backgrounds into action'.[41]

Jeffrey's research dates back to 2004–05. Ten years later, the script remained much the same: the same large pools of unemployed youth; the same feeling of 'timepass'; and the endless wait for something to turn up. But what had changed significantly between 2004 and 2014 was the level of exposure to the media that marked this cohort. The youth of 2014, in addition to the mobile phones and access to the internet through internet cafes that their counterparts in 2004 probably did not have, could now create their own circles of sociality and activism through various social media sites. These were people who came into adulthood in a country where the promise of neo-liberalisation and globalisation to deliver prosperity had constantly been held out from the 1990s, but who had yet to perceive any marked difference to the material basis of their lives.

What was obvious to party strategists, whether in the BJP or AAP, was that young voters constituted a number much larger than earlier assumed, especially after revisions made to the electoral rolls. In 2014, the median age of Indians was twenty-seven. One-third of India's population was under fifteen, more than half under twenty-four; and one in every three urban Indians was between fifteen and thirty-two.[42] In Delhi, what was of particular interest to AAP was the rise in the number of first-time voters. In 2013 the figure stood at 3.49 lakh, but by 2015, another 1.72 lakh had been added. Similarly, the BJP understood well the implications of the fact that of the 810 million electorate in 2014, first-time voters in the 18–23 age group were around 120 million, or almost 15 per cent.[43] The campaigns of both parties privileged the youth factor. Whether through the deployment of communication technologies through apps like Thunderclap, the uploading of selfies displaying the inked finger, or more conventional hooks like catchy songs and skits, the effort at all times was to ignite the imagination and gain the support of a cohort that was notoriously apathetic to civic affairs, and rarely engaged with the issues of the day.

Revisiting the Modi campaign, one observer noted that its technology drive gave it a dramatically new avatar as a party that was holding out the dream of a 'digital democracy'. 'For a younger, aspirational India, this was just the kind of message of hope they wanted to hear from their leadership.'[44] The two themes that figured consistently in Modi's tweets through all the phases of the campaign were 'youth' and 'development'.[45] The data indicated just how successful the party was in getting its youth supporters to vote for it. Sanjay Kumar notes that while the turnout among young voters had been lower than the average turnout in the earlier General

Election of 2009, this time it was higher: a turnout of 68 per cent in comparison to 66 per cent of voters in general (see Table 5.1).

Table 5.1: Turnout of Young Voters: Lok Sabha Elections 2009–14

Turnout amongst	*2009*	*2014*
Young Voters (% votes)	54	68
All-India Turnout (% votes)	58	66

Source: Time Series National Election Survey data/Lokiniti CSDS, 'The Youth Vote Made a Difference for the Victory of the BJP', *Panjab University Research Journal Social Sciences* 22 (2).

Another distinct trend captured by the 2014 data was the manner in which the BJP emerged as the clear favourite for the youth. As Kumar put it,

> This is probably the only election in recent years when the young voters had voted decisively in favour of one political party, the BJP. The vote share of the BJP amongst the young voters was 34.4 per cent more than three percentage points higher, than its average vote share of 31.1 per cent.

He, however, also pointed out that the percentage of young women who opted for the party was lower than that of young men: 32 per cent, as opposed to 36 per cent of men[46] (see Table 5.2).

Table 5.2: Turnout of Young Voters: Lok Sabha Elections 2009–14

Parties	*2009*			*2014*		
	All votes	*Youth*	*Others*	*All votes*	*Youth*	*Others*
Congress	28.6	28	29	18.6	19	20
BJP	18.8	20	18	31.1	34	30
Left	7.5	7	8	4.8	4	5
BSP	6.2	6	6	4.1	5	4

Source: Time Series National Election Survey data/Lokiniti CSDS.

When it came to the correlation between levels of education among the youth and its political preferences, there was a significant rise in support for the BJP among all sections of youth, from 'Uneducated' to 'Graduates Plus', but the shift is most marked among college-educated young voters who are also, of course, likely to be the most exposed to the mainstream and social media (Table 5.3).

Table 5.3: Turnout of Young Voters: Lok Sabha Elections 2009–14

	2009		*2014*	
	Congress	*BJP*	*Congress*	*BJP*
Uneducated Youth	32	16	19	26
Primary School Pass	30	18	21	25
High School Pass	27	18	20	35
Graduates or More	26	25	17	38

Source: Time Series National Election Survey data/Lokiniti CSDS.

Many of the ways in which the BJP reached out to youth were borrowed from AAP's 2013 campaign. But the message was value-added with each successive election. While Kejriwal sold the aspiration of participating in direct democracy to young voters in 2013, Modi expanded it by also promising them a great future in his 2014 campaign. By 2015, AAP was able to ramp up this expectation in an even more sophisticated way, through videos of how party affiliation amounted almost to a job endorsement.

This category of voters will continue to hold relevance for the general election of 2019, when those born at the turn of the century will enter into adulthood and become eligible to vote. It is a cohort estimated to number between 13 to 20 million.

It would seem that going by the evidence of the first half of the second decade of the twenty-first century cited here, elections in India could indeed be won and democracy deepened by the assiduous and strategic harnessing of media convergence. That, however, as we have already noted, would be a hasty conclusion. For one, the universe of communication technologies, and the audiences they create, is in a constant state of flux. For another, a highly mediatised form of electioneering in and of itself is incapable of ensuring victorious outcomes if it is not in sync with the expectations and concerns of the electorate, and does not have the capacity to express a demonstrable representativeness in terms of class, caste, location, ideology, and circumstances.

The verdicts of the polls just reviewed underline the inherently transitory nature of such campaigns. Within five months of AAP's brilliant victory of December 2013 in Delhi, the party failed to win even a single seat in the parliamentary election that followed the following May, with the BJP sweeping all eight Lok Sabha seats in Delhi. Similarly, while the BJP appeared invincible in May 2014, it 'looked old and less credible ... stale rather than new'[47] in February 2015, when it won—let it be remembered—only three seats in an assembly of seventy, while AAP notched sixty-seven.

This would suggest that the instant opinion-making of online conversations, through trending patterns, quick endorsements, rejections, and virality, can both build and dissolve public support in even shorter spans of time. The fragility of political success in highly mediatised contests is also related to a striking paradox. The homogeneity of media practices based on media convergence, including the sameness marking the way information is controlled, comes as a contrast to the great heterogeneity of religious, caste, cultural, and ethnic backgrounds of Indian voters.

As more and more politicians and political parties scramble to try this apparently successful model of mediatised electioneering, there is a curious circularity to this process. In the instances cited here, both Modi and Kejriwal borrowed from the Obama presidential bids of 2008 and 2012. They also borrowed from each other. While AAP adopted media practices from the IAC mobilisation for its first foray into electoral politics in the 2013 Delhi election, the Modi team adapted many of the social media strategies from that AAP campaign for its 2014 general election pitch; and AAP, in turn, drew a great deal from the BJP's 2014 media campaign in order to defeat it resoundingly in 2015.

There is a high probability, therefore, that sooner or later, disenchantment will set in if people's own specific needs and interests are left unaddressed. In the context of the 2014 general election, commentators have pointed to how explicitly caste-based parties suffered in relation to those based on regional identities because the Modi campaign could raise the hopes of gaining private-sector jobs in the industrial and services sectors among the migrating and newly urbanised OBC and lower-caste voters, who 'aspire to join the ranks of the middle class and in Narendra Modi they found an embodiment of their aspirations'.[48] But the possibility, over a period of time, of the splintering of such a support base built on homogenised aspirations is possible if the expectations that are raised are not met.

Such pro forma campaigns are also extremely capital-intensive. Managing information and generating content on the internet require specialist teams working round the clock to flood out negative news with party-friendly material through search engine optimisation. None of this comes cheap. AAP, as a new party in 2013, had self-defined itself as an honest, ordinary person's political formation, yet it outdid its well-established rivals in terms of the money spent. An estimated 67 per cent of its total election expenses went on publicity, amounting to Rs 484.19 lakh on media advertisements, and another Rs 220.42 lakh on publicity material.[49]

The Modi campaign of 2014 was, as we saw, estimated as the costliest in the country's history, if not the world, and the figure amounted to twice the combined spend of the BJP and Congress in the previous general election of 2009.[50] The avalanche of advertisements it unleashed told its own story. The advertising company, Soho Square, is reported to have created 200 TV commercials, 300 radio spots, and over 1,000 press and outdoor displays. Over the course of the campaign, Modi's team ran more than 130,000 ad spots across 226 channels, 9,000 insertions in 295 publications and 16 languages, and 150,000 ads on websites. The morning of every voting day in a nine-phased election had newspapers advertisements customised to the concerned region.

The full costs of such a communications sweep will perhaps never be fully known, but it has significant ramifications for the Indian democracy since it precludes the possibility of a level playing electoral field.

The other consequence of a highly mediatised election is its urban bias. While the AAP elections were fought in a completely urban setting, it is significant that the 2014 general election verdict was secured with the disproportionate support of urban sections of the electorate, far more than in any previous election, following a campaign that had focused largely on the urban elite and middle classes. This was implicit in the fact that the most successful party in this election, the BJP, came to power with a 42 per cent urban vote share—far above its average all-India vote share of 31 per cent. Data put out by the CSDS indicated an interesting aspect of the BJP victory: the party had notched a 28 per cent increase in the vote share of urban seats, as compared to a 5 per cent increase in that of rural seats.[51]

Fake news invariably proliferate in highly mediatised campaigns, with even images of crowds put out in party publicity material artificially magnified through clever multicam angles and the skilful use of software that allows image editing and compositing. Not only are the crowds fake, but the speakers on the podium could also be phantoms! During the 2014 election campaign, the Modi campaign deployed prohibitively expensive hologram projection technology, with the leader beamed to election crowds in over 1,400 locations, reaching an estimated 14 million people. A BJP representative described the experience as something out of ancient legends: 'Just like the Hindu mythology where the God was omnipresent. So he (Modi) is everywhere.'[52]

Highly mediatised campaigns also tend to draw emotional energy from deliberate communal polarisation. The 2014 election had several moments when hatred of minorities, especially Muslims, was deliberately stoked for election dividends. A major instance of this was when BJP president and Modi's right-hand man Amit Shah openly called for 'revenge' against the unstated but clearly understood enemy while campaigning in riot-hit Muzaffarnagar in 2014. His words drew their resonance from the riots that had hit the region a year earlier, lingering long after the campaign ended, and 'continues to thrive outside of election campaign periods among certain groups and is becoming much more evident in daily conversation on social media'.[53] The spate of highly mediatised episodes of Muslims being lynched on the pretext of cow protection, which broke out after Modi came to power, is a tragic and abominable reflection of this.[54]

The severe limitations and negatives of mediatised electioneering apart, it is clear that there can be no going back to old-style campaigning. In that sense, the elections of 2013, 2014, and 2015 together mark a paradigm shift in the practice of electoral politics in India.

FUTURE TRENDS

These developments need to be understood against a global backdrop. The internet has today become a prime site for capitalist development and, as Robert W. McChensey notes, 'monopolistic firms that have capitalized on the digital revolution have grown to world-historical proportions', and now 'sit at the commanding heights of U.S. and world capitalism'.[55] Their growth is being driven by their capacity to aggregate and use data, widely termed as the new oil driving capitalism today.

Take Twitter, which began in 2006—it grew from 49 million users in 2010 to 335 million in 2018.[56] Today, it may lag considerably behind Facebook, which had 2.23 billion users by mid-2018, but it is still among the top ten social media sites in the world. These internet behemoths have benefited immensely from mediatised elections in India, with Twitter even laying claim to General Election 2014 by terming it as India's first Twitter election.[57] From 1 January to 16 May 2014, an estimated 58 million tweets, specifically related to the election, were generated. Modi's tweet on 16 May 2014—'India has won. Bharat ki vijay. Achche din anne wale hain'—was retweeted over 70,000 times, and was demarcated as India's most shared tweet ever.

Since the 2014 general election, however, there have been developments that will have a direct bearing on India's future elections. Among them is the rise in mobile data use within the country, a trend fuelled by the advent of the cheap smartphone and more affordable 4G telecom services—both spearheaded by Reliance Industries in its bid to dominate the telecom market. The Modi government's investment in developing its technological interface with citizens through public initiatives like Aadhaar has also contributed to this phenomenon.

Facebook and its digital properties—WhatsApp and Instagram—have benefited directly from affordable mobile data. Today, this cluster of Facebook, WhatsApp, and Instagram is estimated to account for 95 per cent of social media use through apps in India.[58] WhatsApp, which in 2018 has about 200 million users in India, has emerged as a major election tool. The network that the BJP set up of an estimated 10,344 WhatsApp groups[59] for the Uttar Pradesh assembly election in 2017 is believed to have been a factor in the party's landslide win. These WhatsApp groups working at every level, from the neighbourhood to the district, helped to propagate and amplify party messages, enabling the proliferation of 'news' tailored to party interests.

Future elections could also see a more intensive attempt to capture and use the personal data of citizens in order to map their political sympathies and inclinations, and tailor political messaging accordingly. In early 2018, an international scam involving Cambridge Analytica, where data illegally obtained from Facebook was being used to build voter profiles, caused widespread outrage. It was soon learnt that there was an India angle to the story, with the data of 500,000 Indian Facebook users being 'stolen' by Cambridge Analytica for the purpose of selling it to political parties.

The impacts of such mass digital deception were visible in the Donald J. Trump election of 2016. Not only was a leviathan of a social media site like Facebook deployed for online fundraising, but it also functioned as an echo chamber through which all kinds of information—unverified and unverifiable—circulated endlessly, building opinion, amplifying people's likes and dislikes, and reinforcing prejudices. If there was one conclusion that followed from the wide-ranging post-mortem of that result, it was the erosion of the 'informational underpinnings of democracy',[60] given Facebook's ability to create an informational bubble, customised for the person accessing it. The Facebook News Feed made available to the user is based on the probability 'that you'll like, comment on, or share a story ... the more likely you are to interact with a post, the higher up it will show in your News Feed. Two thousand kinds of data ... get smelted in Facebook's machine-learning system to make those predictions.'[61] The Trump election also saw a proliferation of automated bots on both Facebook and Twitter platforms, which amplified the presence of the prime candidate in order to influence and subvert online conversations.

Facebook's influence and presence in India would indicate that it could, along with other social media platforms, play a similar role in Indian elections of the future. The difference, of course, is that this will play out in a scenario where illiteracy levels continue to be high, where gender and caste inequalities are strongly prevalent, where digital literacy is extremely low, and where financial and digital exclusions are realities. The erosion of the 'informational underpinnings of democracy' in India is a crisis waiting to unfold.

NOTES AND REFERENCES

1. Shaili Chopra, 2014, *The Big Connect* (New Delhi: Random House India), 142.

2. Interview with AAP member Sundeep Narwani, 1 October 2015.

3. Mayank Gandhi, 2018, *AAP & Down: An Insider's Story of India's Most Controversial Party* (New Delhi: Simon and Schuster India), 103.

4. 'Anna Hazare parts ways with Arvind Kejriwal, forbids him to use his name, photo', *The Times of India*, 19 September 2012.

5. Rajdeep Sardesai, 2014, *2014: The Election That Changed India* (New Delhi: Penguin Viking), 191.

6. Saba Naqvi, 2014, *Capital Conquest: How the AAP's Incredible Victory has Redefined Indian Elections* (New Delhi: Hachette India), 107.

7. Simon Denyer, 2012, *Rogue Elephant: Harnessing the Power of India's Unruly Democracy* (London: Bloomsbury), 253.

8. Ibid., 253.

9. Aditya Nigam, 2015, 'Reading the Power Struggle in AAP', *Kafila*, 7 March. Available at http://kafila.org/2015/03/07/reading-the-power-struggle-in-aap/ (accessed March 2016).

10. '13 days on, Arvind Kejriwal still on fast track', *The Times of India*, 5 April 2013. Available at p://timesofindia.indiatimes.com/defaultinterstitial_as.cms (accessed March 2016).

11. Ashutosh, 2015, *The Crown Prince: The Gladiator and the Hope* (New Delhi: HarperCollins), 75.

12. Swapan Dasgupta, 2014a, 'The Papier-mache Mahatma', *The Asian Age*, 1 January. Available at http://swapan-dasgupta.blogspot.in/2014_01_01_archive.html (accessed January 2016).

13. Chopra, *The Big Connect*, 141.

14. Denyer, *Rogue Elephant*, 253.

15. Gandhi, *AAP & Down*, 128.

16. Chopra, *The Big Connect*, 141.

17. Interview with AAP member Sundeep Narwani, 1 October 2015.

18. Chopra, *The Big Connect*, 143.

19. Pratap Bhanu Mehta, 2013, 'Left behind', *The Indian Express*, 9 December.

20. Ashutosh, *The Crown Prince*, 138.

21. Swapan Dasgupta, 2014b: 'A Common Threat—The Congress has closed ranks with the AAP on Modi', *The Telegraph*, 3 January. Available at http://www.telegraphindia.com/1140103/jsp/opinion/story_17741235.jsp#.WDPzM1x8uSA (accessed April 2016).

22. Indrani Basu, 2014, 'In His Own Tweets: Kejriwal's 49 Days in Power', *The 545 Conversations on Indian Elections*, 16 February. Available at http://thefivefortyfive.com/in-his-own-tweets-arvind-kejriwals-49-days-in-power (accessed March 2016).

23. 'India: Concern mounts over anti-corruption party's economics,' *Asia Sentinel*, 25 February 2014. Available at https://asiancorrespondent.com/2014/02/india-election aam-admi-arvind/ (accessed March 2016).

24. Ashutosh, *The Crown Prince*, 139.

25. Sandeep Unnithan, 2014, 'AAPeclipse', *India Today*, 13 June.

26. Ashutosh, *The Crown Prince*, 278.

27. Mohamed Ali, 2015, 'We are sorry for quitting, says an apologetic Kejriwal before going to jail', *The Hindu*, 22 May. Available at http://www.thehindu.com/todays-paper/tp-national/tp-newdelhi/we-are-sorry-for-quitting-says-an-apologetic-kejriwal-before-going-to-jail/article6035401.ece (accessed April 2016).

28. 'Have learned one must never quit the chair, Arvind Kejriwal says', 24 August 2014, *Press Trust of India*. Available at http://timesofindia.indiatimes.com/city/delhi/Have-learned-one-must-never-quit-the-chair-Arvind-Kejriwal-says/articleshow/40860998.cms (accessed April 2016).

29. Rajdeep Sardesai, 2015, 'When Kejriwal Defeated the Media', blog on *Breakingviews*, 12 February. Aailable at http://www.rajdeepsardesai.net/blog-views/when-kejriwal-defeated-media (accessed March 2016).

30. Anant Kumar, speaking at a public discussion on 'Delhi Elections: Impact on National Politics', organised by Centre for Policy Analysis, 2 March 2015.

31. 'Kejriwal apologises for quitting midway', *The Indian Express*, 21 May 2014. Available at http://indianexpress.com/article/cities/delhi/arvind-kejriwal-apologises-to-delhi-for-quitting-midway-seeks-fresh-elections/ (accessed April 2016).

32. Saba Naqvi, 2015, *Capital Conquest: How the AAP's Incredible Victory Has Redefined Indian Elections* (New Delhi: Hachette India), 73.

33. Ibid., 88.

34. Goirick Brahmachari, 2015, 'AAP, Left and Their Cultural Tools', *Economic and Political Weekly* L (8), 21 February.

35. Gandhi, *AAP & Down*, 177.

36. Ibid., 190.

37. 'AAP 2.0 is very different—there's a new coterie, loyalty to Kejriwal matters more: Srirupa Roy', Interview with Amulya Gopalakrishnan, *The Times of India*, 4 September 2016. Available at http://timesofindia.indiatimes.com/home/sunday-times/all-that-matters/AAP-2-0-is-very-different-theres-a-new-coterie (accessed September 2016).

38. Prashant Jha, 2017, How The BJP Wins: Inside India's Greatest Election Machine (New Delhi: Juggernaut), 46.

39. Paul Mason, 2013, *Why it's Still Kicking Off Everywhere: The New Global Revolutions* (London: Verso). 66.

40. 'A Profile of Youth in India', Government of India, Ministry of Health and Family Welfare, 2009.

41. Craig Jeffrey, 2012, *Timepass Youth: Class, and the Politics of Waiting in India* (Foundation Books), 124.

42. Carmen Fishwick, James Walsh, and Emma Howard, 'Indian elections: 10 things we have learned so far', 11 April 2014. Available at https://www.theguardian.com/world/2014/apr/11/10-things-we-learned-about-indian-election-modi-marriages (accessed 8 November 2015).

43. Sardesai, *2014*, xviii.

44. Price, *The Modi Effect*, 243.

45. Joyojeet Pal, Priyanka Chandra, and V. G. Vydiswaran, 2016, 'Twitter and the Rebranding of Narendra Modi', *Economic and Political Weekly* LI (8), 20 February.

46. Sanjay Kumar, 2014, 'The Youth Vote Made a Difference for the Victory of the BJP', *Panjab University Research Journal of Social Sciences* 22 (2).

47. Pratap Bhanu Mehta, 2015, 'A victory of possibilities', *The Indian Express*, 11 February.

48. Christophe Jaffrelot and Gilles Verniers, 2015, 'The Resistance of Regionalism: BJP's Limitations and the Resilience of State Parties', in Paul Wallace (ed.), *India's 2014 Election: A Modi-led BJP Sweep* (New Delhi: Sage Publications), 41–42.

49. 'AAP collected, spent highest funds in 2013 Delhi funds: ADR', *BusinessLine*, 16 April 2015. Available at http://www.thehindubusinessline.com/news/national/aap-collected-spent-highest-funds-in-2013-delhi-elections-ad (accessed August 2016).

50. Devjot Ghoshal and Manu Balachandran, 2015, 'It cost Narendra Modi $100 million to win the Indian election—here's how he spent it', *Quartz India*, 15 January. Available at http://qz.com/327771/it-cost-narendra-modi-100-million-to-win-the-indian-election-heres-how-he-spent-it/ (accessed June 2016).

51. Jaffrelot and Verniers, 'The Resistance of Regionalism', 32.

52. Tom Lasseter, 2014, 'India's Top Candidate Went Full Tupac, Campaigned Via Hologram', Bloomberg Businessweek, 20 May. Available at https://www.bloomberg.com/news/articles/2014-05-13/narendra-modi-indias-election-frontrunner-had-help-from-his-hologram (accessed 5 November 2015).

53. Taberez Ahmed Neyazi, 2017, 'Social media and political polarization in India', *Seminar* November.

54. Delna Abraham and Ojaswi Rao, 2017, 'Cow slaughter row: Since 2010, 97 % of beef related violence took place after Modi govt came to power', IndiaSpend, 29 June. Available at https://www.firstpost.com/india/cow-slaughter-row-since-2010-97-of-beef-related-violence-took-place-after-modi-govt-came-to-power-3752479.html (accessed August 2018).

55. Robert W. McChesney, 2011, *Digital Disconnect* (New York: The New Press), 130.

56. Statista, 2018. Available at https://www.statista.com/statistics/282087/number-of-monthly-active-twitter-users/ (accessed August 2018).

578. 'Twitter releases data around Indian elections', *Social Samosa*, 17 May 2014. Available at http://www.socialsamosa.com/2014/05/twitter-elections-data/ (accessed November 2015).

58. Roopa Kudva, et al., 2017, 'Innovating for the Next Half Billion', Omidyar Network, 18 December. Available at https://www.omidyar.com/sites/default/files/file_archive/Next%20Half%20Billion/Innovating%20for%20Next%20Half%20Billion.pdf (accessed August 2018).

59. Lalmani Verma, 2017, 'BJP's election strategy: 900 rallies, 67,000 workers, 10,000 WhatsApp groups and chopper landings', *The Indian Express*, 12 March.

60. Alexis C. Madrigal, 2017, 'What Facebook Did to American Democracy', *The Atlantic*, 12 October.

61. Ibid.

six

Multiple Changes, Manifold Impacts

The Conundrums Facing a Mediatised India

When hundreds of thousands of demonstrators converge at a particular spot in real time through Facebook posts and live television coverage; when newspapers get their leads from tweets put out by demonstrators ring-fenced by the police; and when an election campaign speech at a rally in rural Madhya Pradesh reaches multiple audiences through WhatsApp, we are talking about radical transformations in the way converged media content is being transmitted, received, negotiated with, and acted upon in India. Digitalisation has shaped and will continue to shape this convergence. It is not just mass action or electoral campaigns that have become so crucially dependent on internet-driven connectivity between various communication devices and platforms; the very fabric of human-to-human interaction is being increasingly woven on its looms.

None of the developments in India considered in this book should be seen in isolation. In many ways, this is a back-to-the-future moment. The present market-fuelled, digital phase of the global media mimics the decade of the 1990s, when television emerged as the most dominant of existing media platforms across continents. Whether the behemoths of the newspaper world had read that earlier moment clearly is difficult to say, but within the next two decades, many of them who had once set the news agenda for the world, had disappeared into oblivion, or are in the process of doing so. In 1966, Gay Talese could choose a title rife with grandiose biblical overtones for his book on *The New York Times—The Kingdom and the Power Behind the Scenes at The New York Times: The Institution That Influences the World.*[1] Today, that same newspaper cannot but breathe in the vapours of mortality arising from the bog of irrelevance, and is desperately searching for ways to reinvent itself to remain in the reckoning.

A quarter century ago, the nature of media content was fundamentally changed by the 24×7 television news cycle, with 'the growing commercialism of the airwaves, partly as a result of the privatisation of global satellite networks and the technological converge between media, computer and telecommunication industries'.[2] Today, with that convergence almost complete and with the internet having become 'the epicenter of our world, the place where virtually everything is done',[3] we are looking at a media landscape caught in yet another vortex of change.

The difference between the earlier churn driven by satellite television and the contemporary scene today is that the very pace of the change has exponentially accelerated, as digital pathways allow global capital to access markets across the world more efficiently than ever. The data gleaned from users will go to fuel the next wave of the information revolution through artificial intelligence (AI). This may bring about an era when large tech companies launch products, not for the revenue they bring through the content they circulate, but through the data generated through such circulation of content, which can then be monetised through other products driven by AI. Non-human processes will raise the speeds at which news/information is generated and it will be tailored to the needs and proclivities of discrete audiences, and delivered to them with an unimaginable efficiency.

If journalism had undergone a complete overhaul with the advent of the age of satellite television, media functioning in the digital age is undergoing multiple, shape-shifting disruptions, all of them occurring simultaneously along different axes.

The positive impacts inherent in these developments are innumerable and profound. A secure internet that is universal in scope and open to all was one of the great aspirations of modernity. The very fact that someone with a smartphone can thumb her nose at the mighty fortresses of mainstream journalism and convey her opinions, views, news to the world is hugely self-affirming; that media networks can, in tandem with uprisings on the ground, deliver change to people on a mass scale is decidedly life-enhancing. New media platforms have helped the socially marginalised to acquire new skills to negotiate their circumstances and deepen their freedoms. The fact that there are opportunities now for people to collectively oppose governmental repression or expose those who seek to defraud them; the possibilities of benefiting from media content that would otherwise be denied to them because of the business models of media conglomerates, have many democratising attributes.

Journalist and author Paul Mason lists twenty reasons why there is revolutionary potential in this moment, because it means 'that a great change in the world's priorities is within people's grasp'.[4] Social networks, he contends, have now become the primary source of information for many, consigning mainstream media with their constructed narratives to second place. Related to this is his argument that tech-enabled horizontalism kills vertical hierarchies, spontaneously allowing social movements access to symbolic space in a manner they had never earlier achieved; allows ideas to arise, get tested, take off, disappear, or self-replicate like genes. In such a situation, the network proves more powerful than the hierarchy. He concludes his list by asserting that technology has in many ways expanded the space and power of the individual.[5]

Whether or not the possibilities outlined by Mason are realised would depend a great deal on who gets to control the new communication technologies and media, and who stands to gain from their existence. The fear that the majority of people, especially those without social and financial capital, could end up being dominated by these controllers of the communication technologies space, rather than being able to assert agency over them, is very real. Such an apprehension is all the more plausible given how immersed users of newer media are in the content they absorb and create, so much so that the separation between their media platforms and they themselves gets blurred, to the point where it almost disappears. Online information then comes to be valued more for the speed of delivery and capacity for instant gratification, rather than any exposition it may provide of everyday realities.

Turning to India, the only thing that can be stated with confidence is that the mediatisation of its society dwelt upon in these pages will only gather pace in the years ahead. There can be no going back to the days when the sole literate elder in the village read a newspaper and shared its insights with everyone. An age when the news bulletins transmitted to a community through government-run radio was all that it knew about government functioning is well and truly behind us.

India is in fact being pulled headlong into the networked space, with internet access growing at a fast clip. According to one estimation, 500 million Indians are projected to access the internet by mid-2018, with the internet penetration of urban India having achieved a level of almost 65 per cent by the end of 2017.[6]

It is the vastness of the Indian market that makes it so attractive, not only for politically well-connected domestic corporations in the digital space like Reliance and Airtel, but also for the giants of Silicon Valley. There is an 'interesting synergy' that is emerging, as Daya Kishan Thussu, a long-term academic observer of the Indian media, highlights: 'an unabashedly pro-business government of Narendra Modi with its "Digital India" programme is strongly supported by hugely influential domestic corporations (Reliance's Jio is a case in point), as well as global digital corporations (Google, Facebook, and Microsoft—to name the most prominent ones).'[7] Digital corporations 'take advantage first and foremost, of network effects which tend to produce "winner-takes-all" markets with almost no middle class of midsized firms'.[8] Google, a search platform, and Facebook, a social media site, had together captured an estimated 61 per cent of the US digital ad market in 2017[9] by acquiring the features of a media company, and going on to purvey 'news', without in fact being a media establishment.

The battle for domination among the giants has fuelled a scramble for global influence, which in turn has direct implications for India. The mediatised half-decade considered here was a forerunner to a series of India-centric initiatives they embarked upon. In November 2015, Microsoft CEO Satya Nadella, speaking in Mumbai, revealed his organisation's vision of creating a 'cloud-first, mobile-first' world. Accessing India's e-commerce market was also something that Microsoft had set its sights on, seeking to partner local start-ups to help them 'use their data in a more effective manner'.[10] During Prime Minister Modi's visit to the Silicon Valley in September that year, Microsoft had also offered 'low-cost broad band' to connect 500,000 villages under Modi's favoured programme, 'Digital India'. A few weeks later Google's CEO, Sundar Pichai, also arrived on Indian shores with plans to deepen his organisation's involvement in the country and assist its small businesses, or so it claimed. Although its project to provide a 360-degree panoramic and street-level imagery of Indian cities through Google Street View was rejected by the Indian government on security grounds, Google has been allowed to team up with the Government of India to develop a 'toilet locator app' to enable people to access public washrooms, which incidentally is in sync with Modi's flagship Swachch Bharat Mission. Google also gained a fairly secure toe-hold in the Indian Railways, through a 2016 partnership to run Wi-Fi networks in railway stations, among other projects. Apple, meanwhile, is anxious to extend the impressive sale of its iPhones in the country, where sales grew in the last quarter of 2015 by 76 per cent at a time when the company's global sales had declined to 0.4 per cent.[11] It is also working on a plan to set up manufacturing bases for these phones in India.

These hard-nosed bids for the market were invariably presented to the Indian public as philanthropic gestures to empower ordinary people. In 2015, Facebook's aborted Free Basics initiative, enabling free but limited access to internet service, was offered ostensibly for the purpose of bridging the digital divide in a poor country. The spirited public campaign to oppose the move flagged several crucial concerns and led to TRAI vetoing it. As a body of Indian scientists had argued at that point, if a private party is allowed to define what is 'basic' and if it were to access the personal content created and used by millions of Indians, it would be a lethal combination 'which will lead to total lack of freedom on how Indians can use their own public utility, the internet'.[12] Call it happenstance or Facebook's overreach, but the Free Basics model provided Indians with an early engagement with concerns that were to flare up a year later, after the Trump election of November 2016, over Facebook's infringement of privacy on a mass scale through aggressive data collection strategies.

Understanding the role of new communication technologies in shaping Indian society involves cutting through a thicket of contradictions. The figure of the boatman plying his vessel on the Ganga, who picks up his battered Nokia phone to complain to Mr Mittal of Airtel fame, which began the story Robin Jeffrey and Assa Doron related about India as the 'Cell Phone Nation', may have been a figment of the authors' imagination, but there are many like that fictional figure in the India of today. Yet, it is also true that if there are 500 million on the internet grid, it also means that there are also hundreds of millions off it, most of them located in rural India. As connectivity grows by leaps and bounds, the gap between the networked and the non-networked continues to widen. As profit-driven monopolies exercise increasingly greater control over the internet, access for all to a wide range of its applications—once seen as its unique promise—could also progressively diminish.

Projecting the scenario of the future would be entering unchartered territory, but three conundrums emerge clearly at the present moment. The first conundrum is the asymmetrical nature of access, largely because it is easier to achieve technological inclusion than social inclusion. The former is driven by market forces eager to extend their spheres of influence; the latter is all about tackling the old, familiar inequalities along lines of class, caste, gender, language, disability and location, in a resource-poor country. The mediatised half-decade considered in these pages constituted a period of rising economic growth for the country, but it also saw a deepening of disparities. The Indian economy took sixty years to achieve a GDP threshold of $1 trillion, but it crossed the $2 trillion mark within the next seven—in 2014.[13] Meanwhile, on most social parameters, change has been slow, and the gains in some sectors even appear to have been reversed. To take an example, the expected years of schooling have remained stagnant since 2011.[14] This would suggest that growth in media presence in India, while greatly benefiting big corporations and those who can directly gain from the market economy, has not brought about commensurate social and economic gains for those located outside that field. Being part of a hyper-connected world—a long-held dream of the Indian elite—could actually mean hyper-exclusion for many sections of the country's population.

Glimpses from a 2017 survey of rural education[15] indicate that while the use of a basic mobile phone is significant—73 per cent of young people in the 14–18 group have used the device 'within the last week'—only 28 per cent and 26 per cent have used the internet and computer in the same time span, respectively, with 59 per cent never having used a computer, and 64 per cent never having accessed the internet. Further scrutiny of these figures reveals other deprivations. Gender is a major divide: while 12 per cent of males have never used a mobile phone, for females, the figure stands at 22 per cent; similarly, while 49 per cent of males have never used the internet, close to 76 per cent of females have never done so. Physical mobility is linked to digital access, and the diktats of family elders and khap panchayats prohibiting—for purposes of moral policing—the use of mobiles and other devices is almost certainly a factor in widening the gender gap. Additionally, school dropout rates were closely correlated to internet and computer use, with those out of school having lower access to these resources.

Affordability and infrastructure are the two primary constituents of digital access. Poverty is certainly a major challenge. 'Even with the low and competitive prices of devices and data plans compared with the rest of the world, internet access in India remains beyond the reach of close to 1.063 billion people.'[16] As for infrastructure, although the Government of India had ambitious inclusion plans for rural areas, the reality has failed abysmally to measure up to the promise. Take the National Optical Fibre Network (NOFN) project, which was licensed to operate from 2013, and aimed to provide last mile broadband connectivity to over 250,000 gram panchayats. By April 2016, only 6,727 panchayats had internet access, or 6 per cent of the total scheduled for Phase 1 of this project.[17] The challenges for rural Indians do not end there. Irregular electricity, poor infrastructural maintenance, and spectrum allocations in the lower frequency coverage bands do not exactly make for an environment of digital inclusion.

Undergirding the class profile and location of those outside the digital space, is the major category of caste. Dalit academics have now been strongly weighing in on this issue, recognising how the use of a potentially liberatory tool like the internet is embedded in the caste hierarchical cultures, privileges, and practices from which it arises. Smita M. Patil, for instance, calls for the 'de-brahmanizing of the online sphere', noting how expressions like 'digital empowerment' and 'the knowledge economy' now lace the neoliberal Indian vocabulary, even while the social composition of those with access to ICTs is dominantly upper caste.[18]

Language too is a great barrier in a country with over 780 languages, including twenty-two official ones. Shalini Narayanan and Anand Pradhan have drawn attention to the fact that India's numerous languages and dialects pose 'another hurdle for access to new media as the primary language for access has been English'.[19] Even something as basic as lack of online content in languages other than English, Hindi, and a handful of other regional tongues is a major inhibiting factor in achieving equality of access.

This leads to the second conundrum. Being digital have-nots does not protect people from the dangers of the internet world, like privacy violations and digital disinformation or fake news. A baseline 2013 survey on the 'Use and Misuse of Internet by Semi-Urban and Rural Youth in India' specifically underlines the low threshold of understanding of concerns like privacy that this cohort of internet users displays.[20] Given its ubiquity and pernicious potential, fake news has become a separate genre of study today, attracting a great deal of academic scrutiny. Scholars in Singapore's Nanyang Technological University reviewed thirty-four papers on fake news published between 2003 and 2017, and concluded that any definition of fake news would need to take into account both 'level of facticity' and 'author's immediate intent to deceive'—both extremely difficult to discern for the ordinary person. The authors also note a disturbing aspect of such disinformation—it needs 'the nourishment of troubled times in order to take root'.[21] It also thrives in scenarios where users, because of their lack of both general and digital literacy and failure to recognise the falseness of the information they receive, are unable to call it out and do battle.

The anonymity with which such information can be produced and circulated in real time is a decisive factor in their proliferation. Like water, such content flows across all media platforms. Take the case of Twitter, which has become an intrinsic part of the converged newsroom of today, and has emerged as the 'most popular social media forum to source news'[22] for Indian journalists. As was apparent in the build-up to the Delhi gang rape, no individual journalist or news organisation, even one with considerable resources, can adequately replicate the coverage of developing news in spatial and temporal terms that can be achieved through Twitter. In an earlier era, the life of the news story, based on facts that were professionally gathered, edited, and fact-checked, ended when the last edition went to bed or the last bulletin was telecast. Twitter disrupted that pattern and extended the news cycle into a 24-hour phenomenon, even as the manner in which news was gathered, disseminated, and consumed was altered forever. Communications professor Alfred Hermida terms this 'ambient journalism', or journalism that is 'constantly on and updated, thanks to the explosion of cable television and the internet'.[23]

The characteristics that make Twitter extremely valuable as a news source are precisely the ones that lead to a deficit in the credibility of its information. Updates of 280 characters arriving in real time are difficult, if not impossible, to fact-check, and do not make for a holistic understanding of social realities. A news anchor indicated how the coarsening of media discourse through Twitter has now become part of contemporary news production strategies: 'We are consciously putting out provocative hashtags to a lead story so that it will then become the talking point of the day. An outrage factory is being created on social media and television news is expected to echo the outrage.'[24] Instances of ordinary people being swayed by spiked information, which is then deliberately made to go viral through the use of hashtags, keep surfacing on a daily basis. A case in point was the sparking of mass panic in rural Jharkhand in May 2017 through a WhatsApp message warning of child lifters in the vicinity, which got amplified by word of mouth and led to the lynching of seven innocents, all of them from the Muslim community.

The third conundrum that confronts a mediatised India is the drive for the control of audiences by a range of actors through various technological devices and strategies. These could include the deliberate creation of information bubbles and echo chambers in order to encourage allegiances, build loyalties, and form constituencies for a broad range of purposes, including the commercial and the political. The electoral triumphs of a politician like Narendra Modi, not only during the general election of 2014 but also in a series of state elections thereafter, were crucially hinged on the creation of hyper-partisanship through the most sophisticated use of media platforms and technologies that the country had ever seen. Its impacts far outlived the elections themselves, with the consequent communal polarisation permeating Indian society and politics, and teams of 'influencers' set up for elections continuing to influence political discourse through interventions like trolling and the coordinated generation of fake news.

In such a scenario, the question arises: How should the democratic dividend inherent in the media in general, and the internet, more specifically, be protected and furthered? If the potentially liberating and inclusive dimensions of mediatisation are to be given free play, society as a whole would need to own the media, recognise these platforms as a public good, and worthy of its attention and critical engagement. McChesney argues strongly for a media reform movement with four components: one, a media policy that reflects the issues of the day; two, active social support being extended to independent media; three, developing media curricula and critique; and finally, building a movement among media producers, especially workers, journalists, and those who contribute through their creativity. Such reform, McChesney argues, 'could just shift some of the power from Wall Street, from advertisers, managers and corporate interests',[25] to the people themselves.

The challenge of these mediatised times for countries across the world, including India, is to understand the hurdles that come in the way of the media and communication technologies being available to everybody, including those in the lowest tier of society. Technology alone cannot ensure social change, it is true. But it must not be allowed to work against the possibilities of achieving such an outcome.

NOTES AND REFERENCES

1. Gay Talese, 1966, *The Kingdom and the Power: Behind the Scene at The New York Times, The Institution That Influences the World* (New York: Random House).
2. Daya Kishan Thussu and Des Freedman (eds), 2003, *War and the Media: Reporting Conflict 24/7* (New Delhi: Vistaar Publications), 118.
3. Glenn Greenwald, 2014, *No Place To Hide* (New York: Picador), 5.

4. John Mason, 2014, *Why it's Still Kicking Off Everywhere: The New Global Revolutions* (London: Verso), 261.

5. Ibid., 269–92.

6. Surabhi Agarwal, 2018, 'Internet users in India expected to reach 500 million by June: IAMAI', *The Economic Times*, 20 February.

7. Daya Kishan Thussu, 2016, 'Foreword', in Sunetra Sen Narayan and Shalini Narayanan (eds), *India Connected: Mapping the Impact of New Media* (New Delhi: Sage Publications), viii.

8. Robert W. McChesney, 2014, *Blowing the Roof off the 21st Century: Media, Politics, and the Struggle for Post-capitalist Democracy* (New York: NYU Press), 228.

9. Derek Thompson, 2017, 'How to Survive the Media Apocalypse', *The Atlantic*, 29 November. Available at https://www.theatlantic.com/business/archive/2017/11/media-apocalypse/546935/ (accessed December 2017).

10. Anushree Singh, 2015, 'Microsoft CEO Satya Nadella's big announcements for India at "Future Unleashed"', *Business Insider India*, 5 November. Available at https://www.businessinsider.in/Microsoft-CEO-Satya-Nadellas-big-announcements-for-India-at-Future-Unleashed/articleshow/49672370.cms (accessed September 2017).

11. Sidhartha, 2016, 'Apple may get to open stores without 30% sourcing norm', Times News Network/Gadgets Now, 20 April. Available at https://www.gadgetsnow.com/tech-news/Apple-may-get-to-open-stores-without-30-sourcing-norm/articleshow/51934783.cms (accessed November 2017).

12. Anita Babu, 2015, 'IIT, IISc scientists dislike Facebook's Free Basics', *Business Standard*, 30 December. Available at http://www.business-standard.com/article/current-affairs/iit-iisc-scientists-protest-against-facebook-s-free-basics-115122900682_1.html (accessed November 2017).

13. Sharad T. C. A. Raghavan, 2015, 'India is now a $2-trillion economy', *The Hindu*, 3 July. Available at http://www.thehindu.com/business/Economy/india-is-now-a-2trillion-economy-says-world-bank-data/article7380442.ece (accessed May 2016).

14. 'India Ranks 130 in Human Development Index: UNDP', *Press Trust of India*, 14 December 2015. Available at http://timesofindia.indiatimes.com/india/India-ranks-130-in-Human-Development-Index UNDP/articleshow/50174190.cms (accessed May 2016).

15. Annual Status of Education Report (Rural), 2017.

16. The Ericsson Consumer Lab Report (2015), cited in *India Exclusion Report 2016* (New Delhi: Yoda Press), 68.

17. Ibid., 82, 83.

18. Smita M. Patil, 2017, 'Debrahmanising Online Sphere: On Large Question of Caste, Gender and Patriarchy', GenderIT.org, 8 September. Available at https://www.genderit.org/articles/debrahmanizing-online-sphere-larger-questions-caste-gender-and-patriarchy (accessed February 2018).

19. Shalini Narayanan and Anand Pradhan, 2016, 'New Media and Social-Political Movements', in Sunetra Sen Narayan and Shalini Narayanan (eds), *India Connected: Mapping the Impact of New Media* (New Delhi: Sage Publications), 117.

20. Cited in Debarati Halder and H. Jaishankar, 2017, *Cyber Crimes Against Women in India* (New Delhi: Sage Publications).

21. Laura Hazard Owen, 2017, 'There's a long list of old-fashioned parallels to today's fake news. Here's one that's actually helpful', Neiman Lab. Available at http://www.niemanlab.org/2017/09/theres-a-long-list-of-old-fashioned-parallels-to-todays-fake-news-heres-one-thats-actually-helpful/ (accessed October 2017).

22. Jennifer Alejandro, 2014, 'How Indian Journalists use social media', Reuters Institute Fellowship Paper, University of Oxford.

23. Alecia Swasy, 2016, *How Journalists Use Twitter: The Changing Landscape of U.S. Newsrooms* (Lanham, MD: Lexington Books).

24. Rajdeep Sardesai, 2017, 'The Venkatesh Chapalgaonkar Memorial Lecture'.

25. McChesney, *Blowing the Roof off the 21st Century*, 147.

Bibliography

Abraham, Delna and Ojaswi Rao, 2017, 'Cow slaughter row: Since 2010, 97 % of beef related violence took place after Modi govt came to power', IndiaSpend, 29 June. Available at https://www.firstpost.com/india/cow-slaughter-row-since-2010-97-of-beef-related-violence-took-place-after-modi-govt-came-to-power-3752479.html (accessed August 2018).

Agarwal, Surabhi, 2018, 'Internet users in India expected to reach 500 million by June: IAMAI', *The Economic Times*, 20 February.

Agnes, Flavia, 2015, 'Why India loves Nirbhaya, hates Suzette', *The Asian Age*, 20 March.

Ahmed, Saifuddin and Kokil Jaidka, 2013, 'Protests against #delhigangrape on Twitter', *JeDem*. Available at http://www.jeedem.org,54.

Ali, Mohamed, 2015, 'We are sorry for quitting, says an apologetic Kejriwal before going to jail', *The Hindu*, 22 May. Available at http://www.thehindu.com/todays-paper/tp-national/tp-newdelhi/we-are-sorry-for-quitting-says-an-apologetic-kejriwal-before-going-to-jail/article6035401.ece (accessed April 2016).

Alejandro, Jennifer, 2014, 'How Indian Journalists use social media', Reuters Institute Fellowship Paper, University of Oxford.

Anand, Jatin, 2013, 'Ranga-Billa redux: How rapists were sent to the gallows', *The Hindustan Times*, 9 January.

Andersen, Walter K. and Shridhar D. Damle, 2018, *The RSS: A View to the Inside* (New Delhi: Penguin/Viking).

Anderson, Benedict, 2006, *Imagined Communities: Reflections on the Origin and Spread of Nationalism* (London: Verso, rev. edn).

Aouragh, Miriyam, 2012, 'Social Media, Mediation and the Arab Revolutions', *tripleC(2)*. Available at http://www.triple-c.at/index.php/tripleC/article/view/416 (accessed February 2015).

Arya, Divya, 2015, 'Reporting Sexual Violence in India: What Has Changed Since the Delhi Gang Rape', *Economic and Political Weekly* l (34), 31 October.

Assange, Julian, 2014, *When Google Meets Wikileaks* (New York, London: OR Books).

Ashutosh, 2015, *The Crown Prince: The Gladiator and the Hope* (New Delhi: HarperCollins Publishers India).

Athique, Adrian, 2012, *Indian Media* (Cambridge: Polity Press)

Atkins, William, 2001, *The Politics of Southeast Asia's New Media* (London: Routledge).

Babu, Anita, 2015, 'IIT, IISc scientists dislike Facebook's Free Basics', *Business Standard*, 30 December. Available at http://www.business-standard.com/article/current-affairs/iit-iisc-scientists-protest-against-facebook-s-free-basics-115122900682_1.html (accessed November 2016).

Bahree, Megha, 2014, 'Reliance Takes Over Network 18: Is This The Death Of Media Independence?', *Forbes*, 30 May. Available at https://www.forbes.com/sites/meghabahree/2014/05/30/reliance-takes-over-network18-is-this-the-death-of-media-independence/#496f98b665c1 (accessed March 2017).

Baishya, Anirban K., 2015, '#NaMo: The Political Work of the Selfie in the 2014 Indian General Elections', *International Journal of Communication* 9, Feature 1686–1700. Available at http://ijoc.org/index.php/ijoc/article/viewFile/3133/1393 (accessed November 2015).

Banerjee, Abhijeet, Donald P. Green, Jeffery McManus, and Rohini Pande, 2012, 'Are Poor Voters Indifferent to Whether Elected Leaders are Criminal or Corrupt? A Vignette Experiment in Rural India'. Available at http://www.hks.harvard.edu/fs/rpande/papers/UP%20Vignette_2012-10-22_final_wfig1.pdf (accessed April 2015).

Bardhan, Pranab, 1997, 'Corruption and Development: A Review of Issues', *Journal of Economic Literature* XXXV (September).

Basu, Indrani, 2014, 'In His Own Tweets: Kejriwal's 49 Days in Power', *The 545 Conversations on Indian Elections*, 16 February. Available at http://thefivefortyfive.com/in-his-own-tweets-arvind-kejriwals-49-days-in-power (accessed March 2016).

Baxi, Pratiksha, 2011, 'In Defence of the Besharmi Morcha', *Women's Feature Service*.

______, 2012, 'We must resist the cunning of judicial reform', *Kafila*, 29 December.Behera, Navnita Chadha, 2012, 'A Perception Survey of

Media Impact on Kashmiri Youth', Institute for Research on India and International Studies.

Berry, Jeffrey M. and Sarah Sobieraj, 2014, *The Outrage Industry* (New York: Oxford University Press).

Bhagat, Chetan, 2010, 'Please don't cheer this loot-fest', *The Times of India*, 29 August.

Bhatia Gautam, 2016, *Offend, Shock, Or Disturb Free Speech under the Indian Constitution* (New Delhi: Oxford University Press).

Bhatia, Rahul, 2012, 'Fast and Furious: The Turbulent Reign of Arnab Goswami', *The Caravan*, 1 December.

Bhattacharya, Tithi, 2015, 'India's Daughter: Neoliberalism's dreams and the nightmares of violence', *International Socialist Review* 97, 1–4 July.

Bunsha, Dionne, 2006, *Scarred Experiences with Violence in Gujarat* (New Delhi: Penguin).

Bijapurkar, Rama, 2013, *A Never-before World: Tracking the Evolution of Consumer India* (New Delhi: Viking/Penguin).

Bourdieu, Pierre, 1998, *On Television*, Priscilla Parkhurst Ferguson (trans.) (New York: The New Press).

Brahmachari, Goirick, 2015, 'AAP, Left and Their Cultural Tools', *Economic and Political Weekly* L (8), 21 February.

Brownmiller, Susan, 1975, *Against Our Will: Men, Women and Rape* (New York: Simon and Schuster).

Brownstein, Ronald, 2008, 'The first 21st century campaign', *National Journal* 19 April. Available at http://freerepublic.com/focus/f-news/2003853/posts (accessed November 2015).

Castells, Manuel, 1994, 'European Cities, the Information Society, and the Global Economy', *New Left Review* 204.

______, 2013, *Communication Power* (Oxford: Oxford University Press).

Chadwick, Andrew, 2013, *The Hybrid Media System: Politics and Power*, Oxford Studies in Digital Politics (Oxford: Oxford University Press).

Chandramouli, C., 2011, 'Houses, Household Amenities, and Assets Data 2001–2011'. Available at http://censusindia.gov.in/2011-Common/NSDI/Houses_Household.pdf (accessed May 2016).

Chari, Chandra and Uma Iyengar (eds), 2015, *The Public Intellectual in India* (New Delhi: Aleph-The Book Review).

Chattarji, Subarno, 2014, 'Culture(s) of Corruption', in Nalini Rajan (ed.), *Covering and Explaining Conflict in Civil Society*' (New Delhi: Orient BlackSwan).

Chattopadhyay, Rohitashya, 2014, *Understanding India* (New Delhi: Sage Publications).

Chaturvedi, Swati, 2016, *I am a Troll: Inside the Secret World of the BJP's Digital Army* (New Delhi: Juggernaut).

Chaudhuri, Maitrayee, 2017, *Refashioning India: Gender, Media, and a Transformed Public Discourse* (New Delhi: Orient BlackSwan).

Chopra, Shaili, 2014, *The Big Connect* (New Delhi: Random House India).

Chotani, Supriya, 2013, 'Television News Media and Facebook as Mediating Spaces of Protest in India', digitmed.wordpress.com.

Couldry, Nick and James Curran (eds), 2003, *Alternative Media in a Networked World* (Lanham, MD: Rowman & Littlefield).

Dabashi, Hamid, 2012, *The Arab Spring: The End of Postcolonialism* (London: Zed Books).

Dagar, Rainuka, 2015, 'Gender Narratives and Elections', in Paul Wallace (ed.), *India's 2014 Elections: A Modi-led BJP Sweep* (New Delhi: Sage Publications).

Dasgupta, Swapan, 2007, 'The Modi Charisma', *The Times of India*, 30 December. Available at http://timesofindia.indiatimes.com/swapan-dasgupta/right-wrong/The-Modi-charisma/articleshow/2661475.cms (accessed April 2016).

______, 2014a, 'The Papier-mache Mahatma', *The Asian Age*, 1 January. Available at http://swapan-dasgupta.blogspot.in/2014_01_01_archive.html (accessed January 2016).

______, 2014b, 'A Common Threat—The Congress has closed ranks with the AAP on Modi', *The Telegraph*, 3 January. Available at http://www.telegraphindia.com/1140103/jsp/opinion/story_17741235.jsp#.WDPzM1x8uSA (accessed April 2016).

De Roover, Jakob, 2015, 'India's Daughter and BBC—Belgian Professor Speaks Out', Niti Central, 11 March. Available at http://www.niticentral.com/2015/03/11/indias-daughter-and-bbc-belgian-professor-speaks-out-306333.html (accessed April 2015).

Denyer, Simon, 2012, *Rogue Elephant: Harnessing the Power of India's Unruly Democracy* (London: Bloomsbury).

Dhar, Ravi K. and Pooja Rana (eds), 2012, *Media in a Swirl* (New Delhi: Pentagon Press).

Dixit, Kanak Mani (ed.), 2014, 'Growing Media, Shrinking Spaces', *Himal* 27 (2).

Dugger, Celia W., 2002, 'Religious Riots Over Indian Politics', *The New York Times*, 27 July. Available at http://www.nytimes.com/2002/07/27/world/religious-riots-loom-over-indian-politics.html?pagewanted=all (accessed April 2016).

Dutta-Bergman, Mohan J., 2004, 'Complementarity in Consumption of News Types Across Traditional and New Media', *Journal of Broadcasting & Electronic Media* 48 (1).

Dyson, Frances, 2009, *Sounding New Media: Immersion and Embodiment in the Arts and Culture* (Los Angeles: University of California Press).

Edwards, David and David Cromwell, 2009, *Newspeak in the 21st Century: Media Lens* (London: Pluto Press).

Fernandes, Leela, 2007, *India's New Middle Class: Democratic Politics in an Era of Economic Reform* (New Delhi: Oxford University Press).

Fishwick, Carmen, James Walsh, and Emma Howard, 'Indian elections: 10 things we have learned so far', 11 April 2014. Available at https://www.theguardian.com/world/2014/apr/11/10-things-we-learned-about-indian-election-modi-marriages (accessed November 2015).

Fioretti, Marco, 2008, 'Indian political party turns to FOSS', *linux.com*, October 20. Available at http://archive09.linux.com/feature/150549 (accessed December 2015).

Fortier, Francis, 2001, *Virtual Check: Power Relations and Alternative Strategies in the Information Society* (London: Verso).

Foster, John Bellamy and Robert W. McChesney, 2011, 'The Internet's Unholy Marriage to Capitalism', *Monthly Review* 62 (10).

Fuchs, Christian, 2008, *Internet and Society: Social Theory in the Information Age* (New York: Routledge).

______, 2017, *Social Media: A Critical Introduction* (London: Sage Publications, 2e).

Gamson, William A., David Croteau, William Hoynes, and Theodore Sasson, 1992, 'Media Images and the Social Construction of Reality', *Annual Review of Sociology* 18.

Gandhi, Jatin, 2013, 'The Modi Mythology', *Open Magazine*, 18 July.

Gandhi, Mayank, 2018, *AAP & Down: An Insider's Story of India's Most Controversial Party* (New Delhi: Simon and Schuster India).

Gangadharbhatla, Harsh and Masoud Valafar, 2017, 'Propagation of user generated content online', *International Journal of Internet Marketing and Advertising* 11 (3).

Geetha, V., 2016, *Undoing Impunity Speech after Sexual Violence* (New Delhi: Zubaan).

Ghosh, Avijit, 2011, 'Anna Hazare's movement is anti-social justice, manuwadi', *The Times of India,* 19 August. Available at http://timesofindia.indiatimes.com/india/Anna-Hazares-movement-is-anti-social-justice-manuwadi/articleshow/9664784.cms (accessed June 2015).

Ghoshal, Devjot and Manu Balachandran, 2015, 'It cost Narendra Modi $100 million to win the Indian election—here's how he spent it', *Quartz India,* 15 January. Available at http://qz.com/327771/it-cost-narendra-modi-100-million-to-win-the-indian-election-heres-how-he-spent-it/ (accessed June 2016).

Gillet, Joss, 2014, 'Measuring mobile penetration: Untangling "subscribers". "mobile phone owners" and "users"', GSMA Intelligence. Available at https://www.gsmaintelligence.com/research/2014/05/measuring-mobile-penetration/430/ (accessed May 2016).

Gladwell, Malcolm, 2010, 'Small Change: Why the revolution will not be tweeted', *The New Yorker,* 4 October. Available at http://www.newyorker.com/magazine/2010/10/04/small-change-malcolm-gladwell (accessed August 2015).

Gore, Sudhir, 2007, 'The write way to earn', *Business Today,* 17 May. Available at http://businesstoday.intoday.in/story/the-write-way-to-earn/1/6327.html (accessed April 2015).

Gowda, Rajeev M. V. and Purnima Prakash, 2014, 'The India Against Corruption Movement', in Ashu M. G. Solu (ed.), *Handbook of Research on Political Activism in the Information Age* (Maverich Technologies America Inc.).

Greenwald, Glenn, 2014, *No Place to Hide* (New York: Picador).

Guha Thakurta, Paranjoy, 2012, 'Media Ownership in India—An Overview', *The Hoot,* 30 June 2012. Available at http://www.thehoot.org/resources/media-ownership/media-ownership-in-india-an-overview-6048 (accessed June 2016).

Habermas, Jurgen, 1989, *The Structural Transformation of the Public Sphere: An Inquiry into a Category of Bourgeois Society,* Thomas Burger (trans.) (Boston, MA: MIT Press).

Halder, Debrati and H. Jaishankar, 2017, *Cyber Crimes against Women in India* (New Delhi: Sage Publications).

Hall, Stuart, David Held, and Tony McGrew (eds), 1992, *Modernity and its Futures* (London: Polity Press, in association with Open University).

Harfoush, Rahaf, 2009, *Yes We Did: An Inside Look at how Social Media built the Obama Brand* (Berkeley: New Riders Press).

Hargreaves, Ian, 2014, *Journalism: A Very Short Introduction* (Oxford: Oxford University Press).

Hasan, Zoya, 2014, 'Manufacturing Dissent: The Media and the 2014 Indian Election', The Hindu Centre for Politics and Public Policy, 2 April. Available at http://www.thehinducentre.com/verdict/commentary/article5843621.ece (accessed June 2016).

Hoffman, David, 2014, *Citizens Rising: Independent Journalism and the Spread of Democracy* (New York: CUNY Journalism Press).

Jaffrelot, Christophe, 2015a, 'What "Gujarat Model"? Growth without Development—and with socio-Political Polarisation', *Journal of South Asian Studies* 38 (4).

______, 2015b, 'The Modi-centric BJP 2014 election campaign: New techniques and old tactics', *Contemporary South Asia* 23 (2).

Jaffrelot, Christophe and Gilles Verniers, 2015, 'The Resistance of Regionalism: BJP's Limitations and the Resilience of State Parties', in Paul Wallace (ed.), *India's 2014 Election: A Modi-led BJP Sweep* (New Delhi: Sage Publications).

Jagannathan, R., 2011, 'Lokpal Fiasco: Post-mortem on a flawed beginning', *Firstpost*, 30 December.

Jaising, Indira and Ritu Menon, 2015, 'Ethics and Theatrics On "India's Daughter"', *Economic and Political Weekly* 50 (13), 28 March.

Jayal, Niraja Gopal, 2004, 'A Malevolent Embrace? The BJP and Muslims in the Parliamentary Election of 2004', *India Review* 3 (3).

__, 2013, *Citizens and its Discontents: An Indian History* (Boston: Harvard University Press).

Jeelani, Mehboob, 2011, 'The Insurgent', *The Caravan*, 1 September.

Jeffrey, Craig, 2010, *Timepass: Youth, Class, and the Politics of Waiting in India* (Palo Alto, CA: Stanford University Press).

Jeffrey, Robin, 2000, *India's Newspaper Revolution: Capitalism, Politics and the Indian-language Press 1977–99* (New Delhi: Oxford University Press).

______, 2012, *Media and Modernity: Communications, Women, and the State in India* (Ranikhet: Permanent Black).

Jeffrey, Robin and Assa Doron, 2013, *Cellphone Nation* (New Delhi: Hachette India).

Jenkins, Henry, 2006, *Convergence Culture: Where Old and New Media Collide* (New York: New York University Press).

Jenkins, Henry and Mark Deuze, 2008, 'Editorial', *Convergence: The International Journal of Research into New Media Technologies* 14 (1), 5–12.

Jenkins, Roy and Anne Marie Goetz, 1999, 'Constraints of Civil-Society's Capacity to Curb Corruption: Lessons from the Indian Experience', *IDS Bulletin* 30 (4), October. Available at http://onlinelibrary.wiley.com/doi/10.1111/j.1759-5436.1999.mp30004006.x/abstract (accessed May 2015).

Jennings, Michael W., Brigid Doherty, and Thomas Y. Levin (eds), 2008, *Walter Benjamin: The Work of Art in the Age of its Technological Reproducibility, and Other Writings on Media* (Boston: The Belknap Press of Harvard University Press).

Jensen, Michael J., 2016, 'Social Media and New Information Dynamics in Political Campaigning'. Available at https://ecpr.eu/Filestore/PaperProposal/c95aab93-e083-4474-8821-e37eb9f98efe.pdf (accessed December 2017).

Jha, Prashant, 2017, *How the BJP Wins Inside India's Greatest Election Machine* (New Delhi: Juggernaut).

Jolly, Joanna, 2016, 'Rape in India: Is the English-language press falling back on stereotypes?', *Columbia Journalism Review* 20 July.

Jose, Vinod K., 2013, 'The Emperor Uncrowned: The Rise of Narendra Modi', *The Caravan*, 1 March.

Joshua, Gitanjali, et al., 2015, 'Locating Hyderbad for Feminism in the Present Struggle against Violence', *Economic and Political Weekly*, 50 (44), 31 October.

Kapoor, Coomi, 2015, *The Emergency: A Personal History* (New Delhi: Penguin/Viking).

Karan, Kavita, 2012, 'E-Engaging India: E-democracy Strategies for Empowerment and Civic Participation', in *Digital Democracy: Concepts, Methodologies, Tools and Applications* (USA: Information Resources Management Association).

Kattayam, J., 2011, 'Social Networking Sites Helping Team Anna', *The Hindu*, 30 August.

Kaur, Raminder and William Mazzarella (eds), 2009, *Censorship in South Asia: Cultural Regulation from Sedition to Seduction* (IN: Indiana University Press).

Kellner, Douglas, 2003, *Media Spectacle* (London: Routledge).

Kirkpatrick, David, 2010, *The Facebook Effect: The Real Inside Story of Mark Zuckerberg and the World's Fastest-growing Company* (New York: Simon and Schuster).

Kohli-Khandekar, Vanita, 2013, *The Indian Media Business* (New Delhi: Sage Publication, 4e).

Krishnan, Kavita, 2014, 'Political Discourse on Gender Hits an All-time Low', The Hindu Centre for Politics and Public Policy. Available at http://www.thehinducentre.com/verdict/commentary/article5968909.ece (accessed April 2015).

Kudva, Roopa, et al., 2017, 'Innovating for the Next Half Billion', Omidyar Network, 18 December. Available at https://www.omidyar.com/sites/default/files/file_archive/Next%20Half%20Billion/Innovating%20for%20Next%20Half%20Billion.pdf (accessed August 2018).

Kumar, Anup, 2014, 'Jan Lokpal Andolan and Alternative Politics', in Taberez Ahmedi Neyazi, Akio Tanabe, and Shinya Ishikzaka (eds), *Democratic Transformation of the Vernacular Public Arena in India* (New Delhi: Routledge).

Kumar, Arun, 2002, *The Black Economy in India* (New Delhi: Penguin Books).

Kumar, Ravish, 2018, *The Free Voice: On Democrcy, Culture and the Nation* (New Delhi: Speaking Tiger).

Kumar, Sanjay, 2014, 'The Youth Vote Made a Difference for the Victory of the BJP', *Panjab University Research Journal of Social Sciences* 22 (2).

Kumar, Sashi, 2014, *Unmediated Essays on Media, Culture, Cinema* (New Delhi: Tulika Books).

Kurup, Pran, 2016, *Arvind Kejriwal and the Aam Aadmi Party: An Inside Look* (New Delhi: Bloomsbury).

Lasseter, Tom, 2014, 'India's Top Candidate Went Full Tupac, Campaigned Via Hologram', Bloomberg Businessweek, 20 May. Available at https://www.bloomberg.com/news/articles/2014-05-13/narendra-modi-indias-election-frontrunner-had-help-from-his-hologram (accessed November 2015).

Louw, Eric, 2005, *The Media and Political Process* (London: Sage Publications).

Levmore, Saul and Martha C. Nussbaum (eds), 2010, *The Offensive Internet Speech: Privacy and Reputation* (Boston, MA: Harvard University Press).

Madrigal, Alexis C., 2017, 'What Facebook Did to American Democracy', *The Atlantic*, 13 October.

Mahurkar, Uday, 2003, 'Modi Makeover', *India Today*, 13 October. Available at http://www.thehindu.com/2003/02/07/stories/2003020705420100.htm (accessed April 2016).

Mander, Harsh, 2009, *Fear and Forgiveness: The Aftermath of Massacre* (New Delhi: Penguin).

Manor, James, 2004, 'The Congress Defeat in Madhya Pradesh', *Seminar* June, 68. Available at http://www.india-seminar.com/2004/534/534%20james%20manor.htm (accessed December 2015).

Marcus, Laura and Lynda Nead (eds), 2015, *The Actuality of Walter Benjamin* (London: Lawrence and Wishart).

Marino, Andy, 2014, *Narendra Modi: A Political Biography* (New Delhi: HarperCollins).

Mason, Paul, 2013, *Why it's Still Kicking Off Everywhere: The New Global Revolutions* (London: Verso).

McCarthy, John D., Clark McPhail, and Jackie Smith, 1996, 'Images of Protest: Dimensions of Selection Bias in Media Coverage of Washington Demonstrations, 1982 and 1991', *American Sociology Review* 61 (3).

McChesney, Robert W., 1996, 'The Global Struggle for Democratic Communication', *Monthly Review* July–August.

———, 2007, *Communication Revolution* (New York: The New Press).

———, 2013, *Digital Disconnect: How Capitalism is Turning the Internet against Democracy* (New York: The New Press).

———, 2014, *Blowing the Roof off the Twenty-first Century: Media, Politics, and the Struggle for Post-capitalist Democracy* (New York: NYU Press).

McCombs, Maxwell and Donald Shaw, 1972, 'The Agenda-setting Function of Mass Media', *Public Opinion Quarterly* 36, 176–87. Available at https://www.unc.edu/~fbaum/teaching/PLSC541_Fall06/McCombs%20and%20Shaw%20POQ%201972.pdf (accessed November 2015).

McNair, Brian, 2006, *Cultural Chaos: Journalism, News and Power in a Globalised World* (London: Routledge).

Meghana, Dilip, 2008, *Rang de Basanti—Consumption, Citizenship and the Public Sphere* (Amherst: University of Massachusetts). Available at http://scholarworks.umass.edu/cgi/viewcontent.cgi?article=1116&context=theses (accessed March 2015).

Mehta, Nalin, 2008, 'India Talking—Politics, Democracy and News Television', in Nalin Mehta (ed.), *Television in India: Satellites, Politics and Cultural Change* (London: Routledge).

———, 2015, *Behind a Billion Screens: What Television Tells us about Modern India* (New Delhi: HarperCollins).

Mehta, Pratap Bhanu, 2015, 'A victory of possibilities', *The Indian Express,* 11 February.

Mehta, Ritesh, 2012, 'Flash Activism: How a Bollywood Film Catalyzed Civic Justice toward a Murder Trial', in Henry Jenkins and Sangita Shresthova (eds), *Transformative Works and Fan Activism*. Special Issue, *Transformative Works and Cultures* 10. Available at http://journal.transformativeworks.org/index.php/twc/article/view/345/271 (accessed April 2015).

Mehta, Vinod, 2014, *Editor Unplugged: Media, Magnates, Netas and Me* (New Delhi: Penguin India).

Menon, Nivedita, 2011, 'We should be there. The Left and the Anna Movement', *Kafila,* 20 August. Available at http://kafila.org/2011/08/20/we-should-be-there-the-left-and-the-anna-moment/ (accessed June 2015).

Mishra, Vandita, 2011, 'Anger after Ramlila midnight is over Govt, netas and reservation', *The Indian Express,* 21 August.

Morozov, Evgeny, 2009, 'Foreign Policy: Brave New World of Slacktivism', 19 May. Available at http://www.npr.org/templates/story/story.php?storyId=104302141 (accessed August 2015).

———, 2011, *The New Delusion: How Not to Liberate the World* (New York: Penguin Books).

Mudgal, Vipul, 2011, 'Rural Coverage in the Hindi and English Dailies', *Economic and Political Weekly* XLVI (35), 27 August.

Mukherjee, Bhaskar, 2009, 'Link analysis of Indian political parties' web sites: A temporal comparison', *Annals of Library and Information Studies* 56, September.

Mukhopadhyay, Nilanjan, 2013, *Narendra Modi: The Man, the Times* (New Delhi: Tranquebar Press).

Muralidharan, Sukumar, 2011, 'Hazare and his children', *Economic and Political Weekly* XLVI (16), 16 April.

———, 2014, 'Civil Society, Media and the Politics of Anti-Politics', in Nalini Rajan (ed.), *Covering and Explaining Conflict in Civil Society* (New Delhi: Orient BlackSwan).

Murray, Joddy, 2009, *Non-discursive Rhetoric: Image and Affect in Multimodal Composition* (New York: State University of New York Press).

Nag, Kingshuk, 2013, *The NaMo Story: A Political Life* (New Delhi: Roli Books).

Naqvi, Saba, 2015, *Capital Conquest: How the AAP's Incredible Victory has Redefined Indian Elections* (New Delhi: Hachette India).

Narayan, Badri, 2011, *The Making of the Dalit Public in North India: Uttar Pradesh, 1950–Present* (New Delhi: Oxford India Paperbacks).

Narayan, Sunetra Sen, 2014, *Globalization and Television: A Study of the Indian Experience, 1990–2010* (New Delhi: Oxford University Press).

Narayan, Sunetra Sen and Shalini Narayanan, 2016, 'An Overview of New Media in India', in Sunetra Sen Narayan and Shalini Narayanan (eds), *India Connected: Mapping the Impact of New Media* (New Delhi: Sage Publications).

Narayanan, Shalini and Anand Pradhan, 2016, 'New Media and Social-Political Movements', in Sunetra Sen Narayan and Shalini Narayanan (eds), *India Connected: Mapping the Impact of New Media* (New Delhi: Sage Publications).

Naughton, John, 2012, *What You Really Need to Know about the Internet: From Gutenberg to Zuckerberg* (London: Quercus).

Neyazi, Taberez Ahmed, 2017, 'Social media and political polarization in India', *Seminar* November.

Neyazi, Taberez Ahmed, Anup Kumar, and Holli A. Semetko, 2016, 'Campaigns, Digital Media, and Mobilisation in India', *The International Journal of Press/Politics* 21 (3).

Nichols, John and Robert W. McChesney, 2013, 'Dollarocracy', *The Nation*, 11 September. Available at https://www.thenation.com/article/dollarocracy/ (accessed November 2015).

Nigam, Aditya, 2011, 'Democracy, Populism and the "Middle Class": The Return of Anna Hazare', *Kafila*, 5 August. Available at http://kafila.org/2011/08/05/democracy-populism-and-the-%E2%80%98middle-class%E2%80%99-the-return-of-anna-hazare/ (accessed June 2015).

______, 2015, 'Reading the Power Struggle in AAP', *Kafila*, 7 March. Available at http://kafila.org/2015/03/07/reading-the-power-struggle-in-aap/ (accessed March 2016).

Nigam, Aditya and Nivedita Menon, 2011, 'Anti-Corruption Movement and the Left', *Economic and Political Weekly* XLVI (37), 10 September.

Ninan, Sevanti, 2007, *Headlines from the Heartland* (New Delhi: Sage Publications).

Ohri, Kapil, 2011, 'How powerful is Anna Hazare on Facebook and Twitter?', *afaqs*, 18 August. Available at http://www.afaqs.com/news/story/31413_How-powerful-is-Anna-Hazare-on-Facebook-and-Twitter (accessed June 2015).

Oomen, T. K., 2013, *Knowledge and Society: Situating Sociology and Social Anthropology* (New Delhi: Oxford University Press, rev. edn).

Owen, Diana, 2009, 'The Campaign and the Media', in Janet M. Box-Steffensmeier and Steven E. Schier (eds), *The American Election of 2008* (Lanham, MD: Rowman & Littlefield Publishers Inc.).

Owen, Laura Hazard, 2017, 'There's a long list of old-fashioned parallels to today's fake news. Here's one that's actually helpful', Neiman Lab. Available at http://www.niemanlab.org/2017/09/theres-a-long-list-of-old-fashioned-parallels-to-todays-fake-news-heres-one-thats-actually-helpful/ (accessed October 2017).

Pandey, Piyush, 2015, *Pandemonium: Piyush Pandey on Advertising* (New Delhi: Penguin).

Pal, Joyojeet, Priyanka Chandra, and V. G. Vydiswaran, 2016, 'Twitter and the Rebranding of Narendra Modi', *Economic and Political Weekly* LI (8), 20 February.

Patil, Smita M., 2017, 'Debrahmanising Online Sphere: On Large Question of Caste, Gender and Patriarchy', GenderIT.org, 8 September. Available at https://www.genderit.org/articles/debrahmanizing-online-sphere-larger-questions-caste-gender-and-patriarchy (accessed February 2018).

Philipose, Pamela, 2002, 'The Portable, Moveable Modi', *The Indian Express*, 25 October.

———, 2009, 'Media and Civil Society', *Infochange*. Available at http://infochangeindia.org/downloads/agenda_17.pdf (accessed April 2015).

———, 2011, 'Aruna Roy speaks of Keeping Intact RTI Law, explains Approach to Jan Lokpal', *Mainstream* XLIX (44), 22 October.

———, 2013, 'Anxieties in the Republic Media: Metamorphosis and Popular Protest', *Economic and Political Weekly* XLVIII (6).

———, 2014a, 'The clamour, the silence', *The Indian Express*, 16 December.

———, 2014b, 'Violence, Just a Click Away: How Communal Violence has a Domain in Cyberspace', *DNA*, 2 September.

———, 2017, 'Tweeting Up the Votes', *The Indian Express*, 17 March.

Prakash, Gyan, 2003, 'Blitz's Bombay', *Seminar*. Available at http://www.india-seminar.com/2003/528/528%20gyan%20prakash.htm (accessed May 2015).

Price, Lance, 2015, *The Modi Effect* (London: Hodder & Stoughton).

Raghavan, Sharad T. C. A., 2015, 'India is now a $2-trillion economy', *The Hindu*, 3 July. Available at http://www.thehindu.com/business/Economy/india-is-now-a-2trillion-economy-says-world-bank-data/article7380442.ece (accessed May 2016).

Rai, Amit S., 2009, *Untimely Bollywood: Globalization and India's New Media Assemblage* (Durham and London: Duke University Press).

Rajagopal, Arvind, 2010, 'Violence, Publicity and Secularism: Hindu-Muslim Riots in Gujarat', in Chris Berry, So-yong Kim, and Lynn Spigel (eds), *Electronic Elsewheres: Media, Technology, and the Experience of Social Space* (Minneapolis: University of Minnesota Press).

______, 2011a, 'Am I Still Anna When Nobody is Watching?', *The Hindu*, 12 September.

______, 2011b, 'Visibility as a Trap in the Anna Hazare Campaign', *Economic and Political Weekly* 46 (47), 19 November.

______, 2014a, 'On the Unexpected Parochialism of Media Studies', in Biswarup Sen and Abhijit Roy (eds), *Channeling Cultures: Television Studies from India* (New Delhi: Oxford University Press).

______, 2014b, 'Two Tyrants in the Age of Television', *Economic and Political Weekly* XLIX (8), 22 February.

Rajan, Nalini (ed.), 2014, *Covering and Explaining Conflict in Civil Society* (New Delhi: Orient BlackSwan).

Ram, N., 2011, 'The Changing Role of the News Media in Contemporary India', Paper presented at the 72nd Session of the Indian History Conference, December.

Ramakrishnan, Venkitesh, 2011, 'Crusaders in the dock', *Frontline* 28 (23), 5–18 November.

Rao, Shakuntala, 2014, *Covering Rape in Shame: Culture, Journal of Mass Media Ethics* (SUNY-Plttsburgh: Department of Communication).

Rao, Ursula, 2010, *News as Culture: Journalistic Practices and the Remaking of Indian Leadership Traditions* (New York: Berghahn Books).

Reddy, Ramachandhra G., 2011, *Crisis of Governance* (New Delhi: Serials Publications).

Reddy, Srinivas K., 2010, 'Facebook to open first Asia office in India', *The Hindu*, 15 March. Available at http://www.thehindu.com/news/cities/Hyderabad/facebook-to-open-first-asia-office-in-india/article245437.ece (accessed June 2016).

Robinson, James, 2010, 'UK and US see heaviest newspaper circulation declines', *The Guardian*, 17 June. Available at https://www.theguardian.com/media/2010/jun/17/newspaper-circulation-oecd-report (accessed May 2016).

Rodrigues, Usha M. 2015, 'Anna's Movement: Social Media Sets Traditional Media's Agenda', in Usha M. Rodrigues and Maya Ranganathan (eds), *Indian News Media: From Observer to Participant* (New Delhi: Sage Publications).

Rodrigues, Usha M. and Maya Ranganathan, 2015, *Indian News Media: From Observer to Participant* (New Delhi: Sage Publications).

Roy, Dhunu, 2010, 'City Makers and City Breakers', in Maya Dayal and Ravi Dayal (eds), *Celebrating Delhi* (New Delhi: Penguin/Viking, 2010).

Roychowdhury, Poulami, 2013, 'The Delhi Gang Rape: The Making of International Causes', *Feminist Studies* 39 (1), 282–92.

S. Rukmini, 2014, 'Modi got most prime-time coverage: Study', *The Hindu*, 8 May. Available at http://www.thehindu.com/elections/loksabha2014/modi-got-most-primetime-coverage-study/article5986740.ece (accessed May 2016).

Sainath, P., 2009, 'Is the "Era of Ashok" a new era for "news"?', *The Hindu*, 29 November.

Sardesai, Rajdeep, 2002, 'Did the media ransack shops, take lives, Mr Modi?', *The Indian Express*, 7 March.

, 2011, 'Media, a double-edged sword for Anna, Govt', *CNN-IBN Live*, 30 December. Available at http://www.ibnlive.com/blogs/india/rajdeep-sardesai/media-a-double-edged-sword-for-anna-govt-11095-746353.html (accessed July 2015).

———, 2014: *2014: The Election that Changed India* (New Delhi: Penguin/Viking).

———, 2015, 'When Kejriwal Defeated the Media', blog on *Breakingviews*, 12 February. Aailable at http://www.rajdeepsardesai.net/blog-views/when-kejriwal-defeated-media (accessed March 2016).

Saxer, Marc, *Fighting Corruption in Transformation Societies* (Bangkok: Friedrich Ebert Stiftung, 2014).

Sen, Biswarup, 2016, *Digital Politics and Culture in Contemporary India: The Making of an Info-Nation* (New York: Routledge).

Sen, Biswarup and Abhijit Roy, 2014, *Channeling Cultures: Television Studies from India* (New Delhi: Oxford University Press).

Sengupta, Shuddabhrata, 2011, 'At the Risk of Heresy: Why I am not celebrating with Anna Hazare', *Kafila*, 9 April. Available at http://kafila.org/2011/04/09/at-the-risk-of-heresy-why-i-am-not-celebrating-with-anna-hazare/ (accessed June 2015).

Seth, Leila, 2014, *Talking of Justice: People's Rights in Modern India* (New Delhi: Aleph Book Company).

Shah, Ghanshyam, 2015, 'Mega Marketing and Management: Gujarat's 2024 Elections', in Paul Wallace, *India's 2014 Elections: A Modi-led BJP Sweep* (New Delhi: Sage Publications).

Shah, Priya, 2010, 'Indian Political Communication and Digital Technology', *Scribd.* Available at http://www.scribd.com/doc/46046810/Indian-Political-Communication-and-Digital-Technology#scribd (accessed December 2015).

Shakil, A., 2013, 'Protests, the Justice Verma Committee and the Government Ordinance', *Economic and Political Weekly* XLVIII (6), 9 February.

Sharma, Arjun, 2013, 'Kashmir separatists using Facebook to revive stone-pelting say intelligence agencies', *India Today*, June. Available at http://indiatoday.intoday.in/story/kashmir-rebels-use-facebook-to-fan-unrest/1/141288.html (accessed June 2016).

Shirky, Clay, 2008, *Here Comes Everybody: The Power of Organizing Without Organizations* (London: Allen Lane).

Shukla, Rakesh, 2014, 'The Rage of Angels: Anger, Fury, Brutal Rape, Protests, Police Action', *International Journal of Applied Psychoanalytical Studies* 11 (2).

Sidhartha, 2016, 'Apple may get to open stores without 30% sourcing norm', Times News Network/Gadgets Now, 20 April. Available at https://www.gadgetsnow.com/tech-news/Apple-may-get-to-open-stores-without-30-sourcing-norm/articleshow/51934783.cms (accessed 25 November).

Singh, Anushree, 2015, 'Microsoft CEO Satya Nadella's big announcements for India at "Future Unleashed"', *Business Insider India*, 5 November. Available at https://www.businessinsider.in/Microsoft-CEO-Satya-Nadellas-big-announcements-for-India-at-Future-Unleashed/articleshow/49672370.cms (accessed September 2017).

Singh, Richa, 2014, *New Citizens' Activism in India: Moments, Movements, and Mobilisation—An Exploratory Study* (New Delhi: Centre for Democracy and Social Action).

SinghaRoy, Debal K., 2014, *Towards a Knowledge Society: New Identities in Emerging India* (New Delhi: Cambridge University Press).

Sirnate, Vasundhara and Nithya Nagarathinam, 2015, 'What enables rape reporting?', *The Hindu*, 25 April.

Smith, Aaron, 2009, 'The Internet's Role in Campaign 2009', Pew Internet, Science & Tech, 15 April. Available at http://www pewinternet.org/2009/04/15/the-internets-role-in-campaign-2008/ (accessed November 2015).

Sonwalkar, Prasun, 2009, 'Citizen Journalism in India: The Politics of Recognition', in Stuart Allan and Einar Thorsen (eds), *Citizen Journalism: Global Perspectives* (New York: Peter Lang).

Sreekumar, R. B., 2016, *Gujarat: Behind the Curtain* (New Delhi: Manas Publications).

Sridhar, Varadhrarajan, 2012, *The Telecom Revolution in India: Technology, Regulation, and Policy* (New Delhi: Oxford University Press).

Subramaniam, Chitra, 2003, 'Sting and Stink in the Tale', in B. G. Verghese (ed.), *Breaking the Big Story* (New Delhi: Viking).

Subrahmaniam, Vidya, 2011, 'It's a long journey: Kejriwal', *The Hindu*, 12 September.

Sundaram, Ravi (ed.), 2013, *No Limits: Media Studies from India* (New Delhi: Oxford University Press).

Suresh, Appu Esthose, 2013, 'Makeover Gurus', *The Indian Express*, 20 October.

Swamy, Praveen, 2010, 'The Ugly World of Online Kashmiri Rebels', *The Hindu*, 24 July. Available at http://www.thehindu.com/news/national/other-states/the-ugly-world-of-kashmirs-online-rebels/article530306.ece (accessed June 2016).

Swanson, David L. and Paolo Mancini, 1996, *Politics, Media, and Modern Democracy: An International Study of Innovations in Electoral Campaigning and Their Consequences* (Westport, CT: Praeger).

Swasy, Alecia, 2016, *How Journalists Use Twitter: The Changing Landscape of U.S. Newsrooms* (Lanham, MD: Lexington Books).

Talese, Gay, 1966, *The Kingdom and the Power: Behind the Scenes at The New York Times, the Institution that Influences the World* (New York: Random House).

Taylor, Astra, 2014, *The People's Platform: Taking Back Power and Culture in the Digital Age* (New York: Metropolitan Books).

Tekwani, Shyam and Kavitha Shetty, 2007, 'Two Indias: The Role of the Internet in the 2004 Election', in Randolph Kluver, Nicholas Jankowski, Kirsten Foot, and Steven M. Schneider (eds), *The Internet and National Campaigns: A Comparative Study of Web Campaigning* (New York: Routledge).

Teltumbde, Anand, 2005, *Hindutva and Dalits: Perspectives for Understanding Communal Praxis* (Kolkata: Samya).

———, 2011, *The Persistence of Caste: The Khairlanji Murders and India's Hidden Apartheid* (London: Zed Books).

———, 2013, 'Delhi Gang Rape Case: Some Uncomfortable Questions', *Economic and Political Weekly* XLVIII (6).

Thussu, Daya Kishan, 2016, 'Foreword', in Sunetra Sen Narayan and Shalini Narayanan (eds), *India Connected: Mapping the Impact of New Media* (New Delhi: Sage Publications).

Thussu, Daya Kishan and Des Freedman (eds), 2003, *War and the Media: Reporting Conflict 24/7* (New Delhi: Vistaar Publications).

Thompson, Derek, 2017, 'How to Survive the Media Apocalypse', *The Atlantic*, 29 November. Available at https://www.theatlantic.com/business/archive/2017/11/media-apocalypse/546935/ (accessed December 2017).

Thompson, John B., 1984, *Studies in the Theory of Ideology* (Cambridge: Polity Press).

———, 1990, *Ideology and Modern Culture* (Cambridge: Polity Press).

Udupa, Sahana, 2015, *News, Publics and Politics in Globalizing India: Media, Publics, Politics* (New Delhi: Cambridge University Press).

Unnithan, Sandeep, 2014, 'AAPeclipse', *India Today*, 13 June.

Vanaik, Achin, 2016, 'India: Liberal democracy and the extreme right', in Leo Panitch and Greg Albo (eds), *The Politics of the Rights* (Monthly Review Press).

Varadarajan, Siddharth, 2002, *Gujarat: The Making of a Tragedy* (New Delhi: Penguin).

———, 2011, 'Satish Sharma aide showed US Embassy employee cash to be used as "pay-offs" in confidence vote', 17 March. Available at http://www.thehindu.com/news/the-india-cables/satish-sharma-aide-showed-us-embassy-employee-cash-to-be-used-as-payoffs-in-confidence-vote/article1544204.ece (accessed April 2015).

Venkat, Archana, 2011, 'For Anna or Against Him. Do I have a choice?', *The Hoot*, August. Available at http://thehoot.org/web/ForAnnaoragainsthimDolhaveachoice/5459-1-1-14-true.html (accessed June 2015).

Verghese, B. G., 2010, *First Draft* (New Delhi: Tranquebar Press).

Verma, Lalmani, 2017, 'BJP's election strategy: 900 rallies, 67,000 workers, 10,000 WhatsApp groups and chopper landings', *The Indian Express*, 12 March.

Verma, Pavan K., 1999, *The Great India Middle Class* (New Delhi: Penguin Books)

Verma, Rahul and Shreyas Sardesai, 2014, 'Does Media Exposure Affect Voting Behaviour and Political Preferences in India?', *Economic and Political Weekly* XLIX (39), 27 September.

Verma, Sudesh, 2014, *Narendra Modi: The Game Changer* (New Delhi: Vitasta).

Vikas, S. N., 2013, 'Facebook India Active Users Up 59% To 71M In Q4-2012', 6 February. Available at http://www.medianama.com/2013/02/223-facebook-71-million-india-users-2012/ (accessed January 2015).

Vilanilam, J. V., 2005, *Mass Communication in India: A Sociological Perspective* (New Delhi: Sage Publications).

Virmani, Arvind, 2006, 'Sustaining Employment and Equitable Growth: Polices For Structural Transformation of The Indian Economy', Planning Commission Working Paper No. 3/2006-PC.

Vise, David A., 2005, *The Google Story* (London: Pan Books).

Visvanathan, Shiv, 2012, 'Janus Shut the Door', *Outlook*, 25–31 December.

______, 2014, 'Narendra Modi's Symbolic War', *Economic and Political Weekly* XLIX (22), 31 May.

Vyas, Neena, 2004, 'Pick up the phone, it may be the PM', *The Hindu*, 25 February.

Wallace, Paul (ed.), 2015, *India's 2014 Elections: A Modi-led BJP Sweep* (New Delhi: Sage Publications).

Wayne, Mike, 2009, *Marxism and Media Studies* (London: Pluto Press).

Weiner, Myron, 1978, *India Votes: 1977* (Washington: American Enterprise Institute for Public Policy Research).

Williams, Raymond, 1976, *Keywords: A Vocabulary of Culture and Society* (Britain: Croom Helm).

______, 1989, *The Politics of Modernism: Against the New Conformists* (London: Verso).

______, 2004, *Television: Technology and Cultural Form* (London: Routledge).

Index

Aaj Tak, 63, 101, 107, 111
Aam Aadmi Party (AAP), 19–20, 81, 119, 211
  Charter of Women's Rights, 92
  Facebook, and Twitter accounts, 220–21, 225–29, 236–44
  media outreach, 21
  preparations for election campaign 2013, 216–25
  use of social media, 225–29, 236–43
  volunteer base, 237
AAP Volunteer Action Manch (AVAM), 242
Adarsh Cooperative Housing Society scandal, 45
Advani, L. K., 31, 160, 162
Afzal Guru's secret hanging, 129
Agnivesh, Swami, 66
Ahmed, Saifuddin, 101
Aiyar, Shankar, 198
All India Progressive Women's Association (AIPWA), 104
Ambani, Anil, 222
Ambani, Mukesh, 214, 222
Anderson, Benedict, 3
anti-corruption campaigns, 33, 51
anti-corruption measures, 32–33
anti-nuclear demonstrations, 47
Antulay, A. R., 30
Antulay's Trustgate scandal, 30
Aouragh, Miriyam, 127
Arab Spring, 47–48
Asaram, 139
Ashutosh, 59, 77, 229, 235
Association for Democratic Reforms (ADR), 36, 52
Association of Victims of Uphaar Tragedy (AVUT), 44

Bachchan, Amitabh, 64, 110
Bagga, Tajinder Pal S., 108
Bahujan Samaj Party, 151
Bajaj, Rahul, 56
Bardhan, Pranab, 33
Bedi, Kiran, 53, 76, 133
Besharmi Morcha, 136
Bhagat, Chetan, 50, 199–200
Bhandare, Namita, 111
Bhanwari Devi gang rape, 134
Bharatiya Janata Party (BJP), 19–20, 80, 157
  innovative media strategies, 21
Bhotmange, Priyanka, 114
Bhotmange, Surekha, 114

Bhushan, Prashant, 53, 66, 234, 244
Bhushan, Shanti, 53
Binny, Vinod Kumar, 234
black economy, 29–30
Blitz, 30
Bofors scandal, 31–32
Bordieu, Pierre, 106
bribe-giving and taking, 31

Cambridge Analytica, 256
capital punishment, 130–31, 134, 137–38
cash-for-votes scandal, 41
caste, 4, 44, 63, 93, 114–15, 151, 198, 252–53, 269
Castells, Manuel, 16, 69, 122
Census 2011, 9, 122, 248
Central Bureau of Investigation (CBI), 32
Central Vigilance Commission (CVC), 32
Chadwick, Andrew, 16
Chagla, M. C., 29
Chandrasekhar, C. P., 50
Chawla, Himanshu, 104
Chawla, Prabhu, 177
Chhokar, Jagdeep, 52
'churnalism', 39
Citizens for Accountable Governance, 193
citizenship, 34
Citizen's Ombudsman Bill, 52
citizens' rights, 31
CNN-IBN, 63, 101, 192, 212
Common Cause India, 36
Commonwealth Games scam, 49–51
communication technologies, 267
  impact on media, 1–7
  in India, 150–51
Congress Party, 79, 157
corruption
  definition, 33, 35
  media coverage, 51
  news breaks on, 40–41
  perception of an all-encompassing, 51
  as theme in Hindi film industry, 42–44
Criminal Law (Amendment) Act 2013, 138
Criminal Law (Amendment) Act 2016, 91
culture, 2

Dabashi, Hamid, 48
Dainik Bhaskar, 11, 62
Dainik Jagran, 107, 112, 189–90
DD News, 101
Delhi city, profile of, 121–22
  gender violence in city, 123
  portrayal of rapists, 129
Delhi gang rape protests, media coverage of
  breaking news, 97–113
  channel headlines, 111–12
  'commodification of "Nirbhaya"', 90
  creative use of extraneous aids, 100
  digital respondents to news report, 98
  Facebook and Twitter campaigns, 102, 105–07, 110, 126, 136
  of family's coping with death, 113

following Jyoti Singh's death, 109–13
India Gate protests, 103, 105–06
by international media, 89–90
Justice Verma Committee Report, 91–92
media's failures, 127–41
Ram Singh's suicide, 113
reasons for framing. *see* framing contexts of gang rape
social media mobilisations, 96
TV coverage, 100–02
Denyer, Simon, 215–16
Desai, Morarji, 32
Deshmukh, Nanaji, 66
Deuze, Mark, 17
Dikshit, Sheila, 224, 228
Doron, Assa, 8, 22, 151
Dreze, Jean, 123

e-commerce market of India, 266
Election Commission of India (ECI), 158
election coverage, 147–52
BJP's general election media campaigns of 2009 and 2014, 200–01
Delhi Assembly 2013, 152
e-campaign, 157
elections of 2013, 2014, and 2015, 244–255. *see also* Aam Aadmi Party (AAP); Kejriwal, Arvind
general election 2009, 157
General Election 2014, 152, 161–66, 189–202, 253–54
'India Shining', 156–57
Modi's use of media, 161–66, 169, 171–88
Obama's presidential campaigns, 152–54

Facebook, 8, 12, 17, 48, 50, 96, 100, 102–05, 118, 126, 189–90, 194, 256, 267
Aam Aadmi Party (AAP)'s election campaign, 220–21, 225–29, 236–44
Delhi gang rape protests, 102, 105–06, 110–11, 126, 136, 140
in IAC protests, 12, 71–77, 81
influence and presence in India, 257
2008 Obama campaign, 152–54
as a tool of protest, 12, 14–15
users in India, 12
Facebook News Feed, 257
Feminism in India, 137
Fernandes, Leela, 5
Foster, Bellamy, 78
fourth-generation (4G) wireless broadband network, 18
framing contexts of gang rape
class and location, 114–15
heroic quality of victim, 115–18
media coverage, 123–27
site of attack, 121–23
timing of incident, 118–21
'Friends of BJP', 160
Fuchs, Christian, 2–3

Gandhi, Indira, 30
Gandhi, Mayank, 243

Gandhi, Priyanka, 198
Gandhi, Rahul, 198
Gandhi, Sonia, 178
gender justice for survivors of sexual violence, 138–39
Ghosh, Jayati, 175
Gladwell, Malcolm, 78
Global Day of Action Against Capitalism, 48
Godhra carnage/Gujarat pogrom, 166–71
Godrej, Jamshyd, 56
Golwalkar, M. S., 171
good governance, 51
Google Plus Hangout, 186
Google Street View, 266
Goswami, Arnab, 58, 131
2G scam, 49, 118
Gujarat Samachar, 168
Gupta, Arvind, 184, 193

Habermas, Jurgen, 2
Hasan, Zoya, 79
hawala scam, 31
Hazare, Anna, 13, 19–20, 35, 59, 63–65, 68, 71, 76, 80, 212
Hegde, Santosh, 53
Hindi-speaking elite, 10
The Hindu, 112
Hindu nationalism, 4
Hindustan Times, 97, 112, 130–31
Hussain, Daood, 132
hybrid media system, 16
'Hyderabad for Feminism' (HfF), 94

IBN Live, 97
Ilmi, Shazia, 223, 234

India Against Corruption (IAC) movement, 11–13, 19, 28, 46, 49–57, 211, 252
- Facebook amd Twitter, role of, 71–77, 81
- film stars in, 55
- genesis of, 52–53
- 'India Against Corruption/ Cricket Against Corruption', 75
- Jantar Mantar fast, 57–60
- mainstream media support, 57–64, 77–78
- mass self-communication, 69
- meltdown of campaign, 65–66, 77–82
- MMRDA Grounds fast, 64–68
- Ramlila Maidan fast and Hazare arrest, 60–64, 76
- social media, role of, 53, 68–72
- support of corporate India, 56

India.com, 97
Indian bloggers, 7
The Indian Express, 30
Indian middle class, 4, 31
Indian National Congress (INC), 41
India Today, 162, 170, 174, 190
India Today Group, 97
Instagram, 8, 189, 194, 238
internet connectivity in India, 151
Internet services, 15
internet use, 12, 15–19, 22, 43, 70, 78, 96, 112–13, 127, 137, 152–55, 157, 270

Jaffrelot, Christophe, 193
Jagran Group, 97
Jaidka, Kokil, 101

Jain, Rajesh, 160
Jaitley, Arun, 55
Jan Lokpal Bill, 52, 57–58, 65, 71
Jayal, Niraja Gopal, 156
Jeffery, Robin, 8, 22, 151
Jeffrey, Craig, 248
Jenkins, Henry, 16–17
Jessica Lal case, 44–45
Jethmalani, Ram, 215
Joshi, Prabhash, 35
'Justice for Jessica', SMS campaign, 45
Justice Verma Committee Report, 91–92, 136–38, 140
Juvenile Justice Act 2014, 138
Juvenis Technologies Private Limited, 70
Jyotipunj, 171

Kapur, Shekhar, 107
Kargil war, 42
Kasab's hanging, 129
Kashmir Valley stone pelting episodes 2010, 14, 95
Kaul, Mahima, 159
Kejriwal, Arvind, 21–22, 52, 57, 59, 65, 68, 71, 80–81, 108, 119–20, 211, 251–52
  AAP's election campaign, 216–25
  appearance on Aap ki Adalat, 213–14
  as chief minister of Delhi, 229–33
  election campaign for election 2015, 236–44
  image creation, 245–47
  mobilisation in IAC protests, 212–13
  tweets, 238–43
  use of social media, 225–29, 243
Khan, Aamir, 55, 73
Khan, Shah Rukh, 55, 72, 110
Kohli-Khandekar, Vanita, 10
Kotak, Uday, 56
Krishnan, Kavita, 104, 135

Ladies Finger magazine, 137
Lal, Ankit, 228
LinkedIn, 189, 194
Lokayukta, 32, 36
Lokpal, 32, 36, 77
Lokpal Bill, 55, 58, 73
Lok Sabha Elections 2009–14, voter turnout, 250

Mahajan, Pramod, 158
Mahindra, Anand, 56
Mahindra, Keshub, 56
Manmohan Singh, 57, 73, 110
Mason, Paul, 264
Mathura rape case, 91
Mazdoor Kishan Shakti Sanghathan (MKSS), 34–35
McChensey, Robert W., 17, 78, 154–55, 255
McComb, Maxwell E., 147–48
media
  agenda-setting potential, 148
  assemblage, 16
  convergence, 16–17
  election coverage, 20–21
  24×7 television news cycle, 263
  understanding of rape culture, 20
media, changing

alternative media platforms, 40–41
business-politics-media nexus, 41
content, 38
credible-informational function, 39
focus on scams and scandal, 40
foreign funding, 37
functions in modern societies, 39
IAC protests, 49–57. *see also* India Against Corruption (IAC) movement
information revolution through artificial intelligence (AI), 263
news breaks on corruption, 40–41
ownership and control, 38
people's mobilisations across world, 46–49

media activism, strengths and weaknesses of, 78–79
media issue attention cycle, 49–50
Medianet, 38
mediatised half-decade, 18–19
Mehta, Deepak, 122–23, 129, 140, 164
Mehta, Ritesh, 45
Mehta, Vinod, 164
Menon, Nivedita, 49
Minorities/Muslims, 167, 175–77, 185, 196, 254–55, 271
mobile phone
'active' mobile users, 11
gender divide in usage, 268
impact on behavioural patterns, 96
ownership in India, 8, 95–96, 151
smartphone users, 2014, 189

Modi, Narendra, 21, 55, 110–11, 119, 160–66, 169, 235, 255, 271
agenda setting, 196
attack on Congress Party, 185, 197–98
blog, 'Letter to my countrymen', 183
Chai Pe Charcha, 199
communication through mainstream media, 178–80
'Digital India' programme, 265–66
election campaign of 2014, 152, 161–66, 189–202, 246, 249, 253–54
Gujarat Model concept, 174–75
handling of Godhra carnage/ Gujarat pogrom, 166–71
handling of Snoopgate story, 188
management of television media, 191–92
NaMo Gujarat television channel, 178–79
personal website, 182
Run for Unity event, 187–88
Seedhi Baat with Prabhu Chawla, 177
self-communication strategies through digital media, 181–88, 193
SMSes, 183
Swachh Bharat scheme, 237, 266
tweets, 183, 194–200
'Two minutes to the truth', 170

Vibrant Gujarat Business Summits, 172–73
'Walk the Talk' interview with Shekhar Gupta, 177
Mozorov, Evgeny, 48
Mubarak, Hosni, 47
Mukherjee, Abhijit, 120
Mundhra scam, 29–30
Myrdal, Gunnar, 29

Nadella, Satya, 266
Nagarathinam, Nithya, 94
Nagarwala scandal, 30
Naidu, Chandrababu, 55
'NaMo' syndrome, 200
NaMo volunteer, 193
Naqvi, Saba, 237
Narayan, Sunetra Sen, 7
Narayanan, Shalini, 7, 269
Narmada Bachao Andolan, 34
Narwani, Sundeep, 71
National Campaign for People's Right to Information (NCPRI), 52, 73
National Democratic Alliance (NDA), 156
National Optical Fibre Network (NOFN) project, 269
Navbharat Times, 62
NDTV 24×7, 63, 97, 99, 101, 104–05, 131, 191
Nehru, Jawaharlal, 29
Netcore Company, 70
Network 18 Media and Investments Ltd, 18
News Broadcasters Association, 112
newspapers
circulation of, 10
interactive websites of, 15
The New York Times, 263
Nichols, John, 154–55
Nigam, Aditya, 49
Niira Radia Tape controversy, 41, 54, 214
Ninan, Sevanti, 10
Nirbhaya Fund, 92
NitiDigital, 193
Nyaya Yatras, 162

Obama elections, 152–55
Occupy Movement, 47
Om Yog Sadhara, 56
Open Source movement, 78
Operation West End, 40–42

Pandey, Gaurav, 132
Pandey, Jyoti Singh, 89, 94
Parivartan, 52
Patel, Keshubhai, 164
Patil, Smita M., 269
Paul, Samuel, 31
Pichai, Sundar, 266
'Pink Chaddi' protest of 2009, 135
Pinternet, 189, 194
Pradhan, Anand, 269
Prahalad, C. K., 36
Premji, Azim, 56
Prevention of Corruption Act 1947, 32
Prevention of Corruption (Amendment) Act 1988, 32
Public Interest Litigation (PIL), 36
Public Safety Act (PSA), 14
public sphere, 2

Radio, 8, 11, 17, 30, 148, 155, 187, 189, 238, 253, 265
Rai, Amit S., 16

Raja, A., 150
Rajagopal, Arvind, 5, 63
Ramdev, Baba, 56, 73, 80, 108
Ram Janambhoomi agitation, 156, 188
Rang De Basanti (RDB), 42–44
Rashtriya Swayamsevak Sangh (RSS), 162, 166, 188
Reliance Industries, 18, 214–16, 233, 256, 265
Resurgent Group of Gujarat, 171
right to information movement, 35–36
Roy, Aruna, 35
Roy, Dhunu, 122
Roy, Srirupa, 247

Sama, Sanghamitra, 98
Sandesh, 168
Santhanam, K., 32
Sardesai, Rajdeep, 59, 188
satellite television, 22
scams during NDA rule (1998–2004), 42
Sen, Amartya, 123
Seth, Justice Leila, 91, 94, 127
Shah, Amit, 188, 247, 255
Shah, Ghanshyam, 185
Shah, Manubhai, 31
Shankar, Sri Sri Ravi, 56, 73, 80
Sharma, Rajat, 191
Shaw, Donald L., 147–48
Shaw, Kiran Mazumdar, 56
Shirky, Clay, 78
Short Messaging Service (SMS), 11, 17, 45, 69–70, 158
Shourie, Arun, 30
Shukla, Rajeev, 163
Singh, Digvijay, 215
Singh, General V. K., 120
Singh, Jaswant, 50
Singh, Manmohan, 73, 110, 186
Singharoy, Debal K., 122
Sirnate, Vasundhara, 94
Sisodia, Manish, 76, 80, 234
social media usage, 11–12, 264
  Aam Aadmi Party (AAP), 225–29, 236–43
  in Delhi gang rape protests, 96
  in IAC protests, 12–13, 68–72
  by Kejriwal, 225–29, 243
  by Modi, 183, 194–200
  role in activism, 12–14
Solanki, Prashant, 160
Star News, 63, 101
State, conception of, 34
student politics and activism, 93
  Delhi University FYUP, rollback of, 93
  Film and Television Institute of India protests 2015, 93
  Jawaharlal Nehru University (JNU) protests, 93
  Rohith Vemula, suicide of, 93
Subramaniam, Chitra, 31
Sukh Ram, 150
Swaraj, Sushma, 111, 120, 131, 139

Tahrir Square, 47, 54, 57, 107
Talese, Gay, 263
TAM India, 157
Tehelka, 40
tehelka.com, 40–41
Telecom Regulatory Authority of India (TRAI), 192
television, 5–6, 9–10, 37, 45
  coverage of IAC, 58–64

coverage of gang rape protests, 99–102, 105–06
coverage of Modi, 186–88
coverage of 2014 campaign, 192–92
coverage of Kejriwal, 213–15
Teltumbde, Anand, 114
Thakurta, Paranjoy Guha, 11
Thapar, Karan, 65, 178
third-generation (3G) services, 7
Thussu, Daya, 4
Times Now, 131
The Times of India, 38, 62, 97, 112, 124, 130, 163, 212, 241
Transparency International (TI), 31
Trump, Donald J., 155, 257
Twitter, 8, 12–13, 48, 50, 56, 96, 102, 126, 189, 255, 270–71
Aam Aadmi Party (AAP)'s election campaign, 220–21, 225–29, 238–44
Delhi gang rape protests, 102, 105–07, 110, 126, 136
Modi's tweeting patterns, 183, 194–200
2008 Obama campaign, 152–54

Udwin, Leslee, 90
Uphaar theatre trajedy, 44

Vajpayee, A. B., 41–42, 171, 214
Varma, Pavan K., 4
Vilanilam, J. V., 4
violence against women, 90, 92, 139
as electoral issue, 92
Viswas, Kumar, 76
Vittal, N., 33

The Wall Street Journal, 176
web-based media platforms, 40
Weiner, Myron, 155
Weinstein, Harvey, 137
WhatsApp, 13, 23, 189–90, 238, 256, 262, 271
Whistleblower's Act, 52
Wi-Fi broadband services, 7
WikiLeaks, 41, 78
Wikileaks, 46
Williams, Raymond, 2, 94

Yadav, Mulayam Singh, 139
Yadav, Yogendra, 234, 243–44
YouTube, 17, 69, 102, 107, 120, 132–33, 135–36, 152, 160, 194, 240
AAP News, 224
2008 Obama campaign, 152–54
Youth, 13, 42–43, 186, 200, 247–51, 268

Zee News, 101